THE ART OF LIBROMANCY

THE ART OF
LIBROMANCY

On Selling Books and Reading Books

in the Twenty-First Century

JOSH COOK

BIBLIOASIS

Windsor, Ontario

FIRST EDITION
2 4 6 8 10 9 7 5 3

Library and Archives Canada Cataloguing in Publication
Title: The art of libromancy : selling books and reading books in the
twenty-first century / Josh Cook.
Names: Cook, Josh D., 1980– author.
Identifiers: Canadiana (print) 20220476187 | Canadiana (ebook)
20220476217 | ISBN 9781771965415 (softcover) | ISBN 9781771965422
(EPUB)
Subjects: LCSH: Booksellers and bookselling. | LCSH: Selling—Books.
Classification: LCC Z278 .C66 2023 | DDC 381/.45002—dc23

Edited by Daniel Wells
Copyedited by Chandra Wohleber
Cover designed by Michel Vrana
Typeset by Vanessa Stauffer

PRINTED AND BOUND IN CANADA

To 'rissa, who worked in offices so I could work in a bookstore

CONTENTS

A READER'S INTRODUCTION TO BOOKSELLING

9

BOOKSELLING IN THE REAL WORLD

22

THE FUTURE OF BOOKSELLING IS BOOKSELLERS

38

ON A MOVING TRAIN

The Possibility of Progressive Bookselling

59

TWO PATHS FOR THE INDEPENDENT BOOKSTORE

70

ADVOCACY AND STEWARDSHIP, PEACE AND DESTINY

Indies Introduce, Faces in the Crowd, *and* The Haunted Bookshop

85

GOOD TASTE IS A THING YOU DO

Reclaiming "Good Taste" from Cultural Authoritarianism

104

THE INDIE BRAND PARADOX

116

SOUR CREAM AND OTHER WHITE MISTAKES

Bookselling and the American Dirt *Fiasco*

128

A SONNET, A MENU, A PLACE
Genre in the Bookstore
148

THE LEAST WE CAN DO
White Supremacy, Free Speech, and Independent Bookstores
162

HOW TO READ EXPERIMENTAL WORKS OF LITERATURE
IN TRANSLATION (AND OTHER WORKS YOU THINK
ARE TOO DIFFICULT FOR YOU)
201

TEAMMATES IN THE GAME OF BOOKS
Lessons for Writers from a Writer Who Sells Books
224

TELL ME EVERYTHING YOU'VE EVER THOUGHT
AND FELT IN THIRTY SECONDS
On Connection, Intuition, and the Art of Handselling
244

THIS IS MY MASK
My Bookselling During the COVID-19 Pandemic
263

ACKNOWLEDGMENTS
295

A READER'S INTRODUCTION TO BOOKSELLING

I f books are important to you because you're a reader or a writer, then how books are sold should be important to you as well. If it matters to you that your vegetables are organic, your clothes made without child labor, your beer brewed without a culture of misogyny, then it should matter how books are made and sold to you. This collection isn't *The Jungle* for bookselling and I don't spend that much time on how the sausage gets made, but I do pull back the curtain a bit on these spaces that are so important to readers and writers. For readers, you'll be able to see some of the discussions and decisions that create these spaces in your communities, as well as some of the debates over how those spaces should be created and maintained. You'll also learn some of the challenges bookstores face, in terms of meeting their individual missions, staying open as individual stores, and staying important and sustainable as an industry. Furthermore, by seeing how stores communicate (or at least try to) with readers through the use of space, stock, events, social media, and via personal conversations, and by learning some of the ideas and terms that dictate and organize our efforts, you'll be a better bookstore customer. It will be easier for you to find what you're looking for. You'll ask better questions and get better answers. You'll be more able to support your local store without having to spend any extra money. For writers,

I think it is important to your careers to have a better understanding of that last link in the chain that brings books from
your brains to readers. I've always believed MFA and other
writing education programs and institutions should spend a
significant amount of time on how books are sold and though
this collection won't provide true professional development
for writers, it will at the very least provide some insight and
perspective on the people actually selling your books.

I hope this conversation will be enlightening, or at least
interesting, to everyone, like sneaking out of a brewery tour
and eavesdropping on the actual brewers chatting about
their latest batch, or taking a wrong turn in the museum and
overhearing the curators discussing their next exhibit. But
those eavesdropped conversations are a lot more interesting
if you have some modest background in what they are talking
about. Below are some common terms, concepts, and discussions in bookselling. Some of these you'll encounter directly
in these essays while others form more of the background
and context. All of them will give you a basic overview of
independent bookselling as it exists today:

AMERICAN BOOKSELLERS ASSOCIATION (ABA)

The American Booksellers Association is the trade association for, well, American Booksellers. According to their
website, "Founded in 1900, ABA is a national not-for-profit
trade organization that supports the success of independent
bookstores. This success is assisted through education, information dissemination, business services, programming,
technology, and advocacy."[1] They provide education through
workshops, panel discussions, and conferences, advocacy
through petitions, form letters, and meetings with publishers
and lawmakers, and other supports through a wide range of
information relevant to keeping a bookstore open. They also
manage IndieCommerce, an online commerce platform for

indie bookstores. (See what I did there?) Bookstores also have regional trade associations that provide similar but more focused services and resources. One potentially important clarification is that it's bookstores that are ABA members, and not booksellers. See how it says "success of independent bookstores" above? So Porter Square Books is a member of the ABA, but I, as a human bookseller, am not. What that distinction means for the services the ABA provides or if it actually has an impact on how the ABA interacts with human booksellers is a topic of ongoing discussion.

FRONTLINE BOOKSELLER

A frontline bookseller is anyone who works on the store retail floor and specifically with customers. The person who checks you out at the register at a bookstore is a "frontline bookseller." The responsibilities of working with customers directly are distinct from "back room" or "office" tasks like receiving, buying, returns, marketing, event coordination, human resources, accounting, office management, and all the other jobs a small business has to do to stay open. Unlike in a restaurant, where chefs often don't interact with customers, or in larger corporations or franchises where management is off-site, most people with office responsibilities at a bookstore also work on the floor. Given that the distinction between "frontline" and "back office," is fluid, most of the time I'll use the term "bookseller" to refer to anyone who works in a bookstore, and will only use the term "frontline bookseller" or "bookstore owner," or other specific job titles when I need to distinguish between employees and management or am talking about specific responsibilities.

HANDSELLING

"Handselling" is the term we use for the conversations we have with readers about specific books that we hope will lead to sales. The conversations are composed of recommendations, of course, but also answering questions, or helping a customer choose between a number of different options, or generally providing information a customer will use to decide whether to buy a book, like the age range the book is geared to, what specific type of book it is within the genre, any potential content warnings, its general vibe, and anything else that might not be described in the information on the cover. Quite literally, handselling is putting a book in a customer's hand to sell it.

SHELFTALKER

The tags, notes, drawings, pieces of paper stuck to shelves recommending books are shelftalkers. They ... talk to you ... from the shelf.

ADVANCE READER COPY/ARC/GALLEY

These are the copies of a book that publishers send out to booksellers, reviewers, other authors, and media to build publicity and solicit reviews before it is released, usually before the book is completely finished. Though there are technical differences between "ARCs" and "galleys," especially for publishers, I've always seen booksellers use them interchangeably and will do so in this collection.

BUYING

"Buying" is the process bookstores use to decide what books they will stock. It is the "buying" of books from publishers, distributors, and wholesalers.

SALES REPS

Sales representatives or "sales reps" or "reps" work for publishers. They introduce forthcoming titles to buyers and bookstores, make recommendations based on past sales and their knowledge of a store's character and community, and provide customer service to bookstores. Essentially, sales reps are booksellers to booksellers. Sales reps are a vital part in the chain from author's head to reader's hands. They work a ton of hours, have a ton of responsibilities, often travel a ton of miles, and very rarely get the credit they deserve.

MARGIN

Margin is the difference between the cost of a book to the bookstore and the price of a book to the customer.

WHOLESALER

Bookstores get the majority of the books they stock from two places: publishers and wholesalers. Publishers only sell the books they publish; wholesalers sell books from many different publishers. They're like massive bookstores that only sell to smaller bookstores. Wholesalers are more expensive to bookstores but are useful for two reasons: They often deliver books faster than publishers do, and they provide access to titles stores can't order from the publisher for some reason.

DISTRIBUTOR

It takes a lot of logistics to get books from a publisher to a bookstore and not every publisher has the capacity or desire to handle those logistics on their own, so they use a "distributor," to "distribute" their books. Some distributors are also wholesalers, some are other publishers, and some are just distributors.

IMPRINT

An "imprint" is a distinct division within a publishing company. It's like how universities are composed of distinct schools or colleges. Sometimes that distinction can be very strong, with the imprint operating essentially autonomously, while other times the imprint is more a way to organize the books being published based on their genre or target market. Regardless of how distinct the imprint is from the publisher, the money still all goes to the same place.

DISCOUNT VS. WHOLESALE

The difference between how bookstores get their books to sell and how most other retail stores get their goods to sell is one of the fundamental differences between bookstores and other retail. Most retail stores buy their goods from wholesalers and producers at a per-unit or wholesale price. For example, a grocery store might buy bananas at $0.23 per pound from a produce wholesaler with some minimum poundage order. Then they are free to charge whatever they want for those bananas, marking them up really high if there is a lot of demand, using them as a loss leader by setting the price low, or something in between. In calculating the price to consumers, they figure in the cost of getting those bananas from the wholesaler to the customer, such as staff time, transportation, utilities, meeting health and safety regulations, etc. Then they'll add something on top of that for profit.

This model allows for price flexibility. Bananas can be different prices in different types of stores or at different times of the year depending on supply and demand and the strategies of the specific retailers. Who knows, maybe you live in a town with a crippling potassium deficiency. If so, your bananas are going to be very expensive.

But that's not how books are sold to bookstores. Bookstores usually pay between 45 and 60 percent of the cover price set by the publisher, no matter what that cover price is. So if the cover price of a book is $35.00, the bookstore will pay something between $15.75 and $21.00 for it. This means that the margin is based on a price set by the publishers regardless of what it costs the bookstore to get the book from the publisher to the reader, and whether or not that particular price is the best for that particular bookstore in its particular market. With bananas, the grocery store gets to figure out their overhead and then tack on more for profit. Bookstores can't do that.

TRADE VS. ACADEMIC DISCOUNTS

"Academic" books or "textbooks," intended to be sold primarily to colleges, universities, highs schools, and in other academic settings have a much lower discount than "trade" books. That discount is often 5 to 10 percent or sometimes even *net*, which means the retailer buys the book at the cover price and must mark it up to make a profit. Academic and university bookstores have a captive customer base of students required to purchase these books and so can manage the slim margin through volume of sales, but most regular or "trade" bookstores lose money selling books with those "short discounts." There are a lot of other reasons why a title might only be available at a "short discount" besides being a textbook, but since it all amounts to roughly the same effect—that most indie bookstores can't stock them—I won't enumerate the reasons here.

RETURNS

Why are books sold at a discount off the cover price set by the publisher and not at a per-unit wholesale price? Unlike bananas (and nearly everything else), unsold books can be returned to the publisher for credit. Essentially, books are sold on consignment. Making books returnable was a Depression-era sales technique developed by John Simon of Simon & Schuster to encourage sales to bookstores. And it worked. Bookstores bought a lot more books from Simon. In fact, it worked so well that most publishers followed suit. In fact, it worked so well that, even after publishers realized it had created a massive amount of inefficiency for them, and even after the Great Depression ended, they were kind of stuck with it. So in essence, bookstores get the ability to return unsold copies and publishers get the ability to set the price.

Though knowing all of those terms will help you talk inside baseball with the booksellers in your life, you can't understand the state of independent bookselling today without understanding two forces: the destructive nature of Amazon and the consolidation of publishers and wholesalers. So, even though they're not terms that can be defined, an introduction to bookselling would be incomplete without some discussion of them.

HOW AMAZON IS DESTRUCTIVE

So if books have this inherent lack of price flexibility, how come Amazon's books are so cheap? Amazon likes to tell a story of efficiency, about how their system and business model reduce overhead and how they pass those savings to their customers. But after spending about a year with Porter Square Books as essentially an online fulfillment center during the COVID-19 pandemic, I can say that fulfilling online orders is extremely labor intensive. It doesn't matter how efficient you are at it, a three-item order requires three different items to be brought together from somewhere. With in-store shopping, the customers take care of that logistic themselves. Furthermore, even though online-only retailers might not have storefronts and the associated cost of managing those, you still have to pay for warehouse space and, if one of your goals is to reduce delivery time, you need to pay for a lot of it in a lot of different places. For some reason, we just seem to assume "online" means "more efficient," perhaps because it feels and often can be more efficient for the customer. But whether you type your credit card number into a field in a browser or tap it on a card reader in a physical store, a physical object was transported from one place to another to you and that takes work.

Of course, Amazon buys at a massive volume, one that, even with the discounting model for books, is going to result in a lower price per unit cost than what independent bookstores get. They are certainly able to pass along part of this as a discount to their customers, though it doesn't come close to the 40, 50, or 60 percent discount you sometimes see. One chunk of their discount comes from the fact that warehouse employees are overworked and underpaid, pushed to their absolute physical limits and often dangerously beyond their limits, as has been reported in numerous articles over the years. Honestly, it seems like at least once a year another article comes out exposing an absolute raft of labor violations that Amazon just seems to…get away with. At time of writing, most recently an Amazon warehouse forced their employees to come to work during a tornado warning and six people were killed when said tornado hit the warehouse.[2]

Amazon is also notoriously predatory in its approach to client relations, using its market power to push for deeper discounts still, while unilaterally establishing co-op and other fees to increase their margin even further. Because they account for almost half of the print book market in the U.S.[3] they can demand better discounts by threatening to remove the "buy" buttons from book listings, by removing books from their algorithms, or by just making it difficult for customers to buy specific books. Finally, sometimes those remarkably low prices that Amazon displays aren't coming from Amazon itself but from used book vendors selling "Like New" titles. It's a way to use their marketplace to make it look like their books are even cheaper than they actually are.

But even then, with all that, we still haven't reached those massive discounts. We all know that Amazon sells stuff besides books, but the reach of their business doesn't always get reported. Did you know about Amazon Web Services? It sells a whole bunch of internet and data services and is the primary source of Amazon's profitability. Did you know they also own over forty subsidiaries, including AbeBooks, Audible, Brilliance Audio, CreateSpace, Diapers.com, Goodreads, IMDb, Amazon Robotics, Ring, Shopbop, Twitch, Whole Foods Market, Zappos, and Zoox. They're now also in the media business with their Amazon Prime streaming service. They also frequently cut other vendors out entirely, selling their own branded products, sometimes even (allegedly) copying those products and then elevating their own versions in search returns and algorithms.[4] All of which generates income for Amazon that has nothing to do with books.

So why are books so much cheaper at Amazon than at independent bookstores? How can they make money on books when their prices are so low? Easy. They don't. Amazon intentionally loses money on books and makes up for those losses through other revenue streams. Amazon's prices aren't cheap; they're subsidized. For a more complete consideration of the threat Amazon poses to society and what you can do about it, check out *How to Resist Amazon and Why* by Danny Caine.

CONSOLIDATION

There used to be many more publishers than there are now. Federal policy starting in the Reagan era has allowed, even incentivized, large corporations to grow larger, often by buying their competition. A very specific and narrow interpretation of existing antitrust regulation has allowed that consolidation to go virtually unchecked, resulting in what looks a whole lot like the monopolies that led to the passage of antitrust legislation in the first place. When I started in bookselling there were the "Big 6," the six largest publishers in the United States, which sold the vast majority of books. Since the 2013 merger between Random House and Penguin created an absolute behemoth of a publishing company, there is now just the "Big 5." Concurrently other large publishers like Houghton Mifflin and Workman were purchased by Big 5 publishers. Though the sale of Simon & Schuster to Penguin Random House was prevented by the U.S. Department of Justice, Simon & Schuster's parent company, Paramount, has made it clear they want to offload it and it's hard to imagine anyone other than a big publisher buying it.

Publishers aren't the only point of consolidation in the industry. Not only is Ingram, by far, the largest wholesaler in the country, it is also a major distributor as well. Its actions, decisions, and changes in policies and procedures have immediate impact on bookstores. It is like the jet stream of bookselling. Ingram and the Big 5 aren't immune to the impacts of consolidation either, as the consolidation of the printing industry has left them with fewer and fewer options for manufacturing their physical books.

The hyperconcentration of wealth and power causes problems in any industry, economy, and society, and publishing is no different, but I do want to mention one specific problem that interacts directly with bookstores and readers. In capitalism, consumers are supposed to be able to influence the economy and society by "voting with their dollars." Essentially, if a business is doing something you don't like, don't shop there. I don't know if that has really ever been effective, but it definitely isn't effective in most of our consolidated economy and it certainly isn't effective in publishing. Every large publisher has a "conservative imprint" (or several) that publishes books written from and for the American right. I (and others) argue that the contemporary American right is inherently white supremacist and actively fascist and so, by publishing works from the American right, all the large publishers are aiding and abetting white supremacy by legitimizing it through publication and providing a revenue stream for white supremacists and fascists. The capitalist solution to this problem would be to boycott the big publishers, but that is essentially impossible. First, it would be cutting off support for plenty of books and authors you like, but, more directly, and more specifically from a bookseller's perspective, it would be very difficult to fill a bookstore of just about any size without at least some books from the Big 5.

Ultimately, consolidation in publishing limits our choices for where to get books, makes us vulnerable to the decisions of more powerful entities, and limits our ability to change the industry.

Reading this book won't teach you everything you need to know to become a successful bookseller because: that's not the goal of the book; I don't know everything there is to know about being a successful bookseller; and there is no one way to be a successful bookseller. Because Porter Square Books is what many people would consider a "traditional indie bookstore," that's the type of store I'm going to write most about, leaving out pop-ups, mobile bookstores, bookstore/restaurant hybrids, online-only independent bookstores, used bookstores, antiquarian bookstores, bookstores that exist only as shelves in other local businesses, book-of-the-month-style stores, publisher-owned bookstores (which one could argue are the most "traditional" bookstores), and whatever someone else is developing now that I haven't encountered or can't imagine. Even within that world of traditional indie bookstores, I wouldn't be surprised if some booksellers disagree with my definitions and descriptions of these basic terms and concepts. "Independent" bookstores aren't just independent from Barnes & Noble and Amazon. They're also independent from each other. You'll get a picture of an independent bookseller from these essays, and that picture will likely be accurate enough for many indie bookstores, but not for all of them.

Furthermore, what it means to be a bookstore and how to succeed at being a bookstore has changed many times over the years and will likely change again in the near future. Many of these terms or my definitions of them could be out of date in the next few years. But armed with them, now, you can at least dip your toe in the conversation. And the next time you walk into a bookstore, you'll have a better understanding of everything that goes on behind the scenes.

BOOKSELLING IN THE REAL WORLD

One easy way to increase the sales of a specific book is to stack a whole bunch of copies of it somewhere in the store. Booksellers call this technique "stack 'em high, watch 'em fly." A stack of copies makes that book noticeable both to people who are looking for it specifically and to people just browsing. For those looking for it, the stack is easier to spot than a spine on the shelf, even when it is in the exact place the customer was looking for it on the shelves. We don't see only with our eyes. We also see with our expectations, so if the spine of a book doesn't match a customer's expectations they might not see it even if their eyes physically pass over it. Yes, I assure you, this happens all the time. Since the stack displays the entire cover, it is less likely (though not impossible) for the customer to look directly at it without seeing it. Seeing the entire cover also makes it more likely a customer who is just browsing notices something enticing about it. The title catches their eye, or the author's name, or something visually striking about the art, or they recognize a name on one of the blurbs. They pick it up, maybe read the cover or jacket copy, and decide to buy it.

In bookselling, there are two types of sales: captured and created. With captured sales, the customer is already intending to buy a specific book and the bookseller merely has to do something so that the purchase happens with them. They capture a sale that was already going to happen. With created sales, the customer was not intending to buy a specific book or maybe any book at all, but something in the experience itself, seeing it on a display, getting a recommendation, becoming intrigued by the cover, convinces them to buy it. The store creates a new sale that wouldn't have existed without their efforts. Stack 'em high, watch 'em fly is so effective because it both captures and creates sales by making a book more noticeable. But it's not just the book we notice when we buy something off a stack.

Humans are social animals. We like to be in groups. One easy way to be in a group is to read the book other people are reading. This social reading is most obvious with smash bestsellers. Eventually, "everybody is reading it" becomes a selling point. Eventually, people start reading it so they don't feel left out. Very few books reach this level of popularity, but the emotional mechanics that turn a snowball of sales into an avalanche are at play when the fact of a stack helps nudge a reader to pick a book up. When people see a big old stack of books, they assume there must be a reason the store has so many copies. They'll guess it's already popular or that the store expects it to be popular, or even that the store wants it to be popular. All three guesses, whether they're correct or not, create the chance for a social sale of that book, adding another level of potential sales to "stack 'em high, watch 'em fly."

From a bookseller's perspective, the stack is often as much a consequence of expected popularity as it is an intentional attempt to juice sales of a given book. When we expect a book to be popular, we buy lots of copies of it. If you're going to have a title taking up stacks' worth of space, you might as well put those stacks where people can reach them. But why would a buyer expect a title to be popular?

Buying is a mix of data interpretation, experience with a community's buying habits, and intuition. The data includes an author's previous sales, sales of similar titles, the number of physical copies the publisher plans to print—which indicates how well the publisher expects the title to sell—and its publicity budget—which indicates how much support the publisher is going to give that specific title. There is a significant limit to what that data shows. Just because the author's previous books sold ten copies each at your store doesn't mean the new one will. Just because a couple of other *Gone Girl*–type thrillers are selling doesn't mean this new one will. Just because the publisher is spending a raft of money on publicity doesn't mean that publicity will connect with a store's specific community. But this data is compromised in another way, beyond natural fluctuations in taste and the idiosyncrasies of individual bookstores. There is other noise that I believe too few publishers, buyers, and booksellers grapple with.

We have this image of the writer alone at a desk, scribbling in a notebook or pounding away on a keyboard, locked in a battle with personal demons and artistic ambitions, struggling with the fickle muses to put a unique vision into the world. Regardless of a specific writer's process and how much scribbling and pounding happen where, writers are not isolated from the world. A writer gets to their desk through a life in society, being acted upon by the same forces that act on everyone else. Some writers, just like some people, think and act against those forces, but that does not wholly free those writers from those forces, nor does that process of opposition necessarily remove all of the unconscious biases and other intellectual and emotional baggage we pick up as we grow into adulthood. Furthermore, as Matthew Salesses shows in his book *Craft in the Real World,* systems of power act specifically on the craft of writing, using a particular pedagogy to promote a particular set of values.

Salesses writes:

Our current methods of teaching craft date back to at least
1936 and the creation of the Iowa Writers Workshop, the first
MFA program. The Workshop rose to prominence under the
leadership (1941-1965) of Paul Engel, a white poet from Cedar
Rapids, Iowa, who was invested in what scholar Eric Bennet
calls "Iowa as the home of the free individual, of the poet at
peace with democratic capitalism, of the novelist devoted to
the outlines of liberty. (pp. xiv–xv)

Salesses goes on to show how these underlying principles influenced the pedagogy that solidified into the workshop model that exists as we know it: a model emphasizing the idea of
"voice," while inherently rejecting forms that don't fit into its
read-and-critique structure and prohibiting the writer being
critiqued from responding even when that critique is rooted
in misunderstanding of unconventional narrative forms or
ignorance of the storytelling conventions of other cultures,
identities, and communities. It's important to place Engel's
concepts in their historic cultural context. What writers were
"free individuals" in the United States in 1941? What writers
had "liberty"? Who could be "at peace" with the economy and
government from 1941 to 1965? Furthermore, what types of
stories and narrative conventions would someone like Engel
see as embodying his vision of literature? What "voice" would
he believe expressed successful writing craft? How would he
and the teachers he led respond to works that critiqued the
United States' version of "democratic capitalism?" In 1961, Michael S. Harper was the only African American writer in the
program.[5] In 2006, Lan Samantha Chang became the first
director of the program who was not a white man.[6] Ayana
Mathis became the first African American woman "to hold
the position of Assistant Professor of English and Creative
Writing," at Iowa after she graduated from the program in
2011.[7] Salesses goes on to say, "The Workshop never meant

craft to be neutral. Craft expressed certain artistic and social values that could be weaponized against Communism." (p. vx) Which is not to say that Iowa was or is explicitly white supremacist, but that its founding principles, and Engel's expressed goals, at the very least, ignore the role of white supremacy in the American culture and the literary values they celebrated as universal and canonized as craft.

Given that many, if not most, MFA programs still use the workshop model without engaging with its ideological imperatives, and that many MFA programs still replicate other attitudes drawn from Engel's vision, like prohibiting the submission of "genre" literature, Engel's ideology still has a significant impact on how the craft of writing is taught, and thus, what types of writing and what types of writers produce works that are submitted to publishers and agents. Furthermore, pedagogy, at least in terms of something as subjective as literature, is also a statement of value. Teaching that certain ways of writing and critique are the "pure craft of writing" teaches that those ways are "correct," which teaches that certain types of books are "correct." Obviously, individual teachers can and have found ways to teach the craft of writing with an openness to form, technique, style, and voice, and many writers who have gone through Iowa-style workshops have been able to write with that openness, but that openness was never part of Engel's vision. He wanted to produce more "American literature," as he specifically understood the concept.

Of course, getting an MFA through an Iowa Writers' Workshop–style program isn't the only way books get written and published, but that is also not the only way systems of power influence how books are written and what books are valued. For example, the *Paris Review* was founded as part of Peter Matthiessen's CIA cover. Its "Art of Fiction/Essay/Poetry" interview series, in which major writers discuss their creative processes, might be the second most influential craft institution in the United States. The relationship between the review and the CIA with its cultural and propaganda warfare against the Soviet Union ran deeper than its founding and lasted after Matthiessen left:

> But the Review's archives...shows a number of never-reported CIA ties...including what one editor described as a "joint emploi" where the Congress [for Cultural Freedom] and the Review would team up to share an editor's living expenses and also to share interviews and other editorial content. In its vast quest to beat the Soviets in cultural achievement and showcase American writing to influence European audiences and intellectuals, the Congress may have even suggested some of the famed *Paris Review* interviews.[8]

Furthermore, outside of any direct editorial influence the CIA and the Congress for Cultural Freedom may have had, the funding the *Review* received through these channels gave it an advantage over literary magazines and journals that were not identified as weapons in the culture war. Regardless of the quality of work being published or readers' receptions to it, this funding gave the *Review* time to grow into the institution it is today, and thus have its values canonized as one of the standard-bearers of American literature.

This cultural warfare was also built into Yale's American Studies program, which "has promoted scholarship on the cultures and politics of the United States."[9] It was co-founded by Norman Holmes Pearson, who recruited[10] Matthiessen to the CIA and was the source of funding for numerous conferences, journals, and other publications, primarily in Europe and eventually around the world. Taken together—and in the context of American white supremacy—it adds up to significant direct institutional support for white writers—in addition to all the institutional supports for white people in general—writing with an aesthetic that promoted a specific vision of "American literature" and within a specific understanding of craft, which helped those writers and those books get published at a far greater rate than books by people of other identities expressing other visions of literature.

At least in part as a result of this, publishing is an artificially white industry, even for the United States. A few years ago, the publisher Lee & Low began quantifying the whiteness of publishing by surveying the racial identities of people working in it. They also looked at the identities of protagonists and authors of published books. Quoting work by another researcher, Lee & Low shares that 31 percent of children's books published in 2017 were "diverse," which was the "highest on record since 1994."[11] Though a sign of progress for sure, that 31 percent still doesn't reflect the racial composition of American society, which is 42 percent "diverse."[12]

But the report goes on to show another problem with that apparent progress. "Even as the number of diverse books increases substantially, the number of books written *by* people of color has *still* not kept pace ... *Black, Latinx, and Native authors combined wrote just ... 7% of [new children's books published]*."[13] (All emphasis in original.) Furthermore, "only 29% of books about African/African American people were by Black authors/illustrators."[14] To me, this disconnect between representation in published works and authors from marginalized communities actually publishing books is evidence of the institutional bias Salesses writes about. This is not to say that white people can't write successful stories centering people from non-white communities, but that the institutional biases in writing and publishing have resulted in more white writers capitalizing on our society's desire for non-white stories than non-white writers.

Lee & Low's own study of publishing revealed that "76% of publishing staff, review journal staff, and literary agents are

White." Editors are even whiter than the industry average at 85 percent. None of this should come as a surprise to anyone. As Salesses writes, "In order to become a writer at all, writing has to seem possible as a career path. Reading has to seem as valuable as work, friends, dating, etc. Where does that come from?" (p. xvii) Whether we're talking about general access to education and books or how white and male the American canon of literature has been and still to an extent is, or how writing education specifically values and supports white voices and perspectives, our society encourages white people to read, write, publish, and critique in ways it does not for other identities.

But even when non-white writers do get published, they face challenges in getting the attention of readers. For example, "Many African American writers and commentators ... critique the practice in the U.S. whereby 'only one' or a few Black writers are elevated by white publishing outlets, while many other authors are ignored." Public Books studied this phenomenon by tracking the mentions of Black writers in the *New York Times*[15]:

> Our findings reveal that many Black writers received at least minimal attention in [that] prestigious media outlet. Even so, the vast divide between those who received extensive coverage and those who did not explains why some Black people express concern about the persistence of the "One Black Writer" idea. Only select Black writers ... appeared in more than 1,000 articles. Fewer than 20 writers from our list of 500 appeared in more than 500 articles. That means that a relatively small number of writers ... appeared in far more articles than hundreds of others.

Anticipating a potential critique, the report goes on to clarify:

Some skeptics might argue that the *Times* simply prefers one or two writers above the rest, no matter their race...While the coverage of [Toni] Morrison far outpaces that of her Black writer peers, that is not the case in comparison with white writers, especially in the Books section of the *Times*. John Updike, Philip Roth, and Norman Mailer have been cited in more articles than Morrison since 1970, though she has been referenced in more articles overall than her generational cohort of women, such as Joyce Carol Oates, Joan Didion, Margaret Atwood, and Susan Sontag. Still, those white women writers are much closer to Morrison in terms of citation than are Morrison's Black women peers. That confirms that among major women writers, Morrison is the only Black one.

These data tell a number of different stories beyond revealing the fact of "one Black writer." There is a story of intersectionality, as not only is Morrison outpaced by Updike, Roth, and Mailer, so are Oates, Didion, Atwood, and Sontag. There is a story about the differences between American and European acclaim as Morrison is the only writer on this list with a Nobel Prize. But the story told by that line "especially in the Books section" stands out to me. The imbalance of attention was particularly pronounced in the specific section of the paper of record most connected to and most influential in the publishing industry. If there's "only one Black writer," in the Books section of the *New York Times* you can forgive some readers for assuming there is "only one Black writer," worth their attention.

Ultimately, we get a self-reinforcing cycle: White people are encouraged to go into publishing, white writers are supported and their visions and voices are validated by the craft of writing pedagogy and a number of literary institutions, white people in publishing publish white writers, white critics and journalists cover white books, white books get the most media attention and so books by white authors sell better than books by other people. Because books by white people sold well in the past, they publish and support books by white writers. Because only one Black author seems to sell with any consistency at any given time, they publish very few Black authors and give significant support to even fewer. That imbalance in support leads to an imbalance of sales and those imbalanced sales are used to make the next round of decisions. In some ways, it feels silly to spend this much time showing that something in the United States is racist. Really, the burden of proof should be showing something isn't. But many booksellers approach publishing data as if it were a clean and accurate representation of the desires of readers and the visions of writers, if they think anything of the numbers beyond how they can be applied to potential sales at their stores.

When booksellers use publisher data—past sales, print runs, publicity budgets—they feed that cycle and perpetuate those values. We buy large quantities of the types of books that have sold well in the past expecting them to sell well again. Those large quantities guarantee the books end up on display, faced out on the shelves, and stacked high, increasing their sales in relation to other books in the store. Those sales are fed right back into the cycle to influence publisher decisions and then, of course, subsequent bookseller decisions. As long as we treat publishing data as "pure," as long as we do not engage with the roles of institutional bias and systems of power in creating this data, we will reinforce those systems and biases. If we want to be allies to antiracism, we need to factor the thumb on the scale into our buying decisions. We need to buy fewer stacks of already popular, already well-supported, already privileged white writers and more books by everyone else. If that sounds like affirmative action for selecting bookstore stock, it is. Affirmative action has been used to help diversify many other institutions, so I don't see why it can't be used to help diversify publishing and bookselling as well.

Some might argue that identity-conscious buying is its own form of discrimination and by centering author identities in our buying decisions we support the fundamental mechanism of white supremacy. They might go on to argue that unless we base our decisions entirely on the quality of the book as it relates to our specific store and community, we are being just as racist as the forces we claim to oppose. But, as with the principles of affirmative action in hiring, college admissions, and elsewhere, "race blind" or "identity blind" practices aren't effective at diversifying cohorts because they don't account for the inherent advantages of certain identities. Worse, by claiming a version of subjectivity, this strategy gives cover to oppression by allowing those systems to claim a kind of equity. I mean, publishing ended up so white because people explicitly and intentionally supported white people, making explicit and specific identity-conscious decisions for centuries. If that's how we got here, I don't see how one could argue that we can't get to somewhere else the same way.

If "stack 'em high, watch 'em fly," works, it doesn't matter much what we stack. We can use that space for books we want to sell as much or more than for books we expect to sell, juicing those sales, and breaking the cycle of bias. Furthermore, there are other pretty standard displays that share the same mechanisms of "stack 'em high, watch 'em fly" that we can rethink as well, like bestseller displays. Just like those stacks, bestseller displays leverage popularity to capture and create sales. They can be valuable displays for many stores. But you don't need to display the *New York Times* or a local major newspaper, or even the Indie Next bestseller list which is determined by sales at independent bookstores. You can display your store's specific list. You don't need to do the top ten or top five in fiction and nonfiction, in hardcover and paperback. You can grab a title from farther down and display it as a store favorite. You can rotate some of the genres or suggested age ranges through your display. You can use shelftalkers to highlight specific books on the list if they don't fit into your physical display structure. The *New York Times* list is curated to some extent, so why shouldn't we curate our displays of it? The same goes for a display of titles featured on NPR or even the Indie Next List.

Without additional curation, these displays support books with a ton of resources behind them. Even the Indie Next List, which is generated through bookseller nominations is, at least in part, a function of which publishers send out the most galleys. The ABA now sets aside a certain number of slots specifically for indie and small presses that can't afford a galley flood to even the playing field a bit, but, as with bestseller lists, we don't need to display the top ten or twenty in order. We don't need to highlight the number one pick. We can use the list as source material for a display that speaks more directly to our community and more explicitly to our values. Same goes for a Heard on NPR display, which can also be an extremely valuable display. NPR covers tons of books across many different programs. Perhaps displaying a title from a marginalized author next to whatever was featured on *All Things Considered* will help create sales for it, while still capturing sales of the more prominently covered title.

Could there be other displays that create more sales than these standards? Could displays that readers haven't seen anywhere else generate as many or more sales than the standards? Could a rotating idiosyncratic display drive traffic to the store as readers pop in to see what you've done this month? You don't see a lot of bestseller or Heard on NPR displays shared by readers on social media, but you do see a lot of clever, quirky, and funny displays. That attention is free publicity. What about letting individual booksellers curate displays? Local authors? Loyal customers? I'm not arguing bookstores need to jettison all the standard practices that have worked well enough for many stores for many years or to completely ignore publishing data, but I am advocating that we engage more directly with what that data actually shows and be intentional in how our stock, displays, and other practices support or oppose oppressive systems of power and societal bias.

All change invites risk. Buying in this way may increase the chance a store runs out of something popular or gets stuck with a lot of inventory it can't move. To me, the primary way to mitigate this risk is to build a community of readers who come to your store first when looking for any books, trust your stock enough to take risks on books and authors unfamiliar to them, always ask a bookseller when they can't find the book they're looking for, and always special order the book if it isn't in stock. With a community like this, you will capture almost all their sales whether you are able to accurately guess those sales ahead of time or not. And you will be able to create even more as they will trust your recommendations, both passive and active, and buy them with consistency.

But even using the data as if it is pure, even using standard techniques for buying and displaying, even outright declaring that you couldn't care less why some books sell as long as they sell from your store, there will still be plenty of stacks that don't move. Maybe the cover is bad or it got a bad review or it ends up next to a killer cover on the table and no one notices it in the shine of the other or it just doesn't sell because some books just don't. There are always stacks that eventually get rotated into overstock and then into boxes to be returned to the publisher. At time of writing, I can picture the stacks of *Carrie Soto Is Back* by Taylor Jenkins Reid under Porter Square Books' new hardcover fiction table. Given that it was her first new book since *The Seven Husbands of Evelyn Hugo* became a smash social media hit, buying it in stacks was a no-brainer. But for some reason it didn't sell the way we expected it to. Good buyers will have a strong enough sense of what their customers want to keep the lights on, but even the best buyers will have plenty of misses. If ignoring the forces that influence what gets published, what gets supported by publishers, and what sells to the public doesn't guarantee a thriving and profitable bookstore, what value does that strategy deliver?

In contrast, what value does a strategy that prioritizes the books booksellers want to sell deliver? How risky is buying twenty hardcover copies of a book from an author with no significant past sales if you know someone is going to be handselling it? How effective will the new releases table be if every bookseller can point to at least one book on it and tell customers they are excited about it? What if a significant percentage of faced-out books had shelftalkers? What if a store's community came to understand simply being on display as a kind of endorsement? I'm not arguing that stores should only stock what their booksellers personally support or that they should never carry controversial authors, or that they should never consider the likely popularity of a book in their buying and displaying decisions. I'm not arguing for any kind of absolute. I am arguing that leaning harder into books booksellers want to sell will make it easier to build a community of readers that leads to long-term sustainability and profitability. I am arguing that if we want to be allies for justice in this country, we need to make our decisions with justice in mind. If we're gambling anyway, we might as well bet on books we believe in.

Matthew Salesses writes:

> There is, of course, a kind of writer who believes art is free from the rest of the world, as if he does not live and read

and write in that world... These tired arguments get trotted out whenever writers are asked to take more responsibility for their positions in the world. But reading and writing are not done in a vacuum. What people read and write affects how they act in the world. If writers really believe that art is important to actual life, then the responsibilities of actual life are the responsibilities of art. (p. 6)

If we believe books are important, and I don't see how someone can be a bookseller without believing as such, then how they are sold is also important. Yet we see the same responses from some booksellers that Salesses identifies in writers. They argue booksellers have a sacred duty not to impose their own tastes and beliefs on the readers they serve. Though there are plenty of situations where a bookseller should keep their opinion to themselves, unless you are able to stock every single book ever written, you are already imposing your tastes and beliefs on your customers. "I stock what sells," is still a belief. "I think this book will sell," is still an opinion.

In a perfect world, the best books for all the different uses of books are published, publishers allocate their support for those books based on their content and not only on their inherent sales potential, and critics cover those books fairly. In a perfect world, writing pedagogy would recognize the vast diversity of narrative perspective and storytelling techniques and account for cultural differences in literary values. In a perfect world, everyone would be encouraged to read and write equally. In a perfect world, past sales, print runs, and publicity budgets would be clean data. In a perfect world, every book would fly out of our stores. But we don't live in a perfect world. We live in the real world. In the real world, a small number of massive companies control the vast majority of books published in the United States. In the real world, book sales are a revenue stream and a platform for the conservative and far right movement, empowering the very people most committed to restricting the right to free expression. In the real world, historical and contemporary institutional biases have created an overwhelmingly white publishing and bookselling industry. And in the real world "the responsibilities of actual life are the responsibilities" of bookselling.

THE FUTURE OF BOOKSELLING
IS BOOKSELLERS

first encountered the phrase "The Future of Bookselling Is Booksellers," at the Bookstore at the End of the World, an online community of booksellers from New York City, Chicago, and elsewhere who were laid off or furloughed near the beginning of the COVID-19 pandemic. They were trying to generate income from bookselling while their stores were closed to in-store shopping. Along with a selection of recommended books sold via Bookshop.org, they sold T-shirts, mugs, and other merchandise. I ended up buying their T-shirt twice—mostly because I forgot I'd already bought it—as well as a coffee mug. I actually got through two and half drafts of this essay thinking I hadn't before the mug turned up in the dishwasher.

One could ask, "What else could the future of bookselling be besides booksellers?" but there is a big difference between booksellers and bookstore owners. Some might bristle at a distinction between the two. For many stores, the person who owns it does everything: manages financials, buys the books, shelves, handsells, runs the register. Especially for smaller stores, the owner is likely to be on the sales floor as much, if not more, than anyone who works for them. Still, there is a fundamental difference between someone who can write checks and someone who can't, between someone who decides what health care benefits to provide and someone waiting on that decision to figure other shit out, between someone who decides what is done with any profits and someone not entitled to even know they exist, between someone with the power to fire people and someone who can be fired.

When I started going to bookseller conferences early in my career, I had a lot of peers; other booksellers in their twenties and thirties. There were also a lot of booksellers in their fifties and older. Now that I'm in my forties, my peer group has greatly diminished, both at the store where I'm the youngest old person or the oldest young person and industrywide. There are still many booksellers in their twenties and thirties and many booksellers fifty and up, but fewer in their forties. There is nothing mysterious about this: Bookselling doesn't pay much, there isn't a lot of room for promotion, especially mid-range, and retail work in general, including bookselling, is profoundly undervalued labor in our society.

It is almost impossible to save up the money to buy a house on a frontline bookseller's salary. It's almost impossible to raise a family on a bookseller's salary. And it is also almost impossible to save up the money required to buy a bookstore on a frontline bookseller's salary. Given that, a lot of people who might be great booksellers don't enter the industry. And many great booksellers leave the industry because they can't live anything close to the home life they want or need if they stay. They make it work for a while, maybe relying on a partner's income, or doing freelance writing or some other side gig, but you can only work sixty-hour weeks and cram four people into a three-bedroom apartment for so long. So at about the moment they would be growing into their skills as great booksellers, they leave. Some are able to stay in books by finding better paying jobs in publishing, libraries, or literary nonprofits, but many, with no place to move up, leave books completely.

Of course, just because there are few promotions available doesn't mean there are no promotions available. Some booksellers can stay in bookstores by becoming event coordinators, buyers, or managers. For a lot of booksellers, that's great. A lot of booksellers are also great event coordinators, buyers, or managers. But not all. Sometimes a promotion takes someone away from the tasks they are best at. Sometimes a promotion burdens someone with responsibilities they do not have the skill set or passion for. Sometimes a promotion can set up a valuable and successful bookseller for failure in a role they didn't particularly want but needed to accept to continue to have any kind of role in the store at all.

The net result of this attrition of frontline booksellers (besides the fact that very few people I work with listened to Soul Asylum when they were teenagers or know about @EvilWylie) is that the people actually making the sale, responsible for putting books into readers' hands, providing the customer service vital to the survival of our industry, are often the lowest-paid, least-experienced, and least-empowered members of the staff. Odds are pretty good they are working other jobs, have other gigs, are going to school, or all three. So they're inexperienced, disempowered, underpaid, and tired.

At this stage in my career as a bookseller, I move fucking units. I upsell like a motherfucker. I can't count all the times I've started a spiel while ringing a purchase at the register and before I can finish the transaction the customer says, "Do you have a copy of it?" I've sold books after eavesdropping a few phrases. I've breezed past customers I know, handing them a book and saying, "This is the one you want," and they bought it and fucking loved that I did that. I've handsold based on T-shirts, tattoos, and Twitter bios. There are people all over the country who buy my picks. One person said I was the only white man they would trust with book recommendations. A *New York Times*–bestselling author described me as one of their favorite booksellers. I know the book you're thinking of, who wrote it, where it is in the store, and two other books in the store right now that would go great with it.

A great bookseller can sell what's in stock. This is one of the truths that seems too obvious to mention, but I think too many bookstore owners either take it for granted, don't recognize the scale of the benefit, or attribute responsibility for many of those sales to buying and displaying. I'll return to this idea a few times and in a few different ways in this essay, but a great bookseller is the ultimate backup. Did the store run out of a smash hit? A great bookseller can replace those sales with sales of other books. Did the publisher not print enough copies and so the store can't restock no matter what? A great bookseller can replace those sales with sales of other books. Did the store run out of copies but there are more on the way? A great bookseller can convince the customer to order it rather than walking out without buying anything. A great bookseller can gather preorders, upsell at the register, find books that have gone missing, figure out what the book with the blue cover is, capture orders, and build a reputation of trust throughout the community so people come to your store first when looking for a book.

We see this most clearly during the holidays. In the last two weeks before Christmas, books go out of stock, deadlines are missed, and a miasma of stress hangs over every retail interaction. Booksellers are faced with customers who will either buy a book right the fuck now or never. For a great bookseller, the desperation of holiday shopping creates an openness to recommendation that is also an opportunity. Readers are ready to try something new. They are willing to take risks. The holiday rush is exhausting but rewarding. But for stores that don't have great booksellers, that rely on the stock to sell itself, a lot of potential sales walk out the door to Amazon or a Visa gift card or whatever store is next door. There are so many sales smashed into the fourth quarter these losses can be hard to see, but everyone who walks into a bookstore in December is a potential customer and every person who walks out without buying something is a lost sale.

The skills and assets needed to be a great bookseller include: knowledge of the stock; ability to read body language and tone of voice; understanding the jargon of publishing to interpret book covers, jacket copy, and blurbs to assess books you haven't read; relationships with publishers, other booksellers, and authors to add to the number of books you are substantively aware of; a cache of readers whose opinions you trust enough to apply to books you haven't read; and an archive of books you have read as the primary source of your recommendations. Every single one of those skills and assets takes time to develop. Though there are some teachable skills, nothing replaces time on the floor interacting with readers, nothing replaces time with other industry professionals online, at conferences, and with your colleagues in the store, and nothing replaces the time it takes to read books. A lot, if not most, of that developmental labor is unpaid, fit in around other jobs, social obligations, and, you know, eating dinner and stuff. This is why, as the American Booksellers Association says in the summary of ABACUS, their annual survey of financial and other store data, "Replacing existing workers costs one-half to two times an employee's annual salary, according to a 2022 Gallup study. The cost in terms of sales can be even greater in an industry in which handselling and the knowledge and passion of booksellers are crucial parts of the business's value proposition." There is a cost to paying frontline booksellers more in terms of wages and benefits but there is also a cost to not paying frontline booksellers more in terms of wages and benefits.

Bookstores face legitimate barriers to paying all their employees the wages that would keep frontline booksellers in the business as frontline booksellers. According to results from the 2021 ABACUS, the average net operating profits for an independent bookstore in 2021 was 1.5 percent. Not a lot of room to maneuver in terms of wages or anything else really. Furthermore, profits are really only part of the story when we're talking about wages. Cash on hand, as in the ability to pay financial obligations as they come due, might be more meaningful in terms of wages than profits. Like all retail, the vast majority of profits come in during the fourth quarter and its pathological holiday shopping. For the rest of the year, bookstores generally either break even or operate at a loss. This compression of sales means that for much of the year, even during a year with strong sales, many stores will not have much cash on hand to pay higher wages even when they are confident of December profits. This can be especially true for newer stores or stores with lower credit limits at publishers. Bookstores are usually given an amount of time, from thirty to ninety days, to pay our bills to publishers after we have already received their books. We buy them on credit with the idea that sales of those books will be used to pay the cost of those books. But that line of credit has a limit and once a store has hit that limit, the publisher will stop sending them books, making it difficult for the store to maintain its inventory. Smaller and newer stores often have lower credit limits than larger and older stores and so often need to pay publishers more frequently and in greater amounts to keep the books coming in.

Furthermore, this compression of sales means that bookstores generally have no meaningful idea what their sales for the year are going to be until the year is nearly over. The store may have been able to afford raises while maintaining their inventory and other obligations because the fourth quarter sales are enough to pay down any debt that might have built up over the course of the year. By that same token, there is also always the chance something happens—bad weather in December, a recession, or a fire or some other damage to the store—that fundamentally compromises December sales. Those higher wages then would result in extreme, perhaps even existential, financial precariousness.

It is a fact that it is very difficult to make significant profits in American bookselling today. It is also a fact that many
bookstore owners are paying their booksellers as much as
they honestly believe they are able to. And it is also a fact that
some bookstore owners use the difficulty of the industry as
cover or apology for exploitative labor practices. It is also a
fact that when confronted by their employees about wages,
unpaid overtime, unsafe working conditions, and disempow-
erment from store decision-making, some store owners de-
flect that criticism by saying "I don't even pay myself." Even
when deployed honestly and in full good faith this is significantly problematic.

No matter how it is intended, it is an act of emotional
manipulation, leveraging the "vocational awe" that by itself
is often used to exploit booksellers, librarians, teachers, and
other creative professionals. You are saying that you are making a sacrifice for the store and implying that your bookseller
is being selfish or unreasonable. At the same time, you are
highlighting a massive power imbalance as, again, no matter
how the statement is intended, you are telling your employee that you don't need to be paid for your labor. As thin as
the distinction is (between a bookstore owner who does all
the labor of a bookseller, and their employees) in terms of
day-to-day work, there might be no bigger distinction in our
capitalist economy than between those who absolutely need
income from a job and those who do not. But for me, having
never personally experienced it, but knowing many booksellers who have, I find it infantilizing. If the store can't afford to
give someone a raise, the store can't afford to give someone
a raise. It's arithmetic and store owners should trust their
booksellers to do arithmetic. If, as a store owner, you don't
think your employees will trust your arithmetic without that
additional act of leverage, well, as the more powerful personal
in the relationship, I believe it is your responsibility to earn

that trust. Finally, if you keep the store profits, and many indie bookstores are profitable, you do pay yourself.

Furthermore, a store of any kind should at some point be able to fund its own management. Obviously, it takes time to build a customer base, time to build a community, time to build the brand recognition to run a profitable bookstore, and the most cost-effective investment in the store during this time might be using one's own capital to replace a manager's salary. You don't pay interest on money you already have. But at some point, if the business model is persistently unable to pay for its own management, if it requires an investment of tens of thousands of dollars every year to stay open, I think you need to reevaluate that business model.

Of course, many store owners do pay themselves a salary and many store owners who don't are actually paying their employees as much as they can while keeping the store open and there really isn't a way for me to know what type of store owner you are. With the exception of very rare public statements, like Nicole Sullivan's dramatic exit from the ABA, in which she used an op-ed in the bookselling newsletter Shelf Awareness to explain why she was leaving the trade association,[16] or reportage about an owner's reaction to unionization attempts, the only way an owner's conduct is known is through a bookseller whisper network that tries to warn prospective booksellers away from toxic work environments. To put this another way, if I'm not talking about you, I'm not talking about you.

That 1.5 percent margin may look dire, but it is actually part of a period of consistent growth. Net income after taxes (NIAT), another figure used to describe a store's profitability, has grown steadily since 2013, from -2.0 percent to 6.4 percent in 2021. We have been talking about this time—after the late 1990s and early 2000s die-off caused by Amazon and the big box stores—as an indie bookstore resurgence. Though catastrophic in the short term, the COVID-19 pandemic made people realize how important bookstores and other small businesses are in their daily lives, resulting in a swell of support. To put this another way, it is much more likely that an independent bookstore would have the resources to take a step toward paying their employees a livable wage in 2023 than perhaps in any other year in recent memory.

Though there is no real replacement for higher wages and more power within the organization, I do think there are other ways stores could work toward retaining booksellers within the financial reality indie bookstores face. Here are a few possibilities drawn from Porter Square Books, other bookstores, and my own brainstorming. Every store is different and what works at Porter Square Books won't work everywhere. To me, the goal is less to get stores to adopt these specific techniques and more to get owners thinking creatively and proactively about staff retention. Perhaps none of my ideas would be possible at your store. Perhaps you've already tried some of them or versions of some of them without success. Some stores, in some markets, will need to explore even more radical options, like becoming nonprofits, to be able to pay a living wage. But there is an answer for your specific store, in your specific community, and with your specific booksellers, and you won't find that answer if you don't look for it.

PROFIT SHARING

Committing to higher salaries might be too risky, but once the profits, should there be any, are in, the profits are in. Given that employees also accept some of the financial risk of operating the store (the risk of being one emergency room visit away from bankruptcy) and given their direct role in the generation of profits, it seems fair that they should reap some reward. Individual stores could structure this in whatever way works for them. For example, a store might structure the profit sharing so it only kicks in when certain financial thresholds are met. It can be tied to years at the store or hours worked over the course of the year. It can be responsive to the store's cash-on-hand needs, contingent on certain debts being paid off, or put on a sliding scale. Even if it's not something you can do right away, progress toward it might help retain staff.

CHRISTMAS BONUS BEFORE CHRISTMAS

Porter Square Books has always given annual bonuses to staff before Christmas. By the first or second week of December, we had enough information that we could reasonably project what the holiday season as a whole would be like. From that projection we would calculate what the store could afford and add a percentage to the staff's check before Christmas. Booksellers are also shopping for the winter holidays. A bonus while they are also in need of spending money can be extremely helpful.

STORE FARM SHARES

Buy a few farm shares and let employees take portions of them or buy farm shares for all of your employees as they have done at Oblong Books. Depending on your area and the size of your staff, an investment of a few thousand dollars can provide your staff with fresh seasonal vegetables in the summer. It might not be enough to significantly reduce the cost of living, but it would be something. Furthermore, it would support another important aspect of your community and perhaps create the opportunity for other partnerships. Farm shares tend to be bought in December and January or right when stores have the most available cash.

CLOSING THE STORE THE WEEK AFTER NEW YEAR'S EVE

Every year, Print: A Bookstore in Portland, Maine, closes for a week after New Year's, giving their employees a paid week off. That week tends to be slow in most bookstores and since it comes after the busiest time of the year, stores are more likely to have enough cash to afford it. It is a tangible and immediate way to thank employees for the demands of retail during the holidays.

A PAID READING HOUR

Add an extra paid hour to every bookseller's week as a way to acknowledge the unpaid labor of reading. Yes, booksellers should be people who are going to read anyway, but just because they are going to read anyway doesn't give you permission to exploit that reading. Furthermore, a lot of booksellers read specifically in service to their jobs. I certainly do. An hour a week is far less than what many booksellers will actually do, but it is an acknowledgment of that labor and a little more change in their pockets.

LONG-TERM BOOKSELLER BONUS

The challenge with higher wages is cash flow. Establishing a long-term bookseller bonus, maybe $5,000 to $10,000 paid over the course of a few paychecks or as a lump sum or through some other mechanism, to booksellers after working a certain number of years gets around the challenge of wages by giving you time to plan for it. You can set up an interest-bearing account specifically for these bonuses. In good years, you put in a little more, in thin years a little less. The bonus can be flat and automatic or you could give your booksellers some control over how it is paid. It can be a one-time thing or something paid out when certain thresholds are met. As with profit sharing, and really every other idea here, there are as many different ways to fund and apply this as there are bookstores.

SABBATICAL

Americans, in pretty much all industries, are dangerously overworked and woefully undervacationed. Essentially, American workers "invest" wear and tear on their bodies, intellectual and emotional exhaustion, and lost leisure, communal, social, familial, and personal time into the businesses they work for. An investment they almost never see a return on. Offering long-term employees a sabbatical, a long vacation from the store that does not count against other vacation and sick time, is one way to pay back the employees that made this investment into your store. As with the long-term bookseller bonus, the opportunity to plan years in advance for paying out sabbaticals could make it viable for many stores.

PROFIT SHARING FACILITATED OWNERSHIP

As thrilled as David Sandberg and Dina Mardell were to purchase Porter Square Books from the founders, they felt as though they weren't really the right people to buy the store. The right people to buy the store were the booksellers who made it such a vital community space. But purchasing the store was well beyond the resources of any of the booksellers. Looking to the future, David and Dina wanted to change that dynamic so that when it is time for them to sell the store, they can sell it to the booksellers. So they essentially loaned a number of long-time booksellers the money needed to buy just under half the store and structured the loan so that it is repaid out of the profits ownership entitled the booksellers to, meaning no bookseller needed to have amassed a significant amount of capital to buy into the store. When Dina and David decide to retire, they'll sell the rest of their share through the same mechanism, again so no bookseller will need to have a massive amount of capital kicking around. This solves both the problem of succession and helps with staff retention. In order to work, of course, the store owner must be able to live without those profits, but at least one other bookstore, Raven Book Store in Lawrence, Kansas, replicated this model, and David has given numerous presentations on it.

DECENTRALIZED BUYING

Smaller stores, often by necessity, tend to share managerial responsibilities across the entire staff. Larger stores, also often by necessity, tend to distribute buying responsibilities across multiple buyers. Both of these facts, I believe, show that an even greater decentralization of buying than I have seen is possible. I believe this would lead pretty directly to higher sales. Through their buying responsibilities, frontline booksellers would have an even greater knowledge of the stock, especially forthcoming titles. Through the time they would now be able to spend on the sales floor, buyers would have a more direct connection with how and why books are selling. Booksellers would also feel a stronger connection to the stock as at least some of it would reflect their individual vision for the store. Furthermore, a lot of buying is moving bits of data from one place to another; from the store's point of sale or inventory to a publisher's, wholesaler's, or distributor's ordering system. Many smaller stores share these skills anyway, but for larger stores, imagine if 70 percent of your staff could increase a frontlist order when they happen to notice a bunch of pre-orders or if they could add a title to the restock after selling the last copy. Even if you don't assume this decentralization would lead to more sales, dispersing the tedious parts of buying throughout almost an entire staff will make sales more efficient and responsive. Finally, this decentralization could create some of those mid-range promotions so rare in bookselling. Maybe you don't have space for a full management position, but you do have space for an assistant buyer.

MORE FULL-TIME POSITIONS

Part-time positions are always going to be a part of retail and a part of bookselling and that's fine. A long-term, part-time bookseller is almost as valuable as a long-term full-time bookseller. But not that many people can commit to long-term part-time positions. Those who can are likely to come from typically privileged identities and communities. That doesn't mean they won't be great booksellers, but it does present a challenge in building a meaningfully diverse staff. Full-time offers more pay, more security, more responsibility, more consistent scheduling. For a lot of people, it will create more free time if they can go from several part-time jobs to one full-time job, even if their total working hours stay the same. It can give them an actual two-day weekend. Do you know how many of your booksellers consistently have two days off in a row?

A SEAT AT THE TABLE

Make space for frontline booksellers in your decision-making process. How that works will depend on the management structure of your store. If your store's management structure is pretty much just you, as is the case for many indie bookstores, make time for regular meetings with your staff. In those meetings, allow booksellers to ask questions, offer suggestions, raise concerns, and respond to possible changes. According to the ABACUS survey, 73 percent of indie bookstores have ten or fewer employees, with 42.2 percent having three or fewer. So the vast majority of indie bookstores are small enough that all-staff meetings would be manageable. For larger stores, with more than a handful of employees, you could have the booksellers elect a representative to sit in on management meetings, almost like a union rep. And of course time spent at these meetings would be paid. I don't think the benefit of including booksellers in decision-making is limited to making them feel empowered. The more minds and the more perspectives working on a problem the more possible solutions you may find for it. Furthermore, every bookseller will have a slightly different experience working on the floor, will encounter different customers, and will have to solve different problems. Consistently getting feedback from your booksellers will give you a much more clear and more complete picture of what is happening at your store and why.

OPEN BOOK MANAGEMENT

Make your finances fully open to all of your employees, including salaries and profits, and give them the tools they need to understand the numbers they're looking at. Not only will this demonstrate your trust in them, it will show your employees exactly what you are working with as you make staffing and wage decisions. You won't need to explain to them why this raise isn't possible or these benefits are out of reach when you can just show them the figures. Open book management is a growing strategy in businesses of all kinds because it "helps your employees think like bottom-line business owners...By helping your employees understand how their actions impact profitability, you increase their accountability and tie their daily efforts to your firm's success."[17] As with involving your booksellers in the store's decision-making process, opening the books brings more minds to the challenges the store faces. Maybe one of your booksellers has a connection to an alternative source of some key office supply. Maybe one of your booksellers is an artist who could make greeting cards but never thought of approaching you because they didn't understand how helpful sidelines can be to a store's bottom line. Maybe one of your booksellers used to work at another store that already solved the problem you're struggling with.

None of the above suggestions are true replacements for a living wage, but they can represent good faith efforts toward that living wage. They can be meaningful mitigations of the financial hardships that come with living off a bookseller's salary, while booksellers and bookstore owners work together to reach the level of sales needed to fund higher paychecks.

Booksellers already accept lower wages to work in your store because they feel a connection to books, because they get value from the labor of selling books. You can increase that general value by giving them specific influence over what books they sell, how the store sells them, and how the store creates and manages its space. Even if none of my specific ideas will work for your store, improving the living conditions and empowering your booksellers will help retain staff, increase the quality of their experience working for you, and bring more creativity, passion, and ideas to the problems your store faces.

But "the future of bookselling is booksellers" isn't only an idea for bookstores. It is also an idea for publishers. There are two ways publishers can compete with the power of Amazon: Transfer sales to other channels so Amazon has a smaller market share, or get as big as Amazon to increase their negotiating power. Publishers who have chosen to do the latter—as most have—aren't really solving the problem so much as they are shifting the consequences of a profoundly destructive economic system to other businesses and people. Furthermore, I'm not sure a publisher of any size could ever truly have balanced negotiations with Amazon because Amazon doesn't really need to sell books to survive. Amazon uses books as a loss leader to capture market share of online retail, not to make money. They'll even feature used books from other sellers in order to make their books look cheaper than they are. Amazon has regularly used removing a publisher's buy button from their book listings as a negotiation tactic because Amazon knows the publisher needs those sales a lot more than Amazon does.

When bookstores have more long-term booksellers working on the floor, bookstores sell more books. When bookstores sell more books, publishers sell more books outside of the Amazon channel. If publishers want Amazon to have less power, they need to support booksellers. Publishers could do that directly, as James Patterson does with the Holiday Bookstore Bonus Program that gives cash directly to booksellers, or by funding staff retention efforts at independent bookstores. They could fund some of the programs I recommend above, or raises, or percentages of raises. They could cover health care costs, or pay a housing stipend, or fund grants to pay off student loans. They could use organizations that already exist like the ABA or the Book Industry Charitable Group or create their own.

For example, $1 million a year could fund an extra $10,000 a year for a hundred booksellers. I can tell you from personal experience an extra $10K would be life-changing for those booksellers and would very likely help retain some significant percentage of them who might have otherwise left the industry. That is up to one hundred stores likely to create or maintain year-to-year sales growth through these retained booksellers. All that growth, of course, would be in the indie bookstore channel, chipping away at the dominance of Amazon.

Of course, $1 million seems like a lot of money and publishing has never seemed like a particularly lucrative industry. Still, Penguin Random House had $2.2 billion in capital available to purchase Simon & Schuster. Not only that, PRH also had $200 million available to pay Simon & Schuster's parent company in the event the sale was blocked by the Department of Justice, as it ultimately was. So failing to spend $2.2 billion buying another publisher still cost PRH $200 million, money they apparently had lying around. Prior to that, Hachette bought Workman publishing for $240 million and HarperCollins purchased the Houghton Mifflin trade division for $349 million. For all the "harsh realities" publishing executives claim when negotiating with their lowest-paid employees and for all the support they so often claim to show independent bookstores, when it comes to spending significant amounts of capital they seem to spend it on buying other publishers instead of on those who actually produce and sell their books.

What about $5 million a year? What about $10 million? Obviously, the way capital is gathered for billion- and hundred-million-dollar purchases is different from the way capital is gathered for salaries and wages. Few banks, venture capitalists, or investors would accept the long-term indirect return on investment these programs would create, but publishers do not need that kind of capital to make this investment. If every Big 5 publisher committed $2 million a year toward "industry development," with $1 million going to booksellers and $1 million used for improving the lot of publishing employees, for a total of $10 million a year—a pittance compared to the sales, profits, and cash these businesses have or can leverage—it would absolutely revolutionize the industry. From the example above, that would allow up to five hundred booksellers a year to stay in the industry and up to five hundred stores to see sales growth and cost savings from that very modest investment. Five hundred bookstores represents about 20 percent of ABA member stores.

I'm not just guessing that retaining booksellers through increasing their wages would increase sales. There is data from Porter Square Books and the ABACUS survey that suggests a strong correlation between the two. The average total personnel expense per full time equivalent employee for an indie bookstore in 2021 was $37,326. For the most profitable stores it was $35,427. For Porter Square Books it was $49,310, which does not include the share of profits co-owners like me are entitled to. The net sales per full time equivalent employee for the most profitable stores was $192, 904. For all stores it was $151,500. For Porter Square Books it was $222,507. So although Porter Square Books' cost is about 30 percent higher than the industry average (which I certainly don't see as a bad thing) our sales are about 50 percent higher. Furthermore, median sales per transaction for all stores is $34.18; for the most profitable stores it is $34.70, and for stores with more than $2 million in sales, it's $36.31. For Porter Square Books, it's $47.58. That right there is me eighteen years in the business, upselling like a motherfucker. Finally, the net profit margin of all stores is 1.5 percent. For Porter Square Books in 2021, it was 8.7 percent.

Are these figures definitive proof that retaining employees long-term through higher wages correlates to higher sales and profits? No. Obviously, the sample size is too small and there are other factors between wages and sales and sales and profits for this to be certain, but Porter Square Books has done a relatively good job on employee retention over the long term, we tend to pay our employees more than the industry average, and our sales and profits are strong. And, data aside, it makes sense that people with more experience selling books will sell more books.

The median salary for frontline booksellers in 2021 at stores responding to ABA's ABACUS survey was $30,000. The average was $28,571. It's just not enough. There are a ton of factors, many of them outside the control of booksellers and bookstore owners, keeping both employee wages and store profits low, from the stagnation of the federal minimum wage to the costs of health care, education, and housing; from the relative lack of public transportation in much of the United States to the discounts and credit schedules offered by publishers. It may be true that in this capitalist economy it is nearly impossible to keep your bookstore open without exploiting your employees to some degree. Though I obviously want there to be as many independent bookstores in the country as possible, I think at some point we as booksellers and bookstore owners need to ask: If this business model can only survive through exploitation, does it deserve to survive at all?

Imagine shopping in a bookstore in which a significant percentage of the booksellers have over a decade of experience. Imagine shopping in a bookstore in which a significant percentage of the booksellers have a direct and personal connection to the inventory. Imagine shopping in a bookstore where all of the booksellers are valued, empowered, and feel a sense of ownership and responsibility for the store's character, the communities it cultivates, and the experiences of every person who comes in. What kind of customer service do you think you'd get at a store like that? One of my favorite things to do at the store is help a customer as they rattle off a series of titles from their phones and find every single one of them without having to look them up. (Yes, I kinda like to show off a bit, but that's not my point.) An interaction that could have taken five, maybe even ten minutes, takes two or three. Imagine if most of a store's booksellers could do that. How many more customers could that store serve during the crush of holiday shopping? How much more time would the booksellers have to accomplish other tasks? How much more time would booksellers have for the longer conversations of handselling that build community? How many more books would that store sell?

Despite the financial risk it may present in terms of cash flow, paying booksellers higher wages so they stay longer in our stores may actually be part of the solution to the problem of low bookseller wages because those wages fund themselves several times over. Many stores already embrace the philosophy "the future of bookselling is booksellers" whether they use the phrase or not. It is likely that many more will at least need to make progress toward those ideas in order to retain enough staff to function. And those that do will out-compete the bookstore owners who insist on replicating exploitative business models. A transition to this model is already happening. You as an owner can be an active participant in this transition and benefit as well, because, even if your slice of the pie is proportionally smaller than it has been, the pie will be much larger; or you can hoard every scrap of margin you can squeeze out of a store that sells fewer and fewer books in comparison to your peers while you lose money as a result of constant turnover and the loss of talented booksellers to the stores willing to support them.

The Bookstore at the End of the World petered out as its various booksellers returned to their jobs or moved on. I don't know if the online-only affiliate sales model they used to try to pay the rent during the pandemic is viable as a long-term business model, even with Bookshop.org emerging as an alternative to Amazon for affiliate sales. But I do think their experiment hit on something, something other booksellers in other contexts and with other resources can experiment with, develop, and perhaps draw on to create new, more viable business models. Ultimately, the future of bookselling is booksellers because it's the booksellers who sell the books.

ON A MOVING TRAIN

The Possibility of Progressive Bookselling

n November 2021, I participated in a panel discussion with booksellers and representatives of PEN America about the complicated relationship between bookselling and free expression. In that conversation Derrick Young, co-owner and co-founder of MahoganyBooks in Washington, D.C., said this:

> I'm a bookseller who is Black, right. I have what is called an "African-American bookstore" and I was just doing some research and the interesting thing about how Black bookstores are perceived is that even on Wikipedia it says that Black bookstores are considered to be radical in terms of what we sell, what we are aligned to, whether it's the Black Power movement, Pan-Africanism, it's already putting us in a corner where we are not the norm. When what we're talking about, the voices that we're making accessible in our community and to others are just telling our stories. And that's what I'm here to do every day. To make sure that my community is heard, that whatever their perspective, whether it's conservative, whether it's liberal, wherever they come from, that they have a book that tells their story, that they can been seen and represented somewhere.[18]

Though this was said while discussing how bookstores should select their stock, it resonated with something else I've believed and argued for a long time. There is no such thing as a "nonpolitical" bookstore. Hannah Oliver Depp, owner of Loyalty Bookstores, expressed a similar idea. As reported in Shelf Awareness, Depp said that "as a Black bookstore owner one never makes a 'business decision in isolation.'"[19] When Black-owned bookstores identify their ownership or even just when their ownership is known, everything they do is assumed to be a direct political statement because our culture and our systems of power treat holding the identity "Black" or "African American" as inherently political. The same goes for LGBTQ2+-owned bookstores, bookstores owned by other BIPOC identities, and to some extent even women-owned bookstores. For some, the simple act of existing is a political statement. If marginalized identities are inherently political, all identities are inherently political. To put this another way, if stores owned by marginalized identities have no choice as to whether or not they are "political," then that choice doesn't exist for any other bookstores either.

There is also a Howard Zinnian "You can't be neutral on a moving train," aspect to this, in which all our decisions that have an impact on our economy, society, and culture have some political content—even when trying to be nonpolitical. Within that, bookstores have additional bookstore-specific politics. Unlike grocery and clothing stores, bookstores deal directly with the substance of human thought. They sell, provide access to, and promote materials people use to form political opinions. People use books to develop their morals, support and test their belief structures, come to conclusions about the state of the world, and make voting decisions. A bookstore elevates what it stocks by making those books convenient for intentional purchase and available for impulse buys. Arguing a bookstore isn't political because it doesn't make overt political statements or endorse specific candidates or specific parties is like saying schools, libraries, museums, and the news aren't political unless they openly affiliate with a political party.

I believe there are three ways bookstores can interact with the inherent political nature of bookselling: radical, conservative, and progressive. Radical bookstores overtly and explicitly support specifically articulated ideologies and identities with their programs and stock. Socialist, anarchist, and overtly feminist bookstores are radical according to my definition. Some women-owned, LGBTQ2+-owned, and BIPOC-owned stores would be radical too, but not all of them. Under my definition, many, if not most, Christian bookstores would be "radical," as they focus their stock and programs around specifically articulated ideologies. Though it isn't necessarily relevant to how I'm using the term "radical" in this context, I think it's important to note that those specifically articulated ideologies are often far to the right of what is considered mainstream in the United States today, and so many Christian bookstores should be considered "radical" in the traditional sense as well. We don't think of Christian bookstores as "radical" because our media and culture see "Christian" as a default, hegemonic identity almost no matter what version of Christianity a person or institution adheres to. So a store filled to the brim with forced-birth literature is just a regular old bookstore, but Young's MahoganyBooks, which curates its selection to speak to a wide range of identities in its community, is "radical."

This is not to say that all specialty stores are radical. There needs to be an idea beyond "we want to sell these specific types of books" to meet my definition of radical. A children's bookstore, a cookbook store, a sci-fi/fantasy store, or a store that focuses on works in translation can be radical, just as Black-owned bookstores can be radical, but not all are.

Conservative bookselling understands bookselling to be amoral, displacing all of the moral aspects of books onto writers for what is written, publishers for what is published, and readers for what is purchased. Somehow, according to their understanding, everyone else in the industry has moral responsibility for the industry except for the bookstores. In conservative bookselling, the bookseller's primary concern is logistics; getting the books customers already want to them as quickly as possible, either by having the books in stock or special-ordering them. Curation is almost entirely a sales-prediction skill. Handselling isn't a conversation, it is a simple input/output exchange where the customer inputs a query and the bookseller outputs an answer or recommendation. Whatever else conservative bookstores do in their community is either peripheral to their bookselling or a marketing technique. I use the term "conservative" because I see this conception of bookselling as backward looking, to an apolitical past that never existed, creating a "tradition of bookselling" that excludes many different types of bookstores in order to support its specific definition of the goals and responsibilities of bookselling. I also use "conservative" because this postured passivity inherently supports existing systems of power, which in the United States means supporting a white supremacist capitalist patriarchy. In this political moment it means standing on the sidelines while a variety of white supremacist, neofascist, vulture-capitalist forces contained under the political umbrella of "conservatives" threatens the very existence of American democracy. When you do nothing to change the direction of things you endorse the direction of things. As they say, you can't be neutral on a moving train.

Between radical and conservative bookselling is progressive bookselling. Progressive bookselling acknowledges the inherent political nature of bookselling, that booksellers' decisions influence and are influenced by the systems of power that surround them, that bookselling exists in a political and historical context, and that booksellers' systems, techniques, policies, procedures, traditions, and "common sense" grew within and reflect that context. With that acknowledgment, progressive booksellers have an active and intentional relationship with that context and those systems of power, making decisions and taking actions with those systems in mind. In the United States of America in the twenty-first century that means being cognizant of white supremacy and other attendant bigotries, contemporary American capitalism, catastrophic climate change, and the resurgence of fascism. A progressive bookstore won't act on a publicly articulated ideology like a radical bookstore (at least not all the time), but it also won't pretend it has no ideology, as a conservative bookstore would.

Though there is no such thing as an apolitical bookstore, that does not mean that all bookstores are political in the same way. Activist bookstores make direct political statements and explicitly support specific causes through events, donation, public-facing statements, and curation. They can even endorse specific candidates and parties. They open their space to specific political organizations and organizing efforts. Obviously, radical bookstores, as I define them, are more likely to be activist than progressive and conservative bookstores, but activism is available to all three types of store. There is, of course, a spectrum of activism. A store that historically has been activist can take time off from the work of organizing and activism and still serve their community. A store can take direct political action in response to a need in its community or because a specific bookseller or number of booksellers has the energy for activism. (Raven Book Store's work in support of the USPS is a good example of this targeted activism.) Though I think there's less of a spectrum between thoughtful engagement with our contemporary system and thoughtlessness, there certainly is a spectrum between progressive and radical bookstores as well, one that reflects the different ways booksellers read and interact with books and the different types of communities booksellers serve. Some stores need to carry an ideologically diverse selection in order to survive in their market no matter what books they would most prefer to stock or not stock, while others can specialize and still succeed. "Radical," "progressive," and "conservative" aren't a series of checkboxes; they are guiding principles that help us decide how to be the booksellers we want to be in the world.

So what does it mean to be a progressive bookstore? What does acknowledging our historical and political context look like in practice? Progressive bookselling starts with a simple question: Can I do more than one thing with this act? Can I promote a book I love and nudge the landscape of American literature? Can I connect a book to the right reader and raise up more marginalized voices on our platform? Can I make a sale and support a publisher that upholds my values? The answer to all these questions is, of course, yes. And I bet many of us, if not most of us, wouldn't need to change our reading habits much to accomplish this. Just actively notice the books we've been reading and if it's been all white writers or men or Americans or straight writers or all anything, intentionally add a few books from other communities to our TBR pile. Same goes for recommending titles. Notice what we have been recommending in person, in shelftalkers and staff picks, on social media, in traditional media, and who we are hosting events for, and if it is skewing toward hegemonic identities, skew it back. This sounds like affirmative action for books, whereby we specifically elevate books from marginalized communities, because it is. Publishing isn't white by accident and it won't reflect the true spectrum of human literary creation by accident either.

If a reader lists a bunch of dead white guys as their favorites, that doesn't mean we can only recommend other dead white guys. I mean, Amazon could do that. Shit, Google could do that. Readers come to indie bookstores to learn something, to discover authors they can't find on their own, to be surprised. This creates space to bring those otherwise marginalized voices to readers. We can do this without being judgmental; we can recognize that people end up with reading lists full of dead white men not because of who they are as readers but because those are the authors our systems make most available and describe as most worthy of attention. We can present books from marginalized communities not as prescriptions for a social disease, but as, you know, good books we think the reader will connect with given the books they've read in the past and the reading experience they're looking for now. We can show respect for readers by listening to what they're asking for and by being honest about the books we're recommending. I've made a lot of sales with pitches that start, "Okay, this isn't exactly what you're asking for, but I love this book and here's why I think you'll love it too." We can also show respect for readers by assuming they are willing to try new things, take risks, and read outside their comfort zones. Readers tend to thank me at least as much, perhaps even more frequently, for riskier recommendations, in part, I think, because it's clear I was the only way they'd have heard about the book. There is a difference between respecting a reader's ability to choose books for themselves and assuming a reader will only accept recommendations for comfortable books. One of those feels vaguely insulting to me.

You could argue that the systems of power I'm fighting against demand more dramatic acts than what is implied by "progressive"; that to dismantle a system as radical as white supremacy and as powerful as contemporary capitalism, you need equally radical and powerful action. Bookseller-to-reader recommendations are great and all, but they're not going to halt climate change or protect voting rights. And I agree with that. But no person is just an activist. No person is just a political radical. No person is "just" any one thing.

Those of us who are readers need books for all parts of us. We need entertainment, escape, and leisure, of course, and we also need art that interacts with other aspects of our world, art that explores the nature of language, the composition of the self, the complex relationships between people, and we need cookbooks and fitness books and gardening books, and we also need books that supply substance to our stakes-less interests. And if you're like me, you want to get those in ways that do as little to support oppressive systems as possible. A progressive bookstore gives you the books you need to feel as fully you as possible without having to abandon any morals or ethics.

I think about younger BIPOC booksellers, younger queer and nonbinary booksellers, younger booksellers in general: the people we often say are the future of bookselling, the people who the ABA and individual stores work—or say they work—to keep in the industry, the people who do a ton of undercompensated publicity and marketing on store social media, who then bring their concerns about specific books, specific authors, specific issues to store owners and managers only to be told, "We don't consider that relevant to our decision making," or "It is actually a betrayal of bookselling to bring personal morals to the job." I've seen some conservative responses be thoughtful, articulate, and respectful, and I've seen some be dismissive, a kind of "kids these days with their cancel culture and their TikToks" disrespect. It's one thing to pay poorly. Lots of industries do that. It's another thing to pay poorly and talk a big game. Lots of industries do that too. (There's a reason why managers talk in the language of family and teammates.) But it's another thing to pay poorly, talk a big game, and then explicitly reject the contributions all that big talk was supposed to be about. Unless, of course, they want the energy but not the perspectives. Unless, of course, they think a diverse staff photograph counts as a diverse industry. If nothing else, I believe progressive bookselling is vital for drawing in and keeping a new and diverse generation of booksellers.

Perhaps what I like most about the term "progressive bookselling" is its sense of motion, its inherent incompleteness, its acknowledgment of imperfection. I am not expecting any bookseller to go through an entire career without hosting a problematic author, recommending a problematic book, supporting a problematic publisher, using an outdated term, or making a mistake. Everyone makes mistakes. What matters is what you do after you've made a mistake. Do you get defensive and act as though being accused of making the mistake is more harmful than the mistake itself? Or do you use the mistake as an opportunity to progress?

Progressive bookselling isn't about solving all the problems of society through selling books but about growing with your community and providing the resources for your community to grow through books. It is about being aware of the past while interacting with the present in hope for the future it could lead to. It isn't about judging the choices of individual readers but about recognizing that everyone in the United States, in both their personal and professional lives, has a responsibility to take the antiracist and antifascist actions available to them. It isn't about prescribing books to readers like a nutritionist, but about leading readers to the vast possibility of books and through those books to the possibilities for life.

Perhaps even more than politics, possibility defines my idea of progressive bookselling. Conservative bookselling does not see any relationship between booksellers and what books do or don't do after they've left the store. It cuts itself off from the possibility inherent in literature, books, and reading. To me, there is something sad, maybe even lonely, to the idea that once the receipt is printed your connection to that book and that reader is over. Radical bookselling articulates and works toward specific possible worlds, many of which I want to see enacted. As important and vital as I think that work is, as important as it is to envision tangible, specific futures, radical bookselling has an active relationship only with slices of that spectrum of possibility. That focus is what makes radical bookselling important and effective, and I wish there were more radical bookstores in the world. Progressive bookselling both acknowledges the fact of possibility and maintains an active relationship with it. It shows readers that the world of books is bigger than what we learned in school, bigger than the canon, bigger than a list of classics, bigger than what is covered in the media. And progressive bookselling recognizes that, as much as there is, there can always be more and it helps that more come into being by supporting the writers who are writing it and the publishers who are publishing it. Finally, progressive bookselling recognizes that possibility grows when we are a community instead of a collection of individuals, when we see the relationship between booksellers and readers as collaborative rather than transactional, and when we see providing the opportunity for growth as one of the key services independent booksellers provide to their customers.

Most of us don't end up with the power needed to make any actual change in this fucking world, and those who do usually get there because they pursued the power itself and not the change. Most of us don't have the money to buy politicians. Most of us aren't politicians. And, also, most of us don't end up with the range of skills to become organizers and activists. Most of us aren't movie stars or bestselling writers or professional athletes with wealth and influence. Many of us can't risk being exposed to tear gas. Many of us have obligations that make civil disobedience impossible. Many of us face plenty of challenges just getting to the end of the day. But we all have something. We can all find something to contribute. Some of us can find that something in our jobs. Booksellers can find something in our jobs. Ultimately, the choice is between being an active member of your community through your profession and in a way that might bend the arc of history toward justice and just going home to your life, leaving the problems of racism and fascism and climate change to other people.

Honestly, I don't see how that is a choice at all.

TWO PATHS FOR THE INDEPENDENT BOOKSTORE

A group of booksellers gather at one of their stores for a drink. Most of them are used or antiquarian booksellers. After some small talk, they settle into their standard debate. Though it is clear they have all made the same arguments in the past and that not a single one had been swayed by the entreaties of the others, they recite their points with all the passion of a first foray into an intellectual wilderness. The question is simple: Should booksellers try to influence what their customers buy either through how they stock their stores or how they present the stock and converse with customers; or should they stay out of the way, leaving the customers to make their own judgments and their own decisions without the opinions of store clerks. One argues, "We aren't literary critics. It's not our business to say what's good and what isn't." [*The Haunted Bookshop*, p. 41.] Another asserts, "It is good business to sell only the best." (p. 43) Another asserts with equal vigor, "Wrong again. You must select your stock according to your customers." (p. 43) While another pushes back a bit saying, "It's rather customary in our shop to scoff at the book-buying public and call them boobs; but they really want good books—the poor souls don't know how to get them." (p. 46)

As of 2023 we are still having the same debate. The terms have changed in the hundred years or so since Christopher

Morley wrote this scene in *The Haunted Bookshop*. The threats of Fox News, a fascist Republican party, and catastrophic climate change to our fragile democracy are different from the era of Jim Crow, the Chinese Exclusion Act, and the Alien and Sedition Acts of Christopher Morley's time, but booksellers are still divided by the same fundamental question: Should we influence what sells in our stores?

For those who answer no, the bookstore is simply the place in the neighborhood where people go to buy the books they already know they want. The responsibility for creating that want in the first place is left to educators, critics, influencers, publishers' marketing efforts, book clubs, friends, and family. In these stores, the fundamental relationship is a transaction, and the fundamental skill is knowing what books customers will want. To me, this approach is almost inherently paradoxical. Believing a book will sell is just that, a belief. It is an opinion. It is a subjective statement of value about a book. Hundreds, maybe thousands of times over the years at Porter Square Books, I've heard customers say, "I wasn't planning on buying anything but I just saw this and had to get it." If that book wasn't in the store, the customer would not have bought it. By ordering that specific title, the buyer influenced the reader's decision. Buyers who believe in this approach will do their best to remove their own personal assessments of the books from their buying decisions, using sales data, analytical tools like Above the Treeline and Edelweiss and their own experience in their communities to answer the question "Will this book sell?" But ultimately, it's still a guess. This is not to say buyers and booksellers should never consider customer preference or the potential popularity of specific titles or that buyers should only order books they personally like, but that, no matter how you make the decision, when you decide to carry one book but not another, you cannot help but exert some influence on what books your customers buy.

Furthermore, I think it's important to recognize how difficult curating a store around expected sales can be. Thousands upon thousands of books are published every year. Tastes change and evolve. Trends surge to market dominance and then vanish in a few months. You can never be sure which authors will get a career-making review in the *New York Times* or an interview on NPR, or which authors will have their first week completely buried by coverage of a national tragedy. Good buyers can respond to customer desires in ways that cultivate a sense of trust in customers, they can capture enough sales from specific customers that the stock begins to create sales as well. But it takes a long time to build relationships like this. Buyers and stores need to collect years' worth of sales data to become truly responsive to the reading trends of their specific communities. In the right location, a store will get the years needed to passively build strong relationships with their customer base. But many stores open with high hopes, hang on for a few years, and then close.

For stores that believe booksellers should influence what customers buy, the bookstore is a place of active connection between readers and the world of books. Booksellers also have the ability, if not the outright responsibility, to create desire for books. In these stores the fundamental relationship is the conversation, in-store, online, and passively through the store's stock, and the fundamental skill is connecting readers to books. Though booksellers will still need to shelve, straighten, receive, process special and online orders, count the cash drawers, take out the trash, and everything else that needs to happen to get a bookstore open in the morning to closed at night, space will be made for conversation. Booksellers will be encouraged to get out from behind the desk and talk to readers. They'll be taught to engage readers as they do other tasks, asking readers if they need any help while shelving, recommending something at the register that goes with the other two books in the purchase, tossing an "I loved that book" to a browser while carrying shipping to the back. The processes and workflow for all the vital tasks will be designed to make sure there is time to talk. These conversations and connections don't just sell books in the specific moment, they help booksellers and bookstores turn a customer base into a community.

In "Reinventing Retail: The Novel Resurgence of Independent Bookstores," Professor Ryan Raffaelli of the Harvard Business School studied the resurgence of independent bookstores between 2009 and 2018, a period of time that saw a 49 percent increase in the number of independent bookstores, as reported by the American Booksellers Association. This growth defied the conventional wisdom, which had expected the big box– and Amazon-driven independent bookstore die-off of the 1990s and early 2000s to continue. Raffaelli identified "3 Cs" that contributed to this resurgence: community, curation, and convening. "Independent bookstores," Raffaelli explained, "promoted the idea of consumers supporting their local communities by shopping at neighborhood businesses. Independent bookstores won customers back from Amazon and other big box players by stressing a strong connection to local community values." This, in many ways, is a direct result of the shop local movement, which touts the long-term economic benefits of spending money at locally owned businesses. But Raffaelli found more than just a simple rational cost-benefit analysis. For "curation," Raffaeli discovered that "[i]ndependent booksellers began to focus on curating inventory that allowed them to provide a more personal and specialized customer experience. Rather than recommending only bestsellers, they developed personal relationships with customers by helping them discover up-and-coming authors and unexpected titles." To put this another way, indie bookstores competed with Amazon and Barnes & Noble by leading customers to books they didn't know they wanted. Finally, for "convening," Raffaelli noticed that "[i]ndependent bookstores started to promote their stores as intellectual centers for convening customers with likeminded interests." Taken together, Raffaelli's "3 Cs" reveal a strategy of engaging with customers not only as customers, but as readers and people.

When you engage with people this way, they start to see your store not simply as a store, but as a part of their lives, perhaps even an aspect of their identity. Your store takes up space in their emotional existence. Your store becomes a fixture in their world and, collectively, they go from being a customer base to a community.

I'm reluctant to list the financial benefits stores can see from creating a community instead of cultivating a customer base. It's not that I'm afraid of seeming duplicitous. It's that I reject the capitalist idea that only that which generates profit is valuable. We should build community because community itself is valuable. But building a community does have financial benefits and I believe those benefits are needed to build a bookselling industry that pays a living wage. Unlike customers, community members think of your store first whenever they want a book, not just when they happen to be in the store; they always ask if they can't find the specific book they're looking for rather than walking out when they can't find it, and regularly place special orders for books you don't have in stock. In other words, it is easier to capture the existing sales of a community member than of a customer. The former often create free publicity on social media and generate sales by asking friends and family to shop for them from your store. They also add a layer of resiliency to the store. They respond when a store in distress puts out a call for purchases, they buy store merchandise, they donate to fundraisers.

There are more than enough readers to support ten times the number of indie bookstores that are open now. There's evidence that, despite clickbait headlines, there are more than enough young readers to sustain indie bookstores for decades. Social media has risen, to some extent, to replace the persistent thinning of book coverage in major media. People are hungry for books. People are starving for community. For all its political divisiveness, I think the COVID-19 pandemic heightened those desires. If we can keep society from falling apart, indie bookstores have an opportunity for abundance. I still don't think many people are going to get rich in bookselling, but if we capitalize on this opportunity, applying the lessons of the indie bookstore resurgence, we can greatly increase the number of independent bookstores in this country and, more importantly, those stores could sell enough books to pay a living wage to all their booksellers. But that abundance isn't going to fall into our laps. A community won't just magically grow up around us. We need to commit to those conversations and connections. We need to talk to people about books.

In the world of the twenty-first century, booksellers don't just talk to people in the store, they also talk to people through store content, social media, newsletters, introductions for events, and displays; all of this, whether it includes the opportunity for exchange or is a response to someone else or not, is part of a conversation. Everything a store sends out into the world is an opportunity to make a connection. But content alone doesn't create connection. A series of announcements, whether we're talking about upcoming events, or basic store information like holiday hours, or even links to staff picks on the website, aren't going to build an emotional connection between the store and your potential community. Humans want to talk to other humans, not to brands.

There are a lot of different ways to apply this idea and I'm sure you could find a marketing or social media consultant to take a whole bunch of your money to provide you with content-production strategies, but it doesn't have to be that difficult. Simply empower booksellers to use their personal voices in creating store content. Let them talk on store platforms in the exact same way and in the exact same voice that they use to talk to customers in the store. Does this mean the store won't have a single "store voice" in its content? Yes, that's the point. People don't talk to stores, they talk to people. Does this mean your store's content won't be consistent, that it will speak to different interests, with different priorities, and even different senses of humor? Yes. Readers have different interests, different priorities, and different senses of humor. Giving booksellers the opportunity to connect with the types of people they would connect with if they met them at a party means the store will build connections with those people too.

Many people over the years have told me, online and even in person, that they love the Porter Square Books' social media. They've told me PSB is their favorite bookstore on Twitter or Instagram or TikTok. Sometimes they're talking about content I've created, but often they're not. They're talking about Mackenzie, Caleb, Shana, Hannah, Katherine, Kayala, or someone else. They're talking about the conversations we have that are actual conversations. They're talking about knowing, not just at a factual level but at an emotional level, that they are talking to a real, specific human being when they are talking with "Porter Square Books."

"Be a nerd, not a brand," I exhorted in a workshop I gave with Austin Kleon, author of *Steal Like an Artist: 10 Things Nobody Told You About Being Creative*. Porter Square Books sells books all over the country. We've been a leader in online sales for indie bookstores for over a decade. We've become a tourist destination. Readers make a point to come to Porter Square Books when they visit Boston. A lot of different currents flow into the success of Porter Square Books, but I believe this

commitment to letting our booksellers be people on all platforms and the communities built through this philosophy are
a major part of that success.

For many stores, creating a space for conversation and
allowing booksellers to be themselves in those conversations
are all they need in terms of direct customer-facing actions
to begin building a community. Events, event series, book
clubs, open mics, crafting clubs, opening store space to community organizations, writing groups, social media games,
creative or narrative displays, all of these, many of which are
long-established techniques practiced, even at stores that
see themselves as fundamentally transactional, add depth,
meaning, and substance to the community.

Furthermore, bookstores can build more than one community. Whether you cast the parameters around geography,
generation, or genre, many different communities centered
on or built through books can be nurtured by single bookstores and their booksellers. There's no reason booksellers
should limit themselves to only one of those communities.
Over the years, Porter Square Books has had strong young
adult, romance, queer sci-fi / fantasy, nature writing, mainstream liberal politics, mainstream literary fiction, and small
press / weird fiction / works in translation communities.
Some of those communities grew as we responded to people
shopping in the store, while others were more actively created by booksellers influencing stock, displays, staff picks, and
social media. Each community will need to be tended to in
its own way, but they'll contribute layers of resiliency and
sustainability to the store.

Though it's not as obvious as conversations or events, Raffaelli made it clear curation is a major part of community
building. What stores stock is a statement, not just about
what books they think are valuable, but also about which
readers are most valuable to them, by demonstrating whose

comfort and representation they prioritize. As Candice Huber of Tubby & Coo's Mid-City Book Shop in New Orleans explained in a Twitter thread:

> "Community" can mean different things to different people, but ultimately, we should all have the freedom to build & care for our specific communities, & curation is a big part of that. My store is a queer bookstore. If I carried anti-queer books, that would erode my credibility within my community. I make curation choices not because I want to suppress, but because I want to SUPPORT my community.[20]

Michael B. Tager, managing editor of Mason Jar Press expressed a similar perspective through this story about a bar:

> So the bartender and I were ignoring one another when someone sits next to me and he immediately says, "No. get out." …I asked what that was about and the bartender was like, "You didn't see his vest but it was all Nazi shit. Iron crosses and stuff. You get to recognize them…you have to nip it in the bud immediately. These guys come in and it's always a nice, polite one. And you serve them because you don't want to cause a scene. And then they become a regular and after awhile they bring a friend. And that dude is cool too. And then THEY bring friends and the friends bring friends and they stop being cool and then you realize, oh shit, this is a Nazi bar now. And it's too late because they're entrenched and if you try to kick them out, they cause a PROBLEM. So you have to shut them down."[21]

Both of these statements are real-world examples of Popper's "paradox of tolerance." In *The Open Society and Its Enemies*, philosopher Karl Popper articulated a powerful idea: In order to protect a free society we must be intolerant of intolerance. If we tolerate intolerant forces, those forces will exploit that tolerance to gain control of systems of power and then use that power to build an intolerant society. Whether we're talking about dive bars, bookstores, or the halls of government, if we allow Nazis into our spaces, our spaces become Nazi spaces. In order to create a platform that is tolerant for the widest possible array of humanity, we must exclude those who practice intolerance. Some communities are inherently incompatible, and it does not serve either of them to try to create a space that accommodates both. Your space cannot be welcoming to both the oppressed and the oppressor.

Which makes me wonder: Has indie bookstore curation created stores as welcoming as we assumed them to be? We know romance readers rarely feel welcome in indie bookstores, and the same is often true for sci-fi / fantasy, comics, and graphic novels readers. Some of this discomfort in our spaces comes from booksellers who treat customers asking for these genres with snobbish disdain, of course, but some of it also results from our stock, both what we don't carry and how we display and categorize what we do. We have made great strides in improving our relationships with all these communities, but I wonder how far we can go when some stores insist on stocking misogynists, racists, homophobes, transphobes, and fascists. What would it feel like to pick out a couple of queer romances, turn a corner, and lock eyes with Mike Pence staring at you from his book faced out in the politics section? To wander around the store a bit after a bookseller recommended *Time Is the Thing a Body Moves Through* by T. Fleischmann and encounter J. K. Rowling's latest Robert Galbraith mystery stacked high on the new-fiction table?

Very few people are going to notice every single book you stock, even the ones faced out and stacked high. And even people hurt by the policies and actions of Mike Pence or J. K. Rowling won't necessarily feel hurt by the fact that their indie bookstore carries books by them. But it is a fact that many people have not and do not feel welcome in many independent bookstores. Furthermore, I think it's fair to ask how many of those "unexpected" titles that Raffaelli mentioned in his point about the value of curation are "unexpected" because they come from marginalized identities that typically do not receive significant support from publishers or coverage from media. Curating your selection based only on what sells and without an awareness of how your stock welcomes some communities while repelling others, will mean only those communities reflected by "what sells" will truly be comfortable and welcomed.

Many bookstores have said their customer bases are too conservative to curate their stores toward other communities, even if they would personally prefer to. They say their state or town or city is too Republican for them to stay open at all without sales from the contemporary American right. Every independent bookstore is different, with its own challenges, strengths, quirks, flaws. So there is only so much I can say about specific bookstores, especially bookstores very different from my own.

I would offer two ideas in response to the assertion that some stores need to tolerate the intolerant in order to survive. First, I believe the size of the contemporary conservative movement is greatly overblown because of the disproportionate representation it has in our elected governments, because of how our political journalism presents our current landscape, because super-rich conservatives use their wealth to influence society, and because the conservative movement is so fucking loud and whiny. Most Americans vote Democrat most of the time. When you break it down issue by issue, policy by policy, specific opinion by specific opinion, polls show that more Americans, often even self-identified Republicans and conservatives, agree with centrist, Democrat, and even liberal opinions than agree with conservative or Republican opinions. However conservative your town is, it is probably not as conservative as you think it is.

Second, even if your area is overwhelmingly conservative, it's not entirely conservative. Odds are, there are people in your community with identities dehumanized by the contemporary conservative movement. They deserve spaces that welcome them. They need havens. Bookstores as centers of community are, have been, and have great potential to be those havens. I'm not saying creating a haven bookstore for marginalized populations in your geographic area would be easy. Along with the challenges all independent bookstores face, haven bookstores can be targets for protest, vandalism, and violence. But it is important to remember that our community building is no longer limited to geography. Through social media and online commerce, our communities can include people anywhere we're able to send books. We can be both neighborhood bookstores and national or even international bookstores. A haven bookstore with a strong social media presence, which tells the story of their haven, can make up for the lost sales of conservative titles with sales of their curated titles to distant readers who want to support their haven. I'm not saying all independent bookstores in conservative areas are obligated to be haven bookstores for the many, many populations actively marginalized and oppressed by the contemporary conservative movement, but that it is a more viable possibility than many would assume.

There is, of course, some risk in focusing your store around community-building and conversation instead of around customer bases and transactions. You will lose sales of some popular books because you have made space for other titles. There will be readers who don't shop with you because your conversation and curation does not connect with them. There will be readers who will feel excluded by your store. There are many booksellers and bookstore owners who run their stores as if there is a scarcity of book sales, as if they are in a red-in-tooth-and-claw competition with Amazon, Barnes & Noble, and each other. They chase every expected sale as if any lost sale could be the one that closes them forever. They underpay their booksellers to keep their overhead as low as possible. They don't push against the systemic forces that keep publishing and bookselling artificially white because they believe they need the sales from those forces.

This sense of scarcity didn't come from nothing. The indies die-off of the 1990s and the 2000s left a mark. Like people who lived through the Great Depression who saved every length of twine long after it might be needed, many booksellers who were booksellers during the die-off are managing their stores and making their decisions through the lens of that collective trauma. They act as though any loss of expected sales at any time could put them out of business because they lived through two decades of catastrophic losses. And of course bookstores go out of business all the time. Small businesses close all the time.

But this fear of scarcity can make it difficult for bookstores to find abundance. If we focus entirely on capturing existing sales rather than on creating new sales and on lowering our overhead rather than investing in booksellers, if we try to create a neutral site of commerce, a personality-less node of exchange, in the right locations and with very talented buyers maybe we can keep the lights on, but I don't believe we will ever reach the level of sales needed to pay booksellers a living wage or build the long-term resiliency needed to consistently survive the boom-and-bust cycle of contemporary capitalism. There may not be enough customers to continue the indie bookstore resurgence, but there are definitely enough readers.

The two paths for the indie bookstore are not as distinct as the two paths for the novel that Zadie Smith identified in her essay *Two Paths for the Novel*. Though not every store encourages conversation between booksellers and customers, I've never heard of a store forbidding it. Furthermore, if someone visits a bookstore with any consistency they'll start to form the type of relationship with the store that can grow into a sense of community, especially if they consistently secure or discover books they want on the shelves. Add author events to that mix and the store is likely to build some community whether its ownership or management believes in community as a business strategy or not. Stores that do strive to influence reader purchases are still going to consider the potential popularity of the books they stock in their buying decisions. Unless they are a specialty bookstore, it would probably be wise to carry some bestsellers if for no other reason than sometimes you need to capture a customer's sales a few times before they are open to created sales. But the closeness of the two paths, even the occasional intertwining of the two paths, is not permission to avoid making a choice.

In *The Haunted Bookshop*, Christopher Morley was not neutral in his presentation of the two paths for the bookstore. His protagonist Roger Mifflin passionately argues booksellers should support the books and literature they believe are valuable. "Let the bookseller learn to know and revere good books, he will teach the customer. The hunger for good books is more general and more insistent than you would dream. But it is still in a way subconscious. People need books, but they don't know they need them. Generally they are not aware that the books they need are in existence." (p. 18) To me, outside of the economic advantages, I can't imagine being a bookseller any other way. I love books. I love the way reading makes me feel. I love what happens in my brain when weird shit in a book totally fucks me up. I want to share this love with people. I want to share these books with people. To me, there is something almost sad about the idea that I should somehow set aside my love for books when I come into the store, that I should turn my brain into an organic books database, to think that I have no relationship to the books on the shelves at Porter Square Books after they've been purchased, to believe that the most important thing I do as a frontline bookseller is total a sale and take payment. Sad and lonely.

Bookstores have to make money, of course. Bookstores do need to capture sales. Bookstores do need to respond to tastes and trends. Bookstores will need to follow a bit, even as they lead. But there are many different ways to make money, capture sales, and respond to readers. Some of those ways allow everyone working at the store to be readers, writers, creators, libromancers. Some of those ways allow everyone working at the store to be people. And some ways make it hard to be anything but a clerk, anything but a buyer, anything but an employee. I know where I'd prefer to work. I know where I'd prefer to shop. Ultimately, humans are social animals. Our most natural state is in community. Bookstores can walk the path of contemporary capitalism that reduces everyone to isolated laborers and consumers, scratching and clawing for every single expected sale, latching on to every scrap of margin, or we can embrace community and access the abundance community creates.

ADVOCACY AND STEWARDSHIP, PEACE AND DESTINY

Indies Introduce, Faces in the Crowd, *and*
The Haunted Bookshop

Humanity is yearning now as it never did before for truth,
for beauty, for things that comfort and console and make life
seem worthwhile. I feel this all around me, every day. We've
been through a frightful ordeal and every decent spirit is
asking itself what we can do to pick up the fragments and
remould the world nearer to our heart's desire.

CHRISTOPHER MORLEY, *The Haunted Bookshop*

The chances a book gets enough attention in the world of readers and media to sell a ton of copies are pretty damn low. They are even lower for debut authors who don't have a brand to build from or a record of past sales to inform marketing and publicity. For many authors, their careers started not with smash bestsellers, but with books supported by some number of independent booksellers who created enough sales, both at their individual stores and through convincing other booksellers to support it, for publishers to offer the authors additional contracts.

Household names like Ann Patchett and James Patterson credit their careers to the nurturing their debut and early books received at independent bookstores. To help turn this support of debut or relatively unknown authors into a formal publicity opportunity for its members, the American Booksellers Association established Indies Introduce. Indies Introduce promotes ten debut books for adults and young readers each year, a slate of books selected by a panel of booksellers. It formalizes that support in ways that benefit publishers, authors, and bookstores. For bookstores, it wrangles all the different ways readers have found a new favorite author at an indie bookstore into a single easy-to-remember term. Though not really an award like the National Book Award or the Pulitzer Prize, publishers and authors can use selection like an award in their own publicity. It also creates points of contact, specific booksellers at specific bookstores who already read the books and support them, who authors and publishers might want to partner with or focus on for events, preorder campaigns, or other publicity.

In summer 2013, I was invited to participate in the inaugural Indies Introduce. By that point in my bookselling career, I saw myself as an advocate. As important as it is to help customers find the books they're looking for, if we only do that, the landscape of literature won't grow and change. The same authors and the same types of books will make tons of money while everything else scrapes by or doesn't. Through staff picks, displays, and handselling, booksellers can raise up marginalized voices, small and independent presses, and other books and authors that don't have the resources to gain the attention they deserve, slowly but steadily pushing the world of published and purchased books closer to the true diversity of books and literature being written today. The Indies Introduce program presented another opportunity for that advocacy. Of course I agreed to volunteer.

Over the next few weeks, dozens of galleys and manuscripts arrived. Some were books I would have been interested in, others I never would have picked up otherwise. The chair of our panel distributed the reading responsibilities so no one had to read every single submission and a significant percentage of every submission was read by several different panelists. We rated the books from one to five, in a spreadsheet. From those ratings, we decided which books would be read by the entire panel. Over conference calls we argued for keeping some books and ditching others; the calls got longer and more difficult as we winnowed the number of submissions. Through this process, the dozens of books became the ten Indies Introduce titles for the season.

Coffee House Press submitted *Faces in the Crowd* by Valeria Luiselli, translated by Christina MacSweeney. To quote my (lightly edited) staff pick:

> *Faces in the Crowd* is a subtle, sophisticated examination of identity, authenticity, and poetry. The narrator, a young married writer and mother of two, shares her struggles to write a novel about an obscure Mexican poet, and the novel-in-progress itself, while remembering the time in her life when she became obsessed with him. Luiselli braids the three narrative currents into a brilliant meditation on the nature of creation. Translation hoax. Ghosts on the subway. The demonstrative vocabulary of a clever toddler. The mix of fact and fiction on the page and in the mind. With her first novel, Luiselli has established herself as a brilliant explorer of voice, self, and art.

Since then, it has been a joy to watch Luiselli's career grow and her art exceed the potential shown by *Faces in the Crowd*. Her second novel, *The Story of My Teeth*, incorporates the structural, stylistic, and semantic experimentation and investigation that makes postmodernism important in understanding our contemporary world, while creating a delightfulness unique in the world of experimental fiction. *Teeth* leverages the excavation of language and unconsciousness that made surrealism important while reveling in the silliness that made Dada (in my opinion) the superior current in experimental art. Some of this balancing act must have come from the writing and translation processes. The Spanish original was written as part of a residency connected with the Jumex juice factory (Jumex is a major funder of the arts in Mexico). Luiselli workshopped the individual chapters with the factory workers. To produce an English edition, *The Story of My Teeth* wasn't just translated. Luiselli—who speaks and writes English—worked with Christina MacSweeney to create a new American edition of the book rather than merely an English translation.

Her next publication, the book-length essay *Tell Me How It Ends*, about translating for children applying for asylum in the United States, is moving and heartbreaking. Using the intake questionnaire as a structure, Luiselli explores what it means when we decide some people are worthy of living in the United States and others are not. Here's what I wrote for my staff pick:

> Luiselli introduces us to one of the forgotten figures and tragic heroes of contemporary America: the child who risked everything to come here. Through stories about specific children and consideration of our immigration system, Luiselli sheds light on what most of us would choose to ignore and gives new meaning to the question: Why are we here? Books like this are like dew on a spiderweb, revealing often forgotten and sometimes ignored threads of humanity that connect us all.

Her most recent novel, *The Lost Children Archive*, extends the humanist project of *Tell Me How It Ends* into fiction, juxtaposing those questions of sorting and worthiness with a struggling marriage, a lovely big brother / little sister relationship, and a road trip that tries to combine a personal exploration of history with the rehabilitation of a relationship. *Archive* is heartfelt, profound, and funny without losing the daring that made Luiselli's previous books so enthralling. Here's my staff-pick text for *Archive*:

> Finishing the book feels like the beginning of your own journey, to track down the literary and historic references, to critique a society and culture that "removes" people, to recover the moments from your own life when you realized how big the world around us is, but without any kind of heavy-handed moralizing or didactic injunctions. The characters are so thoughtful and rich that you're inspired to grow so you can have a conversation with them.

At this point, I am invested in Valeria Luiselli's success as an artist and an author.

*

> *You know how much I live in and for books. Well, I have a curious feeling, a kind of premonition that there are great books coming out of this welter of human hopes and anguishes, perhaps. A book in which the tempest-shaken soul of the race will speak out as it never has before ... There is something coming—I don't know just what!* (*The Haunted Bookshop.*, p. 147)

I have a similar relationship with Karen Tei Yamashita and Renee Gladman. I met Yamashita's work much later in her career. She was established, if not famous, with a number of awards, including a National Book Award Finalist for *I Hotel*. As I say in a blurb I submitted for the tenth-anniversary edition:

> *I Hotel* is a brilliant, vibrantly written exploration of politics, identity, radicalism, and activism. Fusing and bending styles, Yamashita's prose sweeps the reader along with the same

manifestos-at-midnight energy that drove the mass cultural changes of the 1960s and '70s. Over the years since I first read it, *I Hotel* has grown in importance to me as a reader, as a bookseller, as a writer, and as a citizen. It is an absolute masterpiece of twenty-first-century American literature.

Over the years, Yamashita's cultural cachet has grown. She even won a lifetime achievement award from the National Book Foundation, but she is still criminally under-read. Her work speaks to a broad range of American experience, ideology, and mythology with a depth and disruption I haven't seen elsewhere. Even when her books are set outside the formal political borders of the United States, she illuminates ideas and issues like immigration, the frontier, and the "self-made man" in ways that reveal the fault lines and failure points of the American "character." I don't think "the Great American Novel" is a real thing, but if it were, I'd argue it's actually Yamashita's *I Hotel*.

Gladman is a harder sell because her work tears at the very threads of storytelling and narrative. She doesn't often use what most people would call "character" and she rarely tells what most people would consider "stories." Using language and narrative to explore the fundamental mechanics of language and narrative is like trying to chop down a tree with another tree, but Gladman pulls it off. As with Luiselli, with Yamashita and Gladman, I am personally invested in their success.

My relationship with *Ducks, Newburyport* feels different. *Ducks, Newburyport* is a thousand-plus-page stream-of-consciousness novel about a woman living in Ohio who supplements her family's income by baking in her home kitchen. *Ducks, Newburyport* is in direct conversation with *Ulysses* and could be read as a contemporary Molly Bloom soliloquy. Perhaps Lucy Ellmann's greatest achievement in *Ducks* is giving profound literary and emotional substance to the miasma of anxiety so many people, especially women, feel living in the constructed precariousness of the contemporary United States. As I say in my staff-pick text, "Rambunctiously political, tenderly personal, and profoundly humanist, Ellmann's simple respect for her protagonist's thoughts, feelings, faults, and successes is revolutionary." It is an absolutely gigantic book, written by a woman, with none of the overt markers of "upmarket literary fiction," with its North American edition published by Biblioasis, a small press in Canada. For all of its brilliance, I knew *Ducks, Newburyport* was going to be a tough sell. So I committed to selling it. I even made a bet with the internet that if Porter Square Books sold a hundred copies I would get a tattoo. We blew right past that. Along with staff picking it, I made it a part of Porter Square Books' social media culture. I passed it on to another bookseller who also loved it and we ended up appearing on a podcast discussing it. For a couple of weeks, it was all *Ducks*, all the time.

When an author publishes a book, they create two distinct objects: the art object and the commerce object. The art object is, of course, the text and all its meaning, emotions, and potential. The commerce object is the book that is bought and sold. My advocacy uses specific books, like *Ducks, Newburyport*, specific commerce objects, to change, as much as I can, the economic and cultural landscape of publishing. Selling *Ducks, Newburyport* was as much about helping the world be a place where books like *Ducks, Newburyport* sell as it was about bringing *Ducks, Newburyport*, the art object, to readers. With Yamashita, Gladman, and Luiselli, it is less about changing the literary landscape—though that is always part of it—and more about creating a permanent platform in that landscape for these authors and their books. It is less about how I can use commerce objects to talk back to publishing and more about how I can lead commerce objects to readers over the course of a writer's career to ensure those writers always have a platform for their commerce.

I've struggled to articulate this idea, especially with the term I should use to describe it. I could nestle it under "advocacy" but for all their similarities, the conversations I have about books like those listed above feel different. The goals are different. The focuses different. I've had a certain word for this in my head for a long time and even though it has some faults it is still the best term I've come up with: stewardship. It's not that I'm leading or guiding the author in some way or influencing their art objects; it's that I'm helping their commerce objects navigate the capitalist field of authorship, bringing them to places where they are most likely to enjoy enduring success. I still don't know if "stewardship" is the most accurate or best possible term, but it is the word that lives in my head to collect all these actions, emotions, and relationships and to keep them sorted from similar but distinct actions, emotions, and relationships. Regardless of whether it's the best term, my life as a steward started with Indies Introduce and Valeria Luiselli.

*

"'Well,' said Roger, 'when literature goes bankrupt, I'm willing to go with it.'" (The Haunted Bookshop, p. 38)

As grateful as I am for the chance to participate in Indies Introduce, I spent a lot of time reading books I did not connect with. It's important to read books you're not sure you'll like. To quote Anthony Bourdain, "If you don't risk the bad meal, you'll never get the magical one." To me, that means if the most important thing to you when ordering from a restaurant or shopping at a grocery store is that you are certain you will like what you get, you will eat along a very narrow path through human culinary creation. This idea applies to reading as well. If the most important thing to you when picking out your next book is that you are certain you will like it, you'll read along a very narrow path through human literary creation, a path most likely defined by the taste you developed as a child or teenager. If that path feeds you, well, that path feeds you.

But if you want to read more broadly, you will encounter books you don't like. Furthermore, there can be value in investigating why you dislike something, drilling down from a vague distaste to something specific about the text itself. Such an investigation could reveal an unconscious bias, or an aspect of your personal taste you hadn't before articulated, or exercise your empathy as you imagine what it feels like for those who do connect with the book. I'm not saying you need to finish every book you start (I don't), or that you should consistently seek out books you know you won't like (I certainly don't), but that encountering books you don't like proves you are taking the risks you need to read along a wide path and provides other opportunities for growth.

Despite the value of reading books you don't like, it's tough to read a bunch at once or several in a row. By the end of the Indies Introduce process, after we had eight or nine of the ten titles, after all of my favorites were either selected or rejected, I got tired. The big pile of submissions felt more oppressive as I got to the top of it. By the ragged end of Indies Introduce, I was in a strange mental space. I wanted to read and was sick of reading. I needed books and I needed to be away from books. Furthermore, it's not like publishers stopped sending me books. It's not like I was on a sabbatical from the bookstore that left me time to catch up on all the non-debut books I wanted to be familiar with. I summited one mountain of books and, from the top, saw another.

*

"There is no one more grateful as the man to whom you have given just the book his soul needed and he never knew it." (ibid., pp. 18–19)

Near the top of the second pile was a new edition, published by Melville House, of *The Haunted Bookshop* by Christopher Morley. According to the flap copy, the book is written, "[w]ith a deep respect for the art of bookselling," so I figured that given my mood it would be a good place to start. *The Haunted Bookshop* is the story of Roger Mifflin, a second-hand bookseller who has settled in a shop in Brooklyn after years selling books out of what we would call a bookmobile. (Those adventures are told in *Parnassus on Wheels*.) In the plot, a young advertising man makes a cold call at the store at roughly the same time a wealthy business owner places his daughter there in a kind of an internship for something like real work experience. Coincidentally, German terrorists are using *The Haunted Bookshop* in a plot to assassinate Woodrow Wilson. (Written shortly after World War I, there's a fair amount of nationalism and xenophobia.) The assassination is thwarted, though not without casualties, and the story has a happy ending, looking forward to a long future of bookselling for the Mifflins and perhaps even a marriage between our young advertising man and the new bookseller.

Of course, the plot really isn't the point. The heart of the book is Mifflin's pontifications on the art and calling of bookselling. It is an exuberant celebration, filled with beautiful quotes about the power of books and the unique joy that comes from being the last link in the chain that gets a book from an author's head to a reader's hands. I read it with a constant smile. It was the perfect book for me in that moment, obliterating any trace of my frustration and exhaustion.

I had plenty of options, of course, a whole mountain of

them, some of which I ended up eventually reading. There was *Shantytown* by César Aira, in which he turns his imagination, wit, and playfulness on the urban crime noir. When described, the plot about a cop destructively desperate to break up a suspected drug ring sounds right at home with significant currents of crime fiction, but this is Aira so everything is a little twisted and the point is much less about crime and punishment and much more about life and mystery. There was *Silence Once Begun* by one of my favorite writers, Jesse Ball. Coincidentally, *Silence Once Begun* is also a weird twist on crime fiction, one that poses a profoundly unsettling question: If given the choice between the truth and a story that satisfies preconceived notions of crime, which would society choose? Even knowing Ball's penchant for upending narrative expectations, I did not see this ending coming. There was also *The Hanging on Union Square*, a wildly inventive, originally self-published novel of leftist politics in the Great Depression written by Chinese immigrant Hsi Tseng Tsiang, that includes, as a kind of epigraph, snippets of its many rejection letters. I actually bought that one after reading about it, but still haven't gotten to it yet. There was also *Seiobo There Below*, in which László Krasznahorkai brings his endless sentences and even endless-er paragraphs from the rain-drowned, misery-drenched Hungary of *Satantango* to a Fibonacci-sequenced exploration of the horror of perfection through stories set in Japan, Athens, and elsewhere. Krasznahorkai's sentences and paragraphs often move in cycles, repeating words, phrases, and details with an off-settedness like the simulacra breakdown of a too often photocopied image. The result, in *Seiobo* especially, is a sense that the prose is too bright to look at. You need to risk the wrath of perfection to behold the beauty of perfection.

There were a lot of conventional submissions to the panel, books that were competent executions of old tropes, tired plots, and exhausted characters. "Conventional," doesn't mean bad. Sometimes we don't want to be surprised. Sometimes we want our expectations met. Even then, seeing the same things over and over, especially in the reading binges required for the panel, wore me out. There were also a lot of solid opening chapters followed by sputtering plots, untaken twists, unchallenged assumptions, and unasked questions. There were also a lot of books that I felt were a year's worth of editing away from being pretty damn good, maybe even special, but, for whatever reason, they did not get that year. I generally gravitate to the weird, the surprising, the unconventional, so reading so much conventional writing left me particularly in search of the strange and the weird. Furthermore, writing is a skill that one tends to get better at the more one does it. Sometimes a first book captures something, a freshness or a fearlessness or a didn't-know-betterness that creates vibrancy, but there is also something to be said for being in the hands of a professional. Looking back on that moment now, I see that the exhaustion at the end of the panel created several different book-hungers. I wanted something strange, something written by a master, something that revitalized my relationship with reading. *The Haunted Bookshop* spoke to one hunger, *Shantytown* another, *Silence* another, *Hanging* another, and *Seiobo* yet another. But since they were all happening at the same time and all stemmed from the same experience, they collapsed in a single desiring rumble. I had hungers, but felt hunger. By feeding at least one hunger Morley and *The Haunted Bookshop* sated me in that moment, allowing me to move out of that strange space and into a new reading life.

*

"I wish there could be an international peace conference for booksellers, for (you will smile at this) my own conviction is that the future happiness of the world depends in no small measure on them and on the librarians." (p. 145)

Along with a number of the other panelists, I presented the inaugural Indies Introduce list over lunch at Winter Institute 2014 in Seattle, Washington. Winter Institute is an annual educational and social conference organized by the American Booksellers Association to provide professional development for booksellers at all different levels of experience and responsibility, including frontline, nonmanagement booksellers. Publishers and sales reps presented forthcoming books. Authors signed books at a cocktail reception. The first Winter Institute I attended was in Portland, Oregon, and I remember the managers of Porter Square Books at the time sent me almost on an exploratory mission, to see if the institute was worthwhile. It was. Attending several Winter Institutes helped to shape my understanding of myself as a bookseller and as a writer, rather than as a writer who was working at a bookstore. I don't think I was the only one who had that type of experience. The program has been so successful that the ABA had to cap overall registration, limit the number of spots any one store could have, and maintain a wait list every year, often several hundred booksellers long. I made some of my closest connections with publishers at Winter Institute. I met most of my closest friends in bookselling there too.

It was very late in the hotel lobby in Seattle. I'd had dinner with Leslie Jamison and a number of other booksellers. This dinner was part of the publicity strategy for what would become Jamison's breakout essay collection, *The Empathy Exams*. I'd sung karaoke with legendary sales rep Carla Gray, food writer and baking educator Kate Lebo, and former bookseller Michelle Filgate. My Eastern Standard brain was muddled by Pacific Time, churned by the exhilaration of the night, and also drunk. Still, there were other booksellers in the hotel lobby and I wasn't quite ready to go to bed. I settled on one of those weird hotel lobby couches next to a bookseller from Australia and a bookseller from New Zealand. Someone was passing around a bottle of bourbon, not quite discreetly enough for the hotel staff, who asked that it be put away. I don't remember what I talked about with those two booksellers from very far away, but I ended up with the New Zealander's business card in my wallet.

A year and a half or so later, I got married and my partner and I decided to go to Australia and New Zealand for our honeymoon. Our friends and family were paying for it so we figured we'd go as far as we could. I dug that business card out of my wallet and sent an email. I re-introduced myself and asked some touristy questions. Where should we stay? What should we do? Along with answers for tourists, Jenna said we could stay at her place, with her boyfriend Stu, two roommates and cat Eleanor the Catton (named, of course, after the Booker Prize–winning author of *The Luminaries*). Jenna mentioned other lodging options, but we didn't really consider them. When someone offers you their hospitality, you take it. We met for lunch outside Jenna's bookstore, the award-winning Time Out Bookstore in the Mount Eden neighborhood of Auckland, got directions to her place, dropped our luggage off there, and went to the museum. Over the next few days we came and went a bit, but found time to hang out with Jenna and Stu. She made us Pavlova. I made American-style chili. It was just a few days, but in those few days, we became friends. Oddly, we didn't talk about bookselling all that much while we were in New Zealand. It felt more like picking up a conversation we hadn't quite finished the last time we'd hung out, even though we'd never hung out before. I remember in the cab ride to the airport for the flight home being sad that we'd probably never see Jenna and Stu again.

I was wrong. Since then, I made sure I went to Winter Institute in Memphis because Jenna would be there. Even though I didn't attend the actual Institute in Washington, D.C., a few years later she was going to be there too, so my partner and I met her a few days before it started. A two-hour flight to a city we already liked was a very small price to pay for seeing a friend from the other side of the world. We even went to Jenna and Stu's wedding in Las Vegas.

I don't know if the Winter Institute is really Morley's international peace conference for booksellers. We don't always concern ourselves with matters of peace. Our focus is often tighter, on our own industry and our own problems. The most important moments almost always happen at the dinners and parties when booksellers, authors, and publishers make connections that grow into relationships and friendships. But sometimes we do concern ourselves with peace. Sometimes we look beyond our store walls to the future happiness of the world. Sometimes we are driven to those conversations, as happened after Roxane Gay's scintillating and excoriating keynote address at the twelfth Winter Institute in Minneapolis. But sometimes we drive these conversations. More and more booksellers are taking responsibility for what the books they sell do in the world, asking how we can fulfill our responsibilities in service to justice. There are more advocates. There are more stewards. Winter Institutes have often been the primary in-person opportunities for booksellers who advocate and steward to meet other booksellers who advocate and steward, to make the connections that eventually grow into networks, that eventually grow into communities of booksellers focused on using their vocation to make the world a better place.

The "future happiness of the world" will be a team effort. No one nation, group, or industry will determine it one way or the other. But books can be a part of that happiness and if they are, booksellers and librarians will play a major role. So whatever Morley himself would think about it, Winter Institute is probably as close as we are likely to get to his international peace conference of booksellers.

*

Did you ever notice how books track you down and hunt you out? They follow you like the hound in Francis Thompson's poem. They know their quarry...Words can't describe the cunning of some books. You'll think you've shaken them off your trail, and then one day some innocent-looking customer will pop in and begin to talk and you'll know he's an unconscious agent of book-destiny... That's why I call this place the Haunted Bookshop. Haunted by the ghosts of books I haven't read. Poor uneasy spirits, they walk and walk around me. There's only one way to lay the ghost of a book, and that is to read it.
(pp. 112–113)

I would have read *The Haunted Bookshop* eventually. I was too close to Melville House at the time and too connected to Dustin Kurtz, who sent me a copy of it, to let it linger very long after I got it. I loved my work at the bookstore and my growing identity as a bookseller too much to let a book written "with a deep respect for the art of bookselling" molder on my to-be-read pile. I was easy quarry. Perhaps the easiest quarry Morley's love song to booksellers has ever had.

But destiny is a funny idea. You really only know for sure you were destined for something when it happens. Before that, it's just one of many potential occurrences surrounding your life. To me, destiny is more an act of interpretation, a way of making the things that happen in your life part of a story, rather than some predetermined plan the universe has for one's life. Humans are story animals. We want the things in our lives to fit into a narrative. We want events to have meaningful connections to what happened before and what happens after. We want our lives to have plot points and character arcs. Often, you don't know a book was hunting you until you've been caught and only then you remember seeing it on a friend's shelf or on social media or hearing someone talk about it. You become hunted only after you've been caught. Honestly, I've always found the idea of "destiny" to be more palliative than productive, a way to make us comfortable with the state of the world no matter what that state is.

But books are different. They exist to be interpreted. They are stories we are supposed to use for our stories. They inherently serve our need for narrative. Destiny, as palliative and as a productive narrative act, is built into books.

My reading life changed dramatically when I starting thinking of myself as a bookseller. I chose books based on whether I thought I could handsell them. It took an even more coherent direction when I started seeing myself as an advocate and a steward. I seek books to advocate for. I seek authors to steward. I choose the books I read carefully and very rarely stumble into something. I became the hunter. Sometimes I miss my previous reading life. The one without self-imposed reading obligations, when personal desire was the only consideration. Sometimes I look at the books I bought on a whim, like *Temptation* by János Székely or *Monsterhuman* by Kjersti Annesdatter Skomsvold and wish my priorities allowed me to read them right away, instead of keeping them on the unread shelf for years. Which is not to say that I never stumble into books, as happened when I discovered the work of Victor LaValle from a review of *The Big Machine*. Or that I never get to those books I stumble into. Packing up for a move inspired me to finally start *Ash Before Oak* by Jeremy Cooper, another book I first heard about from Dustin Kurtz. But those are exceptions. The vast majority of the books I read, I read intentionally for specific reasons.

When Anthony Bourdain ate at El Bulli, the legendary experimental Spanish restaurant, they presented him with a choice before the meal: "control" or "submit." He didn't hesitate. He chose "submit," because when you are being served by an expert you get out of the fucking way and let them be an expert. For the vast majority of people, they will never choose a better meal for themselves than Ferran Adrià can choose for them. There is a kind of joy that only comes from submitting to the expertise of another. You turn your meal over to destiny. But there is also joy in following one's own expertise. It feels good to be good at something. It feels great to be great at something.

I don't know if I would have been invited to participate in the Indies Introduce panel if I was not reading so intentionally as a bookseller. I don't know if I would have discovered Karen Tei Yamashita or Renee Gladman or *Ducks, Newburyport*. I don't know if publishers like Coffee House Press, Graywolf Press, Dorothy, a Publishing Project, And Other Stories, Biblioasis, Deep Vellum, Sandorf Passage, or any of the other small presses I'm connected to as a bookseller would consistently send me books if I did not read so intentionally. I don't know if I would have picked *The Haunted Bookshop* for that moment in my life if I hadn't already had practice intentionally selecting the next book I would read.

My reading life is much different from the reading lives of most readers. My goals are different, my needs are different, my wants are different. But the same books are meaningful to many different readers. In many ways, handselling wouldn't work without this flexibility. Maybe reading wouldn't work without this flexibility. A reader can both "control" and "submit" to a book. They can give themselves over to the book, submitting to whatever idea of fate they hold, assert their own interpretations, wrestling the book into material for their own personal stories. So Morley's idea of a "book destiny" has a wrinkle to it that I'm not sure Morley himself intended. Every hunter seems "cunning" to the prey that has been caught. How else could a book catch me after all? Luck? Everything in your life could be your "destiny," if you interpret it through that lens. Every book you read could be a book you were destined for. I wouldn't say I was destined to be the libromancer I am today. I wouldn't say my fate was determined after the Indies Introduce panel or the Winter Institutes or reading *The Haunted Bookshop*. But I was on the Indies Introduce panel, I did become a steward for Valeria Luiselli, I attended a number of Winter Institutes, and I read *The Haunted Bookshop*, and here I am, calling myself a libromancer, writing about bookselling. I wonder what Morley would say about all of that. I wonder if he would see the same connections I do. I wonder if he would agree with how I think about bookselling. I wonder if he'd see the love for bookselling that I bring to my critique of it. And I wonder, if the mechanisms of linear time broke down enough for Morley to read *The Art of Libromancy*, if he'd feel caught by this hound and if he would set it on the other readers in his life.

GOOD TASTE IS A THING YOU DO

Reclaiming "Good Taste" from Cultural Authoritarianism

R eaders all over the country seek out my staff picks. They regularly take my recommendations both in-store and online. I can sometimes hand a book to a familiar customer and tell them to buy it with no other explanation and they will. One reader trusts me enough that she purchased a gift card that she keeps at the store so I can buy and set aside for her any book I see that I think she'll like. I think all of that offers evidence that I have good taste in books. I've always thought of "good taste" as the ability to discern aspects of things that other people can't, aspects that have a complexity or subtlety that requires some level of expertise to discern. Through formal training, a lot of experience, and often both, someone with "good taste" can see what other people cannot. Readers thinking you have good taste in books might be the pinnacle of achievement for a bookseller. It means you can sell a ton of books both in general and in terms of the specific titles you want to support. Whether we're talking about "good taste" that is rooted specifically in me as an individual bookseller that is built up over a number of successful recommendations or a more general good taste rooted in the fact that I work as a bookseller at Porter Square Books, "good taste in books" is something I want to have and be known for. But "good taste," even in books, hasn't always been used to help people connect to the things they're likely to enjoy. It has often been used to police access to power, marginalize communities, and reinforce existing privilege, and to argue that some specific experiences, perspectives, ways of creating art, and entertainment are "universal human experience."

Though there are experiences we could describe as universal, though we're all born, we all die, we all eat and drink, people in power have often used good taste to argue that their interpretations or versions or perspectives on those universal experiences are "normal" or the "standard," and to judge art created from different interpretations, versions, and perspectives to be inferior. This idea of a standard version of humanity is wielded as an emotional weapon. Just about everyone has been made to feel like shit because someone with "good taste" declared that something they love is bad. We've been made to feel inferior because someone with authority is shocked we haven't read this book, listened to this band, watched that movie. Which is not to say that people can't be inspired to grow when they are shown a gap in their experience, but that there is a significant difference between presenting a gap in someone's reading to them as an opportunity to grow if they choose and presenting a gap in someone's reading as proof they are inferior. No one wants to feel shitty, so we read that book, listen to the band, watch that movie, and make ourselves like it. (Or least we tell people we do.) This version of good taste, then, acts as a kind of cultural authoritarianism, using positions of power and emotional manipulation to homogenize creative expression in service to the culture of systems of power.

The book-world version of cultural authoritarianism most likely calls up the image of the snooty English professor; an elbow-patched, pipe-smoking, grand arbiter of literary value who is visibly appalled when he discovers one of his students hasn't read Hemingway or Carver. It is one thing for this professor to explain to his student that he designed his course with the expectation his students would have read these authors in previous classes, show them they will have a richer experience in the course if they can catch up on their own, and guide them to the most relevant texts those authors have written. It's another thing to give them poorer marks because they don't get references to these works or to call out the student in class. The former is an act of education, while the latter is an act of power. In the indie bookstore in the twenty-first century, we're more likely to think of the lit bro who is probably fine if you skipped Papa Hemingway, but smirks with condescension when he hears you haven't read Krasznahorkai. He may not have the power to tank your GPA, but he certainly has the power to ruin your trip to the bookstore. As much as I want to have good taste in books, as much as I want to use that status to sell books that I think make the world a better place, as a college-educated, cisgender, heterosexual, masculine-presenting white man, I need to be cognizant of ways people like me have used "good taste" as an act of cultural authoritarianism to manipulate culture, denigrate creations from other identities, and empower themselves at the expense of others.

For me, I think the first step in making sure I don't practice cultural authoritarianism is recognizing a simple fact: No one needs my opinion about books. Even if they ask for it at the store, they don't need to take my recommendation. This might be the biggest distinction between what I want to do as a bookseller and what I want to avoid. Rather than relying on my position as a bookseller at an independent bookstore, or as someone with a college degree in literature, or as a critic who has reviewed books, or as a writer who has written them, to confer authority on my opinions I need to put in the work to make my opinions influential.

The thing is, I love Krasznahorkai. Sure, he's difficult. Sure, reading him has become something of a status symbol. Sure, a lot of white dudes with beards and glasses evangelize for him. Frankly, it's not unreasonable to assume that someone like me recommending Krasznahorkai is going to rely on the emotional manipulation of cultural authoritarianism. But nobody writes sentences the way he does. They move in complex cycles, doubling back on themselves to retread ground in slightly altered ways the second, third, even fourth time around. Rather than straight lines or branches, Krasznahorkai's sentences could be diagrammed as curlicues and spirals. Sometimes, as in *Chasing Homer,* this style evokes a sense of lostness, of turning a number of directions with increasing anxiety before taking a hesitant step. Other times he writes with an almost unsettling precision. Reading *Seibo There Below* feels like watching someone repair the same intricate clock over and over again. Other times, as in *Baron Wenckheim's Homecoming* and *Satantango,* the sentences walk the border between floundering and dancing, so it's impossible to tell a panicked whirl from a precisely executed twirl. Even other writers known for their long sentences don't construct them the way Krasznahorkai does. For example, Proust's long sentences branch out like architectural plans, enfolding wide arrays of tightly organized details and contexts before tapering back to their focus. Reading one of Proust's long sentences is like walking through a perfectly organized museum exhibit from start to finish. To me, this style gives Krasznahorkai's work, no matter how fantastic the events depicted are, a fundamental realism. Most of the time, life doesn't move the way linear, easily diagrammed sentences do. Life moves two steps forward, one step back. Events in our past return to impact our present. We try the same thing over and over again. We make little hesitant changes. We regret those changes. We regret not changing. In a way, stories composed exclusively in linear sentences add artificiality to what they depict through that stylistic choice.

If the paragraph above convinces you to give Kraszna-horkai a try, great. If it doesn't, that's fine too. In contrast with the cultural authoritarian version of good taste, it really doesn't matter what you think about my arguments; the fact that I say Krasznahorkai is worth reading is all it takes. In this good taste, who I am is what matters. This is the difference between influence and authority. This is the difference between a version of expertise that helps people make decisions for themselves and a version of expertise that tells people what to do. This is the difference between a version of good taste that accepts that different works will connect with different people and a version of good taste that is used as a justification for denying certain people access to power, influence, and advancement.

So rather than declaring Krasznahorkai better than other writers, in my job as a bookseller I discern and describe what makes Krasznahorkai different from other authors to help readers decide if they want to give his work a try. Some distinctions between books are easy to encapsulate in the descriptions and summaries publishers include on book covers. Anyone can read the summaries of two books, say a crime novel set in the roughly contemporary United States and a speculative fiction set around the Civil War and decide which one they prefer to read. However, important facets of books are not contained in plot summaries that can fit on the back cover. Plot is only one way that *The Trees* by Percival Everett explores historic and contemporary American racism differently than does Colson Whitehead in *The Underground Railroad*. *The Trees* critiques the police procedural genre in support of a broader interrogation of the relationship between historical narrative and the persistence of white supremacy, while toying with readers' assumptions about what we should consider "realistic" and what we should consider "fantastic." It is overtly weird and through that shows just how weird the ideology of white supremacy is. In contrast, *The Underground Railroad* combines historical and speculative fiction into a story that will feel traditional to many readers only to dramatically undercut plot as a narrative mechanism itself and critique the ability of stories to reflect reality in productive ways. Rather than using strange events to critique reality, it challenges the realism of any story that does not factor in the random shit that happens in the world. The challenge in fighting white supremacy doesn't live in fighting its most dramatic expressions but in deracinating its deep and hidden roots from the mundane aspects of life we barely notice.

To see and articulate these deeper distinctions of narrative between *The Trees* and *The Underground Railroad* one needs to have an understanding of police procedurals, historical fiction, and speculative fiction, as well as some understanding of the techniques of narrative writers use to create emotional and intellectual impacts. It would also help to have read other books by Whitehead and Everett to see these works in the contexts of their oeuvres, along with works by other authors, like Walter Mosley and Toni Morrison, who explore similar themes and experiment with similar techniques. Cultivating this level of discernment requires reading both broadly and deeply to develop a sophisticated understanding of a wide range of books, In other words, to see distinctions deeper than plot summaries you've got to read a ton of books and you've got to read them closely.

Articulating these distinctions does more than just help people make decisions. When I describe a book to a reader, I want to do more than just convince them to buy it. Humans are language animals. We understand the world through language. We experience the world through language. For example, until I started reading and paying attention to descriptions of wine, wine always just kind of tasted like wine to me. I could tell a white from a red from a rosé, of course, but tasted with little subtlety beyond that. Learning wines could be described as having "minerality" or a taste of "graphite" or "grass" unlocked those sensations in my mind. I needed the words before I could taste the flavors. We can't ask for what we can't name. Often, we can't even experience or feel what we can't name. So that articulation of distinction doesn't just help people make choices, it also helps them have richer experiences reading the books they choose by giving them language for those experiences.

Sometimes those distinctions do include value judgments. Sometimes I do want to tell a reader that I think this book is better for what they want than that book. But declarations of quality, declaring this book "good" and that book "bad" is a fundamental aspect of weaponized good taste, one that brings together assumed authority and those incorrect assumptions of "standard" human experiences. Rather than thinking in terms of "good" and "bad," I think about books in terms of "success" and "failure." Does this book achieve the goals I think the author set for it? Does it meet my personal needs? Is it likely to meet the needs of this reader at this moment? What impact could it have on the social, cultural, and literary context in which it exists? When I answer those questions, I do so assuming different readers might answer them differently. "Successful" and "failed" are still value statements. I'm still using my expertise in books to assess the quality of books, but "quality" rooted in specific contexts that acknowledges subjectivity is significantly different from a "quality" rooted in an assumption of universal quality. The former rests on acts of influence, while the latter relies on power and authority.

Ultimately, we're all people with different skills and interests who made different decisions about how to spend our time and so developed different resources. To me, a humane practice of good taste means using the resources I've developed to discern distinctions between books and to articulate those distinctions while being honest about my own subjectivity and cognizant of the specific contexts the books exist in to help other people make good decisions for themselves and have better experiences with what they decide to read. I can do this without denigrating works that I don't find successful or readers who love those books. I can do this so readers who want to are encouraged to strive for deeper reading experiences outside their comfort zones without depicting everyone who hasn't read the books I think are important as bad readers. I can open gates. I can lift up. I can inspire readers to want to be lifted.

One might ask: If "good taste" can be used as a weapon of cultural authoritarianism, why bother creating a humane version of it at all? Why can't we just let people like what they like and find what they find? After all, most of us have access to a near infinite database of books, book reviews, amateur reviews, ratings, and opinions. Perhaps the easiest solution to the historical and contemporary weaponizing of "good taste" is to abandon it all together.

But having a near infinite database isn't always helpful. If you don't know what you're looking for or how to sort that information, it's easy to drown in that ocean of data. With online shopping, library networks that lend across branches, and websites like Project Gutenberg that provide easy access to public domain books, the contemporary reader can choose from damn near every book ever written. The number of choices we face can be so overwhelming that we are more stressed having to choose than excited to enjoy what we've chosen. Psychologist Barry Schwartz calls this phenomenon the "paradox of choice," and it is one of the reasons we so often watch the same movies and order the same things at restaurants. (Not that there's anything wrong with returning to favorites.) Good taste can solve this problem by winnowing down the choices to manageable numbers. If nothing else, "Josh said it was good," is one solution to the paradox of choice.

But I think humane good taste offers more than just a practical solution to the paradox of choice. First, readers "just finding what they find" will usually find the same books other readers have already found; classics, canonical titles, current bestsellers. They'll find books already well supported by existing systems. If what's popular meets your reading needs, that's fine, but if you want to have a broader reading life, you'll need to do some work. If you're willing to put in the time and you have some googling skills, you can dig beyond the books currently being adapted into movies and high school English class staples on your own. Many readers do. But if you don't have those skills or don't want to spend that time, getting a recommendation from someone with "good taste," like a trusted bookseller, will help you get to those underknown and undersupported books without hours of research.

More important, we need to recognize that oppressive forces in our society are not "letting people find what they find." Oppressors in the United States have always sought to control who reads what, from making it illegal to teach slaves how to read to removing topics from school curricula and textbooks to the book bans and attacks on libraries so prevalent in the 2020s. Oppressive forces are doing everything in their power to make sure the only books readers—especially young readers—find are books those forces approve of. By guiding readers beyond the first page of a Google search return and especially by bringing books by marginalized populations to readers, this humane practice can be an antidote to those oppressive forces. It can lead readers to books contemporary conservatives in particular and oppressive forces in general would prefer no one read. It can open what fascists strive to close.

Furthermore, by guiding readers to less mainstream books and books by and about marginalized identities and communities, humane good taste can de-marginalize those populations. The more we read about an identity, community, or experience, the less alien it is to us. Even if those identities are dramatically different from our own, seeing them with frequency removes the sharp edge of difference that conservatives use to create fear and distrust. This can have a general impact on one's life as well. Being comfortable reading about specific different communities and identities makes it easier to be comfortable whenever you read something from outside your typical experience.

Also, the language of distinction itself helps this de-othering process. There are good reasons to be wary of people you've never met or things you've never done. Trying something new can be scary. But new experiences are less scary when you have the tools to understand them. By giving people language to describe what they are reading, those unfamiliar books become more approachable and people are more likely to have a positive experience reading something unfamiliar making them more likely to continue trying new and unfamiliar books.

This isn't about presenting a homogenized version of the unfamiliar so it is more likely to be palatable. That can often do more harm than good. Rather, it is about introducing what is different in positive ways and giving people the tools to have positive experiences with it. The goal isn't to make it seem as though everyone is ultimately the same, but to create a culture that celebrates difference. This, I think, was one of the great triumphs of Anthony Bourdain's work. He never tried to adapt the cultures he was exploring for his audience. He never took the people, the places, or the food out of their local contexts. Rather, he strove to present what makes these places special in ways that celebrated that specialness. Through this openness without appropriation, Bourdain was able to show, more than any other person I've encountered, just how fucking big the world is and just how incredible it is to live in it.

The number of books I've read will always be far, far less than the number of books I won't. It seems like every time I move a book off my TBR pile, three more books have already replaced it. Some might find that expanse of books daunting, perhaps even frustrating. I'm sure many readers feel like their TRB pile will loom over them, scowling with disappointment when they die having left so many great books unread. But I am not daunted by the expanse of books I'll never read. I am thrilled. I think it's beautiful that I could read books forever, and forever encounter the unfamiliar. To me, that proves the breadth, depth, and fundamental substance and significance of the human experience. To me, reading is an infinite journey and I want to bring as many people along with me as I can.

Weaponized good taste argues that only some of us are truly worthy of the power of art and literature. It argues that only some of us are capable of discerning the true quality in books and that everyone else should follow that vanguard. It can be easy to believe many books are out of your reach, that you are only capable of appreciating the most conventional or most familiar books, that challenging books are just for professors or lit bros who want to show off for each other. But if you are literate, you are almost certainly a better reader than you think you are. You have the skills to interpret so-phisticated images. You can be comfortable with ambiguity. You are capable of approaching the unfamiliar with curiosity instead of fear. You can be adventurous in exploring that infinite world of books with or without a guide. And if you want a guide, I need to continue reading adventurously and developing my expertise so I am always worthy of whatever influence I have.

Ultimately, perhaps the biggest difference between the humane good taste I'm trying to cultivate and the weaponized good taste used as a tool of cultural authoritarianism is the latter is something you have and the former is something you do. Humane good taste is a practice. It's not about possessing expertise but about using whatever expertise you have developed to enrich the lives of others. It is not about hoarding whatever influence might come with that expertise but about sharing it with others. It's not about occupying a position of authority but about communicating what I think and what I know in ways that are impactful and evocative to other people. It's about what I do, not who I am. The world of books is so fucking big. If I want to claim I have good taste in books, I have a responsibility to bring as much of that world to as many of you as I can.

THE INDIE BRAND PARADOX

When Porter Square Books reopened for in-store shopping after the COVID-19 pandemic lockdown, we limited capacity and enforced a couple of basic health protocols. This created a new job: a mix of greeter, maître d', and bouncer. Being a masculine-presenting cis white man—the identity in our society most people are most likely to associate with authority—and generally affable and patient, I ended up working "the door" on almost all my floor shifts. Along with keeping track of the number of people inside (I bought a stitch counter) and reciting and enforcing the protocols ("Mask on and over the nose, we're asking folks to limit their stays to about twenty minutes, and grab a little hand sanitizer on the way in."), I also fetched curbside pickup orders for customers who didn't want to come in or had just ordered online ahead of time. We'd offered curbside pickup for online orders almost as soon as employees were allowed back into stores and for several months before we reopened to in-store shopping. (We also added a free media mail shipping option and a local delivery service.) Adding curbside pickup (or "front door pickup," I guess) required significant infrastructure development, including workflow processes and physical shelving. At its height, curbside pickup orders filled two levels of plastic shelving the full length of the café's twenty-or-so-foot bar, a full row of boxes below the bar, two modular metal shelves, a few additional bookcases of various dimensions scrounged from the store, and a separate space for oversize bags, all of which was right at the front door. It wasn't an appealing visual, and it gave the impression of a far greater volume of sales than was actually happening, but every single customer who came into the store walked past visual proof of online ordering.

Working the door also involved a strange additional emotional labor. I had girded myself for customers pitching fits about capacity and masks and such, but almost never encountered any of that viral-video nonsense. (See above about being an affable white dude.) What I did not expect was how many people would gush joy, excitement, and a strange kind of relief at me. For many people in our community, the bookstore was the first elective store they went to after the lockdown. For many people, returning to Porter Square Books was a return to their community, even if it was just for fifteen minutes, even if it was after waiting outside for twenty minutes, even if the booksellers who usually chatted with you as they led you to a book were stuck behind plexiglass frantically fulfilling online orders. It was great in a lot of ways, but I often felt a responsibility to match or at least validate their positivity. After a few weeks of working the front door, it became a strange and exhausting emotional space. I mean, I'd been here the whole fucking time. Eventually I landed on "Welcome back," as my standard response. It was validating and honest and didn't ask any more of them or of me.

A customer came into the store a couple of months after we had been open this way. "This is my first time back," she said with that breath of relief as she walked by me and all those shelves of curbside orders, rubbing the sanitizer dry on her hands. I was about to say, "Welcome back," when she continued: "I'm so glad I don't need to shop at Amazon anymore."

The general indie bookstore publicity strategy in our competition with Amazon is pretty straightforward: Remind people of the value they get when they shop at indie bookstores. That value is composed of service only a human can provide in person: conversation, camaraderie, connection. Handshakes. Dog treats. Safe space for the kids. A free flip through the *New Yorker*. Personalized recommendations developed through conversations and relationships rather than generated by an algorithm tracking sales and searches. That value also includes direct and indirect economic benefits. When you shop locally, more of your money stays in your community through store spending, employee spending, and state and municipal taxes on all of that. To put this another way, indie bookstores compete with Amazon by developing a national brand that associates "indie bookstore" with "community." Professor Ryan Raffaelli, in his paper "Reinventing Retail: The Novel Resurgence of Independent Bookstores," found evidence that the national "community brand" is effective.

However, there is a side effect to the indie bookstore brand. In many customers' minds, the ideas of "community," "personal service," "conversation," and other iterations of the brand are associated with "old-fashioned," while shopping online is associated with "modern," which is itself associated with "convenient." Even though it's the twenty-first century everywhere, customers assume we are unable to provide a lot of services we have been able to provide roughly as long as there have been bookstores or as long as we've had computers. My two "favorite" expressions of this assumption are "Are you able to see if you have a book?" and "Are you able to order books?" Next is "Oh, do you have a website?" and "Can I order books from you online?"

In some ways, this side effect only creates a mild annoyance. Practically, it doesn't really make a difference whether a customer asks "Will you look up a book for me?" or "Are you able to look up a book for me?" because we still look up the book for them. The same goes for ordering books, both in-store and online. But in other ways there is a definite cost. For every customer who asks if we are able to order books there is some number who assume we can't and don't bother to ask. For every customer who asks if we have a website and if one could order books through it, there is some number who assume we don't or assume they can't and don't bother to find out. We met one of them earlier in the essay, our friend who believed she *needed* to shop at Amazon to buy books online. It's essentially impossible to know if this is a significant problem or not. Much like showrooming (customers finding books they want in stores and then buying them on Amazon) we can observe the fact of it, but the scope of it is much more difficult to discern. That said, we also know our friend who thought she *needed* to shop at Amazon is not alone. Amazon's profits jumped 220 percent during the COVID-19 pandemic when virtually all retail shopping moved online.[22] Of course, at the time online shopping was really the only safe shopping available, so some increase in Amazon sales was bound to happen. But many locally owned stores of all types, from bookstores to hardware stores to specialty stores, which either already offered online shopping or quickly added it did not see that same jump in online sales. Instead, they struggled to stay afloat. Too many customers assumed Amazon was their only online shopping option even when they had locally owned alternatives.

Of course, this isn't just about misperceptions. This is also about diversity in business models and first impressions. Even though it is the twenty-first century everywhere, independent bookstores have different relationships to available technology. Some bookstores choose not to sell books online. Selling online requires an investment of time and money and not every store believes they'll get the sales required to justify those investments. So it is absolutely possible to ask a specific store, like Three Lives in New York City, if they sell books online and be told they don't. Furthermore, a decade ago, fewer stores sold online, so your chance of being told no was higher. Even just before the COVID-19 pandemic, many stores that had the capacity to sell online didn't promote that capacity. So for many people, when they formed their personal first impression of an "indie bookstore," its perceived capabilities might have been more limited than they are now or just different from those of other stores.

There is also an inverse to this paradox. "Independent" really only describes the ownership of a bookstore. It says nothing about the quality of the store or its moral, ethical, and social values. When a bookstore says they are "independent," or "indie," all they're really saying is that they are not part of a chain. But there are a ton of different ways to be "not a chain." Those ways include the kind of "mom and pop" locally, family-owned business structures we most strongly associate with the idea of "independent" and "indie," as well as ownership structures like co-ops, employee ownership, and management group ownership that are pretty close to "mom and pop." But those are not the only ways "independent" bookstores are owned. Some are owned by extremely wealthy people whose money came from elsewhere. Some are owned by investment groups. Being owned by someone rich or being owned by an investment group doesn't guarantee a bookstore won't embody "indie bookstore values," but being owned by a local family doesn't guarantee the store will embody those values either. Which is the point. "Independent" isn't really meant to tell you a whole lot about a bookstore.

Perhaps the perfect example of this is the Strand, New York City's iconic city-block-size bookstore. The Strand was founded in 1927 by Benjamin Bass and was able to survive the Great Depression, in part through an informal rent deferment agreement with the landlord. The business passed to Benjamin's son Fred, who was able to purchase the store's building in 1996 for $8.2 million. The current owner is Nancy Bass Wyden, who returned to the store after briefly working at Exxon in 1986 and who became the sole owner after her father died in 2018. She is married to Senator Ron Wyden of Oregon. As I said, just because a store is profitable (enough to afford an $8.2 million building in 1996!) or the ownership has income elsewhere, doesn't mean it won't embody community values, but the Strand's response to the COVID-19 pandemic was profoundly troubling.[23]

"The Strand was approved for a PPP [Paycheck Protection Program] loan of $1-2 million to retain 212 jobs. Given that those jobs were not actually retained, workers in the store want to know where the money went."[24] Those same workers had to fight tooth and nail for the PPE and other equipment they needed to operate safely. Managers took on floor responsibilities even though union contracts technically forbade that. "Most jarringly for the workers she employs, however, Bass Wyden also purchased between $222,010 and $600,000 in Amazon stock." Ama-fucking-zon. A fact that we only know because U.S. senators like her husband need to disclose certain financial holdings. "Some current and former Strand workers suspect their boss isn't particularly interested in running a bookstore at all; instead, it seems she is more driven to leverage The Strand's independent history into a boutique brand, and she is taking the pandemic as an opportunity to do so."[25] After all, she was the manager who "supervised the rollout of The Strand's official bookish merchandise, including T-shirts and totes," long before other bookstores started selling merchandise to compensate for sales lost during the COVID-19 pandemic.[26]

On October 23, 2020, Bass Wyden put out a call for support. She talked about her memories essentially growing up in the Strand and what it meant to her family. She talked about the resiliency the Strand had shown over the previous ninety-three years of its existence. She closed by saying, "We need to mobilize *the community* to buy from us so we can keep our doors open until there is a vaccine."[27] (Emphasis mine.) Bass Wyden didn't mention the fact that she owns Amazon stock and the building, and she doesn't account for the PPP loan. Nor does she mention her personal wealth. According to Open Secrets, in 2018, her husband, Senator Ron Wyden, was worth $6,877,025.[28] Despite being essentially unique in the bookstore world, with, at the very least, the resources to purchase hundreds of thousands of dollars in Amazon stock, Bass Wyden's call for community support could have been written by just about any owner of a long-standing bookstore. The call worked:

> Ms. Wyden said the call for help produced a boom in business on Saturday; a single-day record of 10,000 online orders, so many that the website crashed. That day was also the best single day in the month of October that the flagship store, near Union Square, has ever had and the best day ever at the Strand's Upper West Side branch...In the 48 hours since the plea went out, the store processed 25,000 online orders, compared with 600 in a typical two-day period.[29]

For some sense of scale, though a store the Strand's size is always going to have more sales than most stores, Porter Square Books processed 37,000 online orders for the entire year of 2020. I'm not saying I want the Strand to go out of business, or that it can't have a community, but am noting that the nationally cultivated indie brand that was designed to help stores in much more precarious financial positions compete against Amazon certainly helped their cause and their finances even though the Strand is essentially unique among independent bookstores.

Though the Strand may be the most prominent example

of an "independent bookstore" profiting off their "indie" brand while not upholding all the values typically associated with "indie," there are many independent bookstores that don't pay their workers as well as they could, that fight against minimum wage increases, that maintain unsafe work spaces, that demand unpaid labor (above the standard amount of unpaid labor demanded by the book industry), that fight unionization efforts, and/or that are owned by people who personally support municipal, state, and federal policies through activism, donation, or votes that are harmful to their employees, their environment, and/or the rest of their society and community.

Furthermore, being run by human beings, who can make mistakes and be inconsistent, indie bookstores can also make mistakes and be inconsistent. Tattered Cover's open letter to its community ostensibly defending the right to free speech and the value of making space for different opinions was so poorly timed and so shortsightedly, even callously, articulated that it did significant and potentially irreparable damage to the store's brand, even after the store issued an apology. The response of the ownership of Politics and Prose, another nationally or even internationally respected bookstore, to its employees' unionization effort, in not immediately voluntarily recognizing the union and more significantly retaining the notorious anti-labor law firm Jones Day, displayed a fundamental misjudgment of the context of the contemporary labor struggle. Even though they eventually voluntarily recognized the union, this misstep communicated a disconnect between the ownership and the laborers. And since the vast majority of bookstores are far too small to warrant *New York Times* articles or investigative reporting even on the local level, odds are you'll never know if your local "indie" bookstore is really as "indie" as you think it is. Just to make things more complicated, it is entirely possible for a store owner to conduct themselves and make business decisions from a

Strand-ish perspective while their frontline booksellers, who are in direct conversation with customers, either in the store or on social media, project and uphold those values. That's not a case of the booksellers being duplicitous, but of booksellers upholding their own personal values and commitments in a disempowered position, and owners profiting off the sales generated by that more progressive, or equitable, or just, or "indie" branding of their store.

It's not hard to see the source of these "paradoxes." In a way, the idea of a "national brand" for "independent" stores is a paradox in and of itself. If all the stores are "independent" from each other, how can they create a coherent national brand? If there is enough overlap to create a coherent national brand, how "independent" are they? What does "independent" actually mean if all it tells us is "not Amazon or Barnes & Noble"? Wouldn't it be better if all the stores just cultivated their own brands?

All good questions and all absolutely blown up by the presence and actions of Amazon. As reported in *The Everything Store* by Brad Stone, Jeff Bezos saw the publishing industry and especially smaller publishers as "sickly gazelles" for Amazon to chase down like a cheetah. This took the form of raising prices and removing titles from recommendation algorithms to pressure publishers into better terms. Better terms Amazon used as part of a strategy that involved predatory pricing, sales tax avoidance, and lobbying for preferential policies and taxes at all levels of government, to almost wipe out bricks-and-mortar bookstores. This perspective speaks to a kind of perversion of the economy. Though capitalism is (ostensibly) driven by competition, competition is not an inherently predator/prey relationship. It isn't (or at least it shouldn't be) about devouring your competition but outperforming them, generating profit because what you make is better and what you do is better than other businesses offering similar goods and services. Seeking growth through predation in some ways undercuts the entire ideology behind free market capitalism, all but guaranteeing that it's not the people and businesses with the best ideas that succeed, but the people most willing and able to undercut their competition.

Physics gets really weird around black holes. That much mass distorts space so things stop working the way we expect them to. In a lot of ways, yes, a "national brand for independent bookstores," makes no sense. Yes, it would probably be better if all independent bookstores created their own individual brands. But Amazon is such a massive and destructive force in the economy that coping with it will generate some weirdness. Furthermore, Amazon is not the only black hole–equivalent entity in the book industry. Though big publishers may not be as overtly aggressive as Amazon, the continued consolidation of publishing into fewer and fewer massive publishers impacts indie bookstores and the book industry in general. Indie bookstores need to do something, and coping with the confusion of a paradoxical "national brand of independent bookstores" is far preferable to a continuation of the indie bookstore die-off.

One possible solution is to collapse the already artificial separation between "convenience" and "community." The baseline convenience we enjoy today, the speed and ease of procuring goods and services, would look like a torrent of fucking miracles to people not just centuries ago, but in, like, the 1950s. And that ease and speed are having dire consequences for our environment, with the fuel and packaging needed to ship stuff that quickly all over the planet pouring carbon dioxide into the atmosphere. Outside of any argument over where to shop, there are good arguments for everyone slowing down. It is actually a positive thing for a book to take an extra few days to arrive and/or to be picked up at the store instead of being shipped directly to your home in a day or two.

Furthermore, books are not avocados. A book that gets to you in three days is exactly the same as the book that gets to you tomorrow, which is exactly the same as the book that gets to you in three weeks. I know there are birthdays and holidays and such, but the book is exactly the same whether it arrives on the date of the party or later. We can live in a world that isn't overheating, that isn't dominated by massive corporate behemoths, that is full of small businesses and vibrant downtowns *and* in which we can get almost anything we could ever imagine wanting, as long as we're able to be just a little more patient than we have been recently.

This excising of the idea "as fast as possible" from the idea of "convenience" will go a long way in helping build (or rebuild) an economy in which a national indie brand isn't needed, in which we don't have to unify under slogans like "shop local" in order to individually survive, a books ecosystem in which "independent" can return to being meaningful if not particularly informative, and in which if one independent bookstore doesn't share your values, you can conveniently shop at another that does. Though consumer choice plays a role in creating a more just system, at this stage in the economy "consumer choice" as a political act is more palliative than productive. Amazon, Apple, Walmart, and Disney all exist how they exist today because of policy decisions made at all levels of government. From property tax breaks to low minimum wages to the capital gains tax; from very narrow interpretations of existing antitrust legislation to the labyrinthine tax code to enforcement decisions: Elected officials, government bureaucrats, and those empowered to make, interpret, and guide economic policy used all these elements to shape an economy that rewards consolidation. We didn't shop our way into this and we're not going to shop our way out. As valuable as shopping locally and supporting independent businesses is for the health of your specific community, it needs to be paired with activism and voting to have a systemic impact.

As long as there is a multinational competitor and as long as we are dealing with multinational publishers, bookstores need a unified response to create the volume needed to be heard at all, regardless of what the message is. As long as we have that national response and national brand, some stores who don't really fit that brand or perhaps even oppose that brand will benefit, while customers will continue to make incorrect assumptions about what specific bookstores can and can't do. In terms of individual bookstores, the answer to this paradox is the same as the answer to many of the other challenges facing independent bookstores: Cultivate your customer base into a community of readers who know what your store is capable of, who always ask for a book if they can't find it and always order it from you if it's available, and who see you as a vital part of their community and their lives.

SOUR CREAM AND OTHER WHITE MISTAKES

Bookselling and the American Dirt *Fiasco*

The threat of backlash stalks everything that reaches a certain level of hype. Maybe that backlash is driven by envy, cynicism, snobbery. Maybe all three. Maybe publicity machines build up impossible expectations. Maybe we take satisfaction in knocking someone down a peg. Whatever the exact mechanism, time and time again, books, movies, TV shows, and people built up by hype come crashing down. Some works endure that backlash. Others don't.

Before it was released, *American Dirt* by Jeanine Cummins was a "Most Anticipated Book" in the *New York Times, O, The Oprah Magazine, Vogue, Marie Claire, Real Simple, Elle, Entertainment Weekly, Woman's Day, Literary Hub, Parade, Chicago Tribune*, the *Washington Post, Fast Company, Forbes, Esquire, USA Today, POPSUGAR, Bustle*, and the *New York Times Book Review*. Being a "Most Anticipated" book doesn't mean a whole lot about the content of the book, only that people in book media expect it to reach a level of some renown. But it also had blurbs from Oprah (the person, not the magazine), Ann Patchett, John Grisham, Stephen King, and many more. It was an editor's choice in the *New York Times Book Review* and a January Library Reads pick. It was an Oprah's Book Club book, the absolute pinnacle of book hype. It was also a number one Indie Next List pick. The Indie Next List is selected by independent booksellers around the country. Being number one on the list means the book got more nominations than any other book coming out that month. You could make a case that *American Dirt* had some of the most prepublication hype of any book in recent memory. Before anything else happened, before I knew anything about it, I felt *American Dirt* had reached that precarious level of hype. It is easy to teeter on a pinnacle. I mean, Don Winslow called it "a *Grapes of Wrath* for our times." How could it possibly live up to that?

Then I noticed something else about the hype around *American Dirt*. Even though it was "the book" independent booksellers were buzzing about, none of my bookseller friends were buzzing about it. I tend to read books from small presses, experimental books, books in translation, and other books I think need active advocacy from booksellers to reach their audience. That's not the only way to read as a bookseller or the best way, but it's my way. And most of my bookternet friends read that way too. That's part of why we're friends. But not all of them do, and even those that do often read beyond their preferences because they're buyers or event coordinators or they want to cultivate a broad awareness of publishing or, just, you know, contain multitudes. So while Flatiron, an imprint of Macmillan, was never going to send me a galley, and a book with that level of hype was unlikely to be a topic of conversation among my friends, it struck me as odd that I didn't really hear about it until a couple of weeks before publication. To me, it was nowhere and then it was everywhere.

American Dirt is the story of Lydia, a Mexican mother and bookseller living in Mexico. Her husband is a journalist who covers crime and the drug cartels, a very dangerous line of work. Her life is going well, as many lives do at the beginnings of novels, and she's even made a new friend, a suave older gentleman who frequents her store and buys the books she recommends.

But a brutal massacre at a quinceañera forces her to flee to the United States with her son, Luca, "the love of her life" we're told by the publisher's copy. She ends up along the same path as the thousands of other people fleeing cartel and gang violence in Mexico and Central and South America that compose the refugee crisis at the United States' southern border. *American Dirt* was supposed to be *the* novel that would humanize the refugee crisis at the border, *the* novel that would inspire emotional and empathetic connections between the privileged and the marginalized, and that would drive true social change.

And then something else set my spider sense tingling. From what I saw, no booksellers of color were talking about *American Dirt*. Not just those in my friend group, but none at all. When I finally started hearing about it, from what I observed, only white booksellers were hyping a book about the refugee crisis on the border between Mexico and the United States written from the perspective of a Mexican mother and bookseller. At the time, it just made me nervous about some of the enthusiasm other white booksellers at Porter Square Books felt about it, especially since, in large part because of that enthusiasm, we were co-hosting an early event in Cummins's book tour with WBUR, the Boston-area NPR affiliate. Given the risk of backlash I thought *American Dirt* faced, I believed it would be risky to throw the store's weight behind it in any further official capacity.

And then the critical reviews started rolling in: from David Schmidt, Myriam Gurba, David Bowles, and many others. Schmidt, Gurba, and Bowles wrote thorough critiques, quoting heavily from the text to show its cultural mistakes and exploring the problems, both large and small, with it. David Schmidt opens his review in The Blue Nib with:

> I do an excellent British accent—as long as you don't ask
> anyone who is British…anyone from the U.K. can immediate-

ly identify an extremely poor imitation of their voices ... The same could be said for Jeanine Cummins' novel about Mexico. As someone who has spent half a lifetime in Mexico and on the border, I can only pray that this book doesn't go down in history as "the great migrant novel."[30]

David Bowles points out, "Cultural references are often missed and Lydia Quixano Perez (what a name, huh) is ignorant of things that *any* Mexican knows," before specifically exploring Lydia's misunderstanding of the image of "La Lechuza."[31] (Parentheses and emphasis per the original.) Bowles explains that a "lechuza" is a screech owl that Mexicans have long seen as "harbingers of death," and yet Lydia says, "Owls aren't scary." "And this is just one of literally dozens of examples," Bowles says. Gurba writes in her savage review for Tropics of Meta, "Despite being an intellectually engaged woman, and the wife of a reporter whose beat is narcotrafficking, Lydia experiences shock after shock when confronted with the realities of Mexico, realities that would not shock a Mexican."[32] Because of this, Bowles argues in a subsequent opinion piece for the *New York Times*, "*American Dirt* has now largely been rejected by the very Mexicans and Mexican Americans it was meant to foreground."[33]

While all three of the reviews critiqued *American Dirt* at the macro level, exploring the stereotypes Cummins employs, the formulaic plot, the bigger inconsistencies (like why a woman who could afford a quick plane ride to Canada would use La Bestia), and even the unsettling similarities between *American Dirt* and its self-identified source material, it was the little mistakes they identified that stuck with me. David Schmidt points out, "Ostensibly Mexican characters eat typical American cuisine that is foreign to much of Mexico; sticky and sweet BBQ sauce, black licorice drops, tacos with heavy sour cream." Though Cummins peppers the dialogue with Spanish terms that are italicized even though Spanish should not be treated as a foreign language in a book set in Mexico, the cultural references are American. For example, Cummins describes the narcos as "modern bogeymen," but as Gurba points out, "Mexicans don't fear the bogeyman. We fear his very distant cousin el cucuy." Similarly, as Schmidt points out, "When Lydia comes to the route of the freight train, she ponders: *The freight tracks stretch out across the Mexican landscape like a beanstalk migrants must climb.* Never mind that *Jack and the Beanstalk* is a folkloric reference as foreign to Mexico as *La Llorana* is to most British people." Finally, going back to Schmidt again, "The surname *Quijano* has not been spelled with an X since medieval Spain, and the correct Spanish version of the name 'Luke' is *Lucas.*" Because of these cultural errors, the book isn't really set in Mexico, but in "El Sur," an ersatz Mexico that would only seem authentic to someone (like me) who doesn't know what authentic Mexico looks like.

If Cummins can't get the sour cream right, how can we trust her with La Bestia? Or as Schmidt says, "When even the protagonists' names are butchered, what can one expect from the rest of the book?" A lot of people tried to make this fiasco a debate about who earns the privilege of telling certain stories, but the problems posed by *American Dirt* aren't about authenticity but competency. Imagine if a writer from California wrote a book set in Providence, Rhode Island, and had the characters put ketchup on a hot wiener. Sure, that's not the most important detail in the world and the culture of Providence is a lot more than hot wieners, but if you can't be bothered to get a simple, objectively verifiable detail correct, how can you possibly be trusted with the city's complicated relationship between former mayor Buddy Cianci, who was extremely popular at times despite his well-known connections to organized crime? Whether you have the "permission" to write a story is beside the point when you fuck it up. There is a debate to be had about who gets to tell what stories, a debate that needs to be cognizant of the history of cultural appropriation, the decision-making structures in publishing, and the wider systems of power in our society, but *American Dirt* simply does not do enough of the easier work of fiction to be an object in that much more difficult conversation.

Just as it is physically possible to put ketchup on a hot wiener, it is possible to explain away the identified problems with *American Dirt*. We can imagine a family hanging on to or returning to that *x* in "Quixano" for some reason, and no culture or nation is a monolith so I suppose we can also imagine a relatively wealthy Mexican woman having a lower awareness of the strife plaguing her nation. Along those same lines maybe we can accept that it is plausible her husband hid from her the worst of what he had discovered in his job, and I suppose we can forgive the whole "Luca" nonsense as artistic license. The American cultural references could be reasonable given that it was written for an American audience (though, I find that insulting to that American audience as it assumes they will reject works with different cultural references). I guess it's reasonable to believe many Mexicans, and especially someone who is supposed to be a reader, would have a broad awareness of American and European folklore and culture, but that is a lot of explaining and that still doesn't get to the othering created by including Spanish phrases in the text and putting them in italics and the sour cream on the tacos and the other stereotypes and clichés. If you are doing that much work to apologize for a book you didn't write, what exactly are you apologizing for?

Furthermore, "artistic license" is not a morally neutral concept. When someone from a more powerful identity exercises "artistic license" in stories about a less powerful identity, space in the discourse gets taken from the less powerful identity, too often negative stereotypes are promulgated or empowered, and too often the product of the "artistic license" comes to define that less powerful identity rather than it being defined by artistic creations by and from that identity itself. If someone from Providence got everything else right about Providence, one could argue characters putting ketchup on a hot wiener is a potentially powerful act of artistic license, but if someone from California does it in the context of putting Venda Ravioli in the wrong place or talking about Tufts University as being in Rhode Island that's not "artistic license," that's a mistake. There is a debate to be had over the differences between artistic license, cross-cultural influence, and appropriation, but *American Dirt* just doesn't get enough of the basics right to be an object in that debate either. As Christian Lorentzen says in a review in the *London Review of Books*:

> Writing a self-portrait and transposing it across a politically fraught border zone—in theory there's no reason to think it couldn't work. The trouble with Cummins's writing isn't that she gets Spanish wrong, which she does (she also misuses it— why call a soccer ball a *balon de futbal* in a book that converts pesos to dollars?), or that she borrows bits from other writers, such as Luis Alberto Urrea, and deploys their material clumsily; it's that her simplistic worldview, split between the cutesy and the cruel, can't handle subject matter of any seriousness, whatever the colour of her characters' skin.[34]

Americans and white Americans should write about the refugee crisis at the southern border because it is an American crisis, one that white Americans have a stake in, are responsible for to some degree, and are impacted by in practical and moral ways. (Just as white Americans need to write about race and slavery and immigration, just as men need to write about patriarchy and sexism.) I believe that can potentially include writing from the perspectives of other less powerful communities and identities as part of the long conversation literature allows different groups of people to have with each other. There was an opportunity for a powerful conversation through a book written by a white American about the southern refugee crisis and perhaps even from the perspective of a refugee or refugees, so it is a tragedy that we have to talk about *American Dirt* instead.

I'm struck by how easy it would have been for the *American Dirt* we have to be much closer to the *American Dirt* we could have had. From the sour cream to the names to the muffed cultural references to the stilted Spanish to the fucking presence of Spanish at all when everyone is speaking Spanish, much of what makes *American Dirt* problematic could have been fixed during editorial. That no one bothered to check on these things is disrespectful, even insulting, to readers. Either the publisher thought no one would notice or nobody involved in the production of the book knew enough about Mexico to notice themselves. But even then, it's like, I mean, you paid a million fucking dollars for this book; hire somebody who knows enough about Mexico.

Once I start questioning the authenticity of the setting, I start to question other aspects of the book. To me, there is no lazier way to create emotional content in media than putting a child in danger. Which is not to say that all books, movies, TV shows, or whatever that include children in danger are lazy or employ the trope cynically, it's just for those that use it, I personally need to see something else from the work that earns my trust. Why should I trust that Cummins has earned the emotional content of a child in danger if she hasn't bothered to get simple things right? "Narco kingpin as supervillain" is a trope and too often a stereotype. That doesn't mean all narco kingpins in fiction are stereotypes, but, again, why should I trust this specific author to do something meaningful with the trope? If no one involved in the process thought, Wait, are you sure they put sour cream on tacos in Mexico? or Why is the Spanish in italics? It's not the foreign language in this narrative, why should we believe Cummins and everyone else involved was trying to create an experience of empathy and not capitalizing on a contemporary moment by trying to fit a formulaic crime narrative into a politically potent setting?

Independent booksellers and bookstores have been talking a big social justice game for years. We applauded the keynote speakers, hosted the panels, formed the committees, added new language, invited people to the table. White booksellers, by and large, adopted the diction and posture of social and racial justice. We were certainly happy to make antiracist reading lists when flooded with orders for antiracist books in June 2020. And some work has been done. Some good things have been accomplished. Some progress seems to have been made.

But how did many white booksellers respond to *American Dirt*? They made it the number one Indie Next List title for February 2020. And how did many white booksellers respond to critique of *American Dirt* from the marginalized voices of Myriam Gurba, David Bowles, and other critics and activists? How did we respond when those people we claimed to be uplifting actually used their uplifted voices? Dismissal, denial, and defensiveness. We used Isabel Allende (who is Dominican) and Sandra Cisneros (who was born in Chicago) as human shields. We centered Cummins's Puerto Rican heritage, which, as Gurba shows, Cummins had not previously centered in her career. Cummins had previously identified as white. "I am white. The grandmother I shared with Julie and Robin was Puerto Rican, and their father is half Lebanese. But in every practical way, my family is mostly white."[35] We quoted Cummins's description of her research process.

We repeated the publisher's copy that Cummins was married to an undocumented immigrant without interrogating that copy—Cummins's undocumented immigrant husband is from Ireland. We circled the wagons. We said no one who hadn't read the book had any right to critique it. We argued that critiques were a kind of cultural gatekeeping, wokeness policing free expression. We claimed some of the responses were acts of censorship. Those same booksellers attending the educational panels and committing to diversity simply refused to hear practical, specific, antiracist critique when we felt it was directed at a book we liked.

Looking Mexican and Mexican American critics, readers, and authors in the face and saying, "You do not know if a book is racist against Mexicans," is a racist act. I know I would not have caught those fatal mistakes and I don't expect most other white readers to have caught them either. But there was a chance for white booksellers to recognize their own reading limitations and actively value the thoughts, critiques, and experiences of a marginalized community. There was an opportunity for growth, a chance to use *American Dirt* as material for a productive conversation, almost in spite of itself. Space to say, "You know what, I really do think it was an effective thriller and I really connected with Lydia, but I understand how it failed to authentically represent Mexican culture and the experience of asylum seekers and immigrants at the border." There was space to say, "I was wrong." Instead we said, "My personal reading experience is more valid than your critique." Much like issues around white supremacy in publishing and bookselling, white booksellers with an honest general commitment to social and racial justice were blind to the specific consequences of their actions and their preferences.

One of the strangest manifestations of this blindness, that I observed, was the reaction to Lauren Groff's review[36] in the

New York Times.[37] Much like the Isabel Allende and Sandra Cisneros blurbs, I saw Groff's review wielded like a powerful counterargument, as if any one person's opinion could be definitive. But even if it were, Groff's opinions about *American Dirt* are complex and relatively conflicted.

　Groff opens her review with an experience of profound sympathy: "As the anxiety-riddled mother of an 8-year-old—as a person who has nightmares after every report of a mass shooting—I felt this scene in the marrow of my bones." In the next paragraph Groff wonders if she "was the wrong person to review this book," in part because she could "never speak to the accuracy of the book's representation of Mexican culture or the plight of migrants." Given that the explicitly stated goal of the book in the publicity and in Cummins's afterword is the creation of empathy for this exact population, the assignment of this review to Groff raises questions as well. Regardless of Groff's overall opinion of the book, she makes it clear, right at the beginning of her review, that she does not believe she is qualified to critique the accuracy of the book's presentation of its setting. This conflict Groff feels shows itself throughout the review. She finds the book so "propulsive" she didn't "think [she] could have stopped reading." At the same time, she says it "contains few of the aspects that I have long believed are necessary for successful literary fiction." She mentions the "tremendous research" that Cummins describes in the afterword but also acknowledges Gurba's critiques. She recognizes that the book was written for white American readers and that the emotional core of it, the engine of all that breathless page turning, is the relationship between an individual mother and her individual child and not the refugee crisis surrounding them. Though she doesn't use the specific terminology, Groff describes *American Dirt* as an effective thriller that happens to exist in the space of a potent contemporary issue. But whether or not *American*

Dirt speaks to the actual experience of Mexican immigrants at the border in a way that promotes Cummins's stated goal, Groff, as she made clear, can't say. "In the end, I find myself ambivalent. Perhaps this book is an act of cultural imperialism; at the same time, weeks after finishing it, the novel remains alive in me."

Groff has a lot of positive things to say about *American Dirt*, but they are always qualified. Groff frames her perspective so it is clear what she feels she has authority to speak on and what she doesn't. She also frames her review to allow space for other perspectives. Given all that, I think it's a fair and respectful review, even if other critiques have called some of Groff's points into contention. In some ways, Groff actually models a decent response to *American Dirt*; she is open about what she likes and why she likes it, acknowledges her limitations as a reader, and respects the critique of others. Readers who liked *American Dirt* can find a lot of support in Groff's review, but it isn't a counterargument to issues raised by Bowles, Gurba, Schmidt, and others, and it was never intended to be.

I have heard it said that it is unfair to critique and take any kind of action as a bookseller, like returning all the store stock or removing it from store displays, in response to *American Dirt* without reading it, and if my critique were based on the book's prose style or narrative structure, then yes, I would need to have actually read it or a significant portion of it to voice a critical opinion. But I am not critiquing its prose. I am listening to critics like Gurba and Bowles, who would know whether the book is racist, telling me it is racist. I am believing the voices we are supposed to lift up. I am trusting the experts. I don't need to read the actual study that shows a vaccine is safe and effective if my doctor tells me a vaccine is safe and effective, and so I don't need to read *American Dirt* to believe what Mexican and Mexican American readers tell me about it.

I have also heard it argued that the seven-figure advance Cummins received for *American Dirt* was a primary motivator for the critique the book received. My response to that is, yes, of course. Advances are statements of value. An advance says, in as clear a way as possible, what the publisher believes will sell and what they believe will raise their prestige or support their brand. Some books are more about sales and some books are more about prestige, but a seven-figure advance is clearly both. Flatiron (Macmillan) believed they would sell a ton of copies of *American Dirt* and that it would raise their prestige, making them more attractive to agents and authors. Once you spend a million dollars (or more) on a book, you're going to spend a shit ton on the marketing and publicity that's required to make that back in sales. To quote your dad, "Money doesn't grow on trees." Because so much money went to *American Dirt*, other authors got lower advances and other books published by Flatiron did not get the publicity support they needed to succeed. Perhaps three, five, or ten books simply did not happen or did not sell well in exchange for this one. Three, five, or ten books that could have been written by actual Mexicans or actual Mexican Americans.

I have also heard it argued that the reaction to *American Dirt* has as much to do with the publicity as the text, and that critics would have had a different reaction to it if it were marketed differently. To which I reply, yes. Exactly. Also correct. But that doesn't absolve the text, or the author, and certainly not the publisher. Sure, authors don't have a ton of control over how their books are marketed, but the tone of the publicity exactly matched the tone Cummins set in her afterword. She could have written anything there but she chose to write herself as the white savior for the "faceless brown masses." (I guess I can see what she was attempting but, my god, what made her or anyone else think she could get away with that phrase?) She also could have just...not written an afterword and let the book speak for itself. And just because she may have wanted an afterword explaining herself, her publisher didn't have to go along with it. Even if her publisher asked her for an afterword, she didn't have to write what she wrote and they didn't have to publish it as it was written. In some ways, I think the marketing of *American Dirt* makes the whole endeavor seem even more cynical. Everyone involved in *American Dirt* could have marketed it as a conventional crime novel in a contemporary setting. (As Don Winslow's books are marketed.) They could have presented it as a thriller that intersects with current affairs. They could have emphasized the aspects of the book that Groff found compelling.

A conventional thriller has different requirements to be successful. It doesn't necessarily need to build the same kind of trust with readers to employ the trope of a child in danger or the trope of the suave narco supervillain, because someone reading a conventional thriller is reading to be thrilled, not to critically engage with pressing contemporary political issues or build empathy for marginalized communities. Furthermore, a conventional thriller has a different degree of willing suspension of disbelief than a social realist novel. So "El Sur," could be an acceptable setting for a thriller. This is not to denigrate the thriller genre but to be clear that successful thrillers are successful in different ways and through different techniques than successful social realist novels.

But *American Dirt* was marketed as a powerful novel of social justice, a profound act of empathy, a new *Grapes of Wrath*, a work of literature that might change the world, surrounded by blurbs that described it as a "moral compass," "rich in authenticity," and that said it "will no doubt spark conversation," and "proves that fiction can be a vehicle for expanding our empathy." Why?

And once I've asked myself that initial "why" and asked it in the context of the text's many simple mistakes, why does the story need to interact with the refugee crisis at all? Lydia could have run in many different directions. Why does it need to take place in Mexico? There is organized crime all over the world. Though I'm sure most, if not every, person who worked on this book honestly believed in it (which is its own problem), once I start asking the questions it's hard to stop. Why is Lydia Mexican? A lot of the problems aren't problems if she's an American married to a Mexican journalist. Also, why is Lydia a bookseller?

American Dirt was billed as, promised as, celebrated as, supposed to be an act of empathy, but was, in fact, an exploitative work of sympathy. To quote directly from the publisher's copy: "Even though she knows they'll never sell, Lydia stocks some of her all-time favorite books in her store." I mean, that is just fucking catnip for booksellers. In fact, Lydia has far more in common with white American booksellers than she does with the typical person seeking asylum at our southern border. If I squint I can make the argument that Lydia was written that way to lead readers from sympathy to empathy, but this still doesn't account for the simple mistakes and, personally, I find that insulting to the target audience since it assumes bits of themselves need to be dangled in front of them as treats to get them anywhere near empathy for a marginalized identity. White booksellers and white readers connected with *American Dirt* on such a powerful level because Lydia, its hero, is a white bookseller. They responded the way they did to critiques because they felt attacks on *American Dirt* were attacks on themselves. That so many white booksellers did not recognize their own reflection in the book and then read their sympathy as empathy, that so many did not examine what their own defensiveness in response to the critiques of the book says about Lydia and the book, that it did not seem to occur to them—even after Mexican and Mexican American critics and readers cataloged the book's flaws—that their initial reading could be limited, shows that even among professional readers, whiteness can be a powerful barrier to interpretation and critique.

Because white readers see their experience as universal, whenever we connect with a white character, we do not see shared whiteness as the source of that connection. Jess Row describes this phenomenon in his collection of essays *White Flights*, as the "white autonomy of the imagination," which is "a Kantian principle, derived from the *Critique of Judgment*, that assumes only certain people are capable of truly universal, disinterested aesthetic or artistic perception."[38] Which is not to say that all connections white people feel to white characters come through whiteness but that white people are conditioned to not see whiteness as the source of the connection. So we interpret our emotional connection to Lydia without whiteness—through motherhood or love of books— even as she did things—like be shocked by the actions of the narcos—only a white person, or at the very least, an American would do, and even as she used cultural references that were specifically comfortable to white people. The strength and ease of the connection white readers felt to Lydia should have given us pause. Empathy requires work, imagination, and often discomfort. If you felt none of these things while reading Lydia, did you really feel empathy?

This empathy gap is particularly potent, even destructive, when we're talking about the refugee crisis at our southern border. Can an American feel true empathy for the plight of Mexican, Central, and South American migrants and asylum seekers, especially those fleeing cartel violence, if we do not also feel responsibility? Much of the crises south of us are caused by American imperialism and the American "war on drugs." Our attention was drawn back to the border with renewed focus because Americans elected Donald Trump president after he kicked off his campaign with a speech explicitly racist against Mexicans, empowering him to separate asylum-seeking families and build an absolutely pointless and environmentally devastating wall to assuage racist fear. I don't know if empathy and responsibility are inherently connected, but, in this case, they sure as fuck are. And as Parul Sehgal writes in a review for the *New York Times*, "[*American Dirt*] is determinedly apolitical. The deep roots of these forced migrations are never interrogated; the American reader can read without fear of uncomfortable self-reproach. It asks only for us to accept that 'these people are people,' while giving us the saintly to root for and the barbarous to deplore—and then congratulates us for caring."[39]

To return to Groff's review, in the closing paragraph she writes, "When I think of the migrants at the border, suffering and desperate, I think of Lydia and Luca, and feel something close to bodily pain." She does not think of the other people riding La Bestia, the other people at the border seeking asylum, all the refugees from Central and South America, the bodies in the desert, or even the bodies in the book's massacre; she thinks of the mother and her child. "An anxiety-ridden mother," thinks of a mother and her child. There is nothing wrong with sympathy or with leveraging sympathy for emotional impact, or with using sympathy as an emotional stepping stone to empathy. The problem comes from mistaking sympathy for empathy, from believing you have connected with a different person when you have only found another way to connect with yourself. In some ways, you could ascribe some of the failure or slowness of social and racial justice movements to white people consistently confusing sympathy for empathy and concluding from that confusion that if they feel better, things must be better.

Porter Square Books was closed to in-store shopping from the middle of March 2020 to the middle of July 2020, which means we were closed when the Black Lives Matter protests after the murder of George Floyd created an unprecedented surge in online shopping at independent bookstores, specifically for antiracist books. That massive surge in sales buoyed Porter Square Books and likely kept many independent bookstores in business after several months of catastrophic sales losses. We had a lot to do to get ready for letting customers back in the store, including updating our bestsellers display. We use the IndieBound bestseller list, which tracks sales specifically at independent bookstores. I nearly fell on the floor when I saw the July 2020 post–George Floyd bestseller list. There, despite everything, after six months, was *American Dirt*. Just a few feet from *White Fragility*. Not censored. Not canceled. A bestseller. In hardcover. At independent bookstores. For months.

I'm not angry at anyone for loving *American Dirt* when they read it as a galley. I'm not angry at anyone who still loves it. But just because you love something doesn't mean you can't acknowledge its flaws. Your love of something does not invalidate the reasons someone else might critique it. And most important, just because you love a book does not mean you need to use your platform to create sales for it. You may have loved *American Dirt* when you read it as a galley. You may have staff-picked it. You may have pushed for your store to host an event for it. You may have suggested it to your book club. I am not angry at you for any of that. Everyone makes mistakes. What matters is what you do after your mistake has been exposed. How did you respond to critique? What did you learn from the critique, even the parts that you disagreed with? Did you stack a big pile of *American Dirt* on your new-paperback-fiction table? Did you sign up for the virtual event Macmillan organized for the paperback release?

A lot has happened between when *American Dirt* came out and now. #DignidadLiteraria met with Macmillan to develop a plan for better representation moving forward that some seem satisfied with, at least as a place to start. Though at the time of writing, it's difficult to see if any progress has been made from that start. There's been a pandemic and violent insurrection. It might seem strange to rehash these challenging, even painful conversations, but I believe we need to learn from this fiasco as much as we can and we're not going to do that if we just move on. If books are as important to culture as booksellers say they are, if bookstores are as vital to literature and discourse as we say they are when we are asking readers to support us with purchases or donations, then how booksellers and bookstores handle our own problems with social and racial justice will have an impact on the broader struggle for social and racial justice. It will impact which books are published, which authors are read, what book clubs read, which books and authors get coverage in media, who makes money from books, and through all of that, which ideas are discussed and adopted in wider society.

For all I know, many, if not most of the people whose actions and reactions I've critiqued have changed their perspective on both *American Dirt* in particular and the problems it reflects more generally. But I won't be able to see that change. Nobody will. For white people especially, a lot of the good work that we need to do is invisible. There will be no single, public redemptive act that allows us to celebrate our growth into better white people. Instead, there will be a slow accumulation of decisions and actions that accrue into different habits, behaviors, and interactions. Furthermore, a lot of the most practical and productive contributions white booksellers can make in bending the arc toward justice is by not doing things. Does this white author already have tons of galleys floating around, a high publicity budget, and a number of confirmed appearances on major media? Don't staff pick their book, don't nominate it for the Indie Next List, don't nominate it for regional awards, don't select it for store-run book clubs. Don't run for a board position if there's already a ton of white people on it. Don't appear on panels that are all white people, especially if you've been on panels before. And of course, don't fall for this shit again. And if we do fall for this shit again—which we probably will—react differently the next time. And live with the fact that the only person who is going to know or notice whether you have made this growth in your life and your career is you.

A SONNET, A MENU, A PLACE

Genre in the Bookstore

Genre means something different to writers than it does to readers and it means something different again to booksellers. For writers, genre provides potential guidelines for what type of story to tell and how to tell it; guidelines they can adhere to, play with, reference, or even critique. In some genres, these guidelines are strict, even definitive, while others allow for more play. To a writer, genre is akin to poetic forms like sonnets or villanelles but for plot and setting rather than rhymes and meter. Poets interacting with the sonnet form can replicate the meter and rhyme scheme of Elizabethan (aka Shakespearean) or Petrarchan sonnets, experiment with the very nature of "meter," "rhyme," and "forms" as in the works of Diane Seuss, and any mix of adherence, play, and critique in between, like the sonnets of Wanda Coleman, Terrance Hayes, and many others. Prose writers can do the same with genre. Some writers will start with a specific genre in mind, while others will discover or decide on their project's genre as they write. For some, genre will be a primary focus, while others will have a general awareness of it even if it isn't a direct or intentional influence on their specific work. And of course, as poets play with a variety of forms, writers will mix genres, telling mysteries in space or setting their romance in a fantasy world. As with poets, they can also explore the contradictions and complexities that exist in all definitions. Genre can be the most important factor in a writer's process, one of many currents in the process, or something completely outside the process that gets applied by readers and critics through interpretation.

Genre tells the reader, roughly, what they can reasonably expect a book to contain. Think about the different "genres" of restaurants. Knowing a restaurant is "Chinese" or "Italian" won't tell you exactly what will be on the menu and certainly won't tell you whether it's good, but, if you're in the mood for, I don't know, eggplant parmesan, you know an Italian restaurant is far more likely to have it than a Chinese restaurant. Likewise, if you're in the mood to read about robots and spaceships, you know a work of science fiction is much more likely to contain robots and spaceships than a mystery. Ultimately, knowing the genre of a book doesn't tell readers a whole lot, but it can help a reader choose the book they want to read right now.

All writers are also readers and many readers are also writers, so these uses for the idea of genre aren't mutually exclusive or even absolutely distinct. Furthermore, just as readers of poetry can use the poem's form as a tool for interpretation and critique, readers can use the guidelines, traditions, and techniques of genre as a tool for their own interpretation and critique. For both writers and readers, genre is also an interpretive framework they can apply to literature while they're reading.

But to booksellers, genre is a place.

To booksellers, genre answers the question: Where the fuck do I put this book? For all the abstractions that swirl around it, for all the fuzziness at the edges of all definitions, ultimately, genre is where a book is placed in a bookstore. To answer the question, "Where the fuck should I put this book?" booksellers grapple with two follow-up questions: Where does the book "belong"? And: Where do most readers *think* the book "belongs"? Sometimes the answers to both questions are the same. Pretty much all readers will think books by Agatha Christie belong in Mystery because, well, she's the Queen of Mystery. Plato in Philosophy, Butler in sci-fi / fantasy, Tuchman in History. Easy, right? Unfortunately, the answers to those two questions sometimes disagree. Here's an example. Where would you put a work of fiction that imagines wealthy elites maintaining a farm of their own clones whose organs they harvest as a way to extend their health and life? Given that the technology required for this kind of human cloning doesn't—at time of writing—exist, this book most likely "belongs," in Science Fiction. But Porter Square Books keeps it in Fiction and I would bet most other bookstores do too. Why? Because it's by Nobel Prize–winning novelist Kazuo Ishiguro. Most of Ishiguro's other work and certainly his most famous other work, *The Remains of the Day*, are firmly in Fiction, and so we expect most readers would look for all his books there, even those like *Never Let Me Go* and maybe *The Buried Giant*, which really belong in Science Fiction or Fantasy.

In theory, this should be fine. In theory, genre in fiction should not have political content. In the exact same way knowing a restaurant is "Italian" doesn't tell you anything about its quality, knowing a book is "romance" doesn't tell you anything about its quality. In theory, the nature of the attention given to books in Fiction, should be the same as the nature of the attention given to books in Sci-Fi / Fantasy. But of course, our long history of elitism and gatekeeping, of elevating works written and valued by a specific identity as "literature" and denigrating everything else, means shelving a book in Fiction instead of in one of the other genres can be interpreted as a statement of value. A store's Fiction section can often be understood to be essentially the "literature" section, which means a political statement is made when you shelve

Never Let Me Go with the rest of Ishiguro's "literature." You are reinforcing the idea that "some books transcend genre," the idea that certain plots, certain settings, and certain types of characters are inherently more powerful than others, and the idea that some books and some writers are "serious," and others are not.

Of course, even having a section labeled Fiction with other sections labeled by genre—Mystery, Romance, Science Fiction, and Fantasy—creates a problem. It presents the books in a store's Fiction section as the standard and implies that everything is somehow derivative of that standard. It plays into the perception that certain books are "literature" while other books are lesser forms of expression. One's first instinct might be to rename the section Realistic Fiction so that it has some distinguishing label like the other genres. The problem is that a lot of what is in and what probably belongs in a bookstore's Fiction section isn't realistic. And not just in the "it really should be in science fiction, but it's by a Nobel Prize winner" sense. I mean stories that feature phenomena that do not happen in reality but don't fit into Science Fiction, Fantasy, or Mystery.

You could, of course, just keep creating genres and have a Realistic Fiction section and a Fantastical Fiction section. But where would you put thrillers? The events depicted in most thrillers aren't really realistic, but their emotional impact relies, at least in part, on getting the reader to react as if what they're reading is actually happening. Okay, so we have a Thrillers section. That same tension between what could actually happen and what needs to feel like it could actually happen applies to a lot of spy, military, and action-forward fiction so we should probably create at least Military and Spy sections as well. (I once saw it argued that any work that features a single person defeating multiple armed opponents in hand-to-hand combat should be considered fantasy.) And westerns? Are we putting historical fiction in with Realistic or should it have its own section? Are we putting horror in Fantastical Fiction or should it have its own?

Could a highly genred bookstore work? Sure. I could see a store doing this really well. The store would need to be designed to introduce this slightly unexpected layout. The booksellers would need to have a strong grasp of the store's genre taxonomy to answer questions and lead customers to the right places. With those supports, it could be a very satisfying browsing experience. Customers are always asking for thrillers, historical fiction, and spy fiction, and at Porter Square Books at the time of writing all of those are in the Fiction section. I've often wished I could just bring them to a shelf rather than taking them on a tour through the fiction section based on what I remember of the genres within the larger genre. But genre is a physical space. Allocating attention through genre is about getting customers to specific physical locations in the store and moving them from place to place as they browse or search. Each new genre requires a label, some kind of physical demarcation, and a record in the store's inventory. Depending on the size of the store and the design of the shelves, highly genreing your fiction might eat up so much shelf space that you're forced to carry fewer books and titles than you otherwise would. It also creates a much different browsing experience than the standard approach. The physical experience of moving your attention through several dozen feet of fiction is much different from the physical experience of moving your attention through a handful of feet of historical fiction, then a few feet of thrillers, then a few feet of spy fiction. Some customers might struggle to figure out what genre the book they want fits in, especially if it lives in an atypical or unfamiliar one. Furthermore, this still doesn't solve the problem of authors writing in multiple genres or books that have recognizable elements of several genres.

The real solution to this problem is, of course, the culture-wide disentangling of prestige and power from genre, recognizing that art and entertainment (as well as success and failure) aren't inherently tied to types of stories. With genre disentangled from prestige, "fiction" is no longer a possible synonym for "literature," and becomes "fiction without an obvious established genre," with no implied worth, quality, or "seriousness." With literature taught, treated, and interacted with as an ever-evolving, ever-changing, ever-mutating conversation with no inherent bedrocks, no natural expressions, no immutable cornerstones, "fiction without an obvious established genre" communicates nothing more than that. It's probably the place you'll go for stories about dissolving marriages, but you'll find lots of other stuff there too.

Given that the entanglement of prestige and genre comes from many different currents in our society, including how literacy and literature are taught, how books are marketed and publicized by publishers and authors, and how books are covered (or not covered) in media, and given how at least some of those currents impact people before they are bookstore shoppers, there's only so much bookstores can contribute to the untangling of prestige and genre. But that doesn't mean we can do nothing. At the very least, we can stop taking actions that entangle things further. This means being conscientious not just of where we shelve books, but of how we talk about them both in the store and on social media, how we display them both in their sections and on more intentional displays, and how we give books more or less space on our platforms. How often do you host events for genre authors? You don't need to be a store that specializes in romance or sci-fi to host romance or sci-fi authors. How often do genre books show up on your new releases tables? Do your booksellers who read genre fiction feel empowered to share the books they're excited about on the store's social media?

Of course, just talking about genre books isn't necessarily going to contribute to that disentanglement. How you talk about genre matters. Saying a book "transcends genre" as a way to pitch it to potential readers isn't the praise you hope it is, as it implies there is a limit to the types of stories certain genres can tell. "Guilty pleasure" implies that people should feel guilty for reading the book or genre for some reason. We also need to be cognizant of what terms mean to readers and writers of the genre. For example, given that the term has historically been used in reductive and pejorative ways, you probably don't want to describe a romance novel as a "bodice ripper" unless you have already demonstrated a knowledge of and connection to the genre so that romance readers can trust that you're not using the term in a stereotypical fashion. (As we can trust the owners of the romance bookstore the Ripped Bodice.) This awareness and intentionality in our language needs to happen everywhere on our platforms: shelftalkers, tweets, blog posts, online staff picks, signage, newsletters, event introductions, and, of course, in our conversations with readers. If this seems burdensome, well, if your genre-reading booksellers are already engaged and empowered on a store's platforms all the manager really needs to do is get out of the way. If you don't have an expert in a given genre on staff, but still want to support a book or an author for whatever reason, take a moment to google any specific terms you're thinking of using. A few extra minutes of research could have a big impact on the efficacy of your message and could save you the potential headache of dealing with readers you may have offended.

You could, of course, just put *Never Let Me Go* in Science Fiction where it "belongs." I'm sure there are stores that make it work there, but a lot of stores would lose sales because customers would assume all of Ishiguro's fiction would be together and then assume the store doesn't have it if they don't see it with his other fiction. Time and time again I'll see a customer clearly looking for a specific book. I know this because I hear them talking to their friends, I've seen text messages on phones, I've even seen customers looking at our website on their phones. So I ask if I can help them find anything. Some say, "Yes, I'm looking for *Never Let Me Go*," some say, "No...actually, yes, I'm looking for *Never Let Me Go*," and some say, "No thanks," then look around a little longer and leave. There are a lot of different reasons why someone might say, "No thanks," many of which are well-intentioned, but still, it is amazing, just staggering, how many people come into the store with the intention of buying a specific book and leave when they don't find it without asking a bookseller for help.

Another option would be to put a copy of the book in every genre it could arguably belong to. That would solve both the problem of the politics of genre and reduce the problem of customers not finding and not asking for the specific book they want. But every copy of a book on your shelves means some other book is not on your shelves. To have double the number of copies of *Never Let Me Go* means you would have fewer copies of other books or fewer titles. You do this for every work of genre written by an author more known for fiction, or vice versa, or every work that has significant elements of multiple genres, and you end up with a very limited stock. A highly limited stock does not necessarily mean highly limited sales. Smaller stores and specialty stores are successful with highly limited stock.

Another radical solution to this conundrum is to have no genre at all. Alphabetize by author or title. For everything. If you know the author or the title, you'll find the book easily. If you're not looking for anything in particular, you could encounter some very interesting juxtapositions. What would it be like to see all of the *The Girl and The* ...novels in one place? To see Jane Jacobs next to Roy Jacobsen? To stumble from Renee Gladman to Malcolm Gladwell? To see Jacqueline Woodson's writing for all ages all together in one place? But if you're in the mood for a mystery but not looking for a specific mystery novel, good luck. As with the highly genred store, the right design could create a really interesting book buying experience, especially if the store uses rotating displays and shelftalkers to highlight genres customers might be looking for. Furthermore, a store organized like this directly acknowledges one of the problematic truths of genre: Genre is not inherent in the books themselves. It is an agreement among writers and readers about what aspects of a book we consider definitive and how we describe those aspects. We could just as logically genre books by who dies, how many characters it has, if meals are described, what job the protagonist has, where it's set, whether it's "dark" or "light," what primary emotion it elicits, what order the events are narrated in, forever and ever amen. To put this another way, the book doesn't care where you put it. A thriller won't burst into flames if you shelve it with mystery. This genre-less store simply throws out that agreement and presents books in a different context.

One might argue that bookstores and booksellers really only need to concern themselves with figuring out where most customers will expect a book to go and leave the consideration of where a book "belongs" to librarians, publishers, teachers, and critics. After all, one might argue, readers go to bookstores to buy books, not to engage in intractable political dialogues. There is some truth to that, of course, but we need to recognize two limitations to that argument. First, often we don't really know where most people will "expect" a book to be. We can only make guesses that are more or less educated. Customers frequently say, "I never would have looked here," when I show them how we've genred a book. (They almost always say that when I bring them to Sociology.) More important, we need to recognize Matthew Salesses's point from

Craft in the Real World that something becomes normal as a result of people doing it, not the other way around. Those "expectations" were born in our society and in our cultural and political context. "Alphabetize by author's last name" may feel as logical as any law of physics to most of us, but "last name" is not an absolute unit of meaning. It is a cultural construction. Where do you shelve Gabriel García Márquez? Miguel de Cervantes? Dante Alighieri? Does last name mean "family name," or "final name when read from right to left"? Does "family name" mean "patronymic" or "matronymic"? And who gets to decide? What does it mean when you impose what you assume your customers' expectations are on an author or culture who would shelve their books differently? And of course, where do those expectations come from? As Salesses says, "Expectations are not universal, they are standardized." [40]

The real solution to this problem of genre for bookstores (well, besides society getting its shit together) is to cultivate a community of customers who always ask when they can't find a book and who read your genreing generously, understanding you might do things differently if you had an infinite amount of space, and who see genre and genreing as an ongoing conversation the bookstore is participating in rather than a pronouncement the bookstore is making. Any of the potential solutions to the problem of genre can work if you bring your community along with the one you choose. My goal here isn't to solve the problem of genre for every store but to show it to be an idea ripe for critical reevaluation. Just because a store has always been genred in a particular way does not mean it has to stay that way forever. Just because a book has been in a particular genre for as long as you can remember doesn't mean it has to stay that way for all time. And perhaps most important, just because you might not have the answers to the political questions posed by genre and to the oppressive stratifications genre has been used for does

not mean you are absolved from responsibility for their continuation. Genre is a challenge, but it is also an opportunity.

Genre might also be a tool to solve one of the vexing challenges of bookselling in our contemporary political moment.
As Alex Shephard writes in the *New Republic*, "Fact-checking
would, it's also worth pointing out, make it impossible to publish a great many conservative books ... being forced to tell
the truth is not an existential issue for most of publishing; it
is for conservative imprints."[41] I have argued elsewhere that
simply not stocking these books and only selling them as special orders is the best solution to the problem publishing the
contemporary American right poses to booksellers, but genre
might be another possible response. Could a store that sub-
divides their politics section by left, right, and center better
serve their community? Mainstream, left, and right? What
about political science, politicians, and pundits? Political science and political opinion? Ultimately carrying a book is an
endorsement of some kind for the book and stocking that
book in a nonfiction genre says that the bookstore believes
it reaches some level of truth in the context of that genre.
You wouldn't put a book arguing the earth is flat in the Science section, so what should a store do with the books Alex
Shephard is describing? A more intentional engagement with
their content by creating genres might be one solution to the
problem these books present.

Bookstores need to think about how they shelve and how
they use the tool of genre to communicate with, inform, and
help their customers both find and discover books. For a
long time, many of us hid from this responsibility behind a
particular interpretation of free expression and a particular
interpretation of what influence bookstores should have over
what books are read in their communities. But we are facing
the rise of fascism in this country because a specific group
of ideologues has been actively pursuing its advancement

with whatever techniques they can get their hands on, and everyone else—bookstores and booksellers (and myself) included—has been at best participating in a debate or at worst getting out of the way. What do we do when we allocate any customer attention, let alone some form of "balanced" allocation of customer attention, to books that we know are full of bullshit ideas? How is that "fair"? How is that "balanced"? How is that "respecting our customers"?

What do we say when we say an independent bookstore is important to its community? We often talk about how much bookstores give back to their communities through donations and other community engagement, but plenty of local businesses do the same. We also talk about providing a "third place," a place that is neither home nor work, where people can gather, but just about any store that allows browsing and doesn't hound customers can be a third place. We talk about the importance of conversations that happen around and through books, but you can have rich, vibrant conversations around and through beer, bikes, spices, clothes, toys, fruit, cheese, and really anything that people create and buy. If the conversations at a bookstore are more likely to be rich and rewarding than at other stores because books are such naturally rich and rewarding sources for conversation, the distinction lies not with the store, but with the books. The difference, then, really, is the books themselves.

There are a number of arguments independent bookstores make in our competition with Amazon and one of them is that we actually make buying books more convenient because, through our professional judgment, we have filled our stores with books that bring value to our community. However we define "value," we sell our judgment to our community. We say, "These books are works of history about World War II." We say, "Out of all the books of World War II history that are available in the world, these are the few we have picked out for you." But we can't sell our judgment without accepting responsibility. You can't say, "Shop with us because of how we choose our books" and, "Our choices express no other information about the book besides the choice itself." We can't have it both ways: We can't tell our community to trust our stock and also that we have no official opinion about it.

You walk into a bookstore looking for something to read, maybe starting with the bestsellers or staff picks, maybe spending time at the seasonal or thematic displays. You move into the aisles of bookcases. Sometimes being surrounded by books feels like being embraced by books. You wander through the shelves, narrowing your search, using the walking time to listen to your thoughts about what you want and need for the day. You walk through Mystery. You walk through General World History. You walk through Music. A faced-out book calls to you, so you pull it down and read the summary. An author's name on a spine catches your eye and you try to remember if this was the writer your friend who's read everything told you about. Every physical book you see in every specific place involves a series of decisions, first by writers, then by the editors, marketers, and sales reps working for the publisher, and finally by booksellers. Some of the decisions are more intentional than others. Sometimes despite our best intentions, we end up putting a book where the physical copies of it will physically fit on our shelves. Sometimes, if you ask why this book is in this place, we'll say, "Well, there are a few different places it could go but we had to choose one." Because no matter how playful it is, how multifaceted it is, how directly it questions or critiques the very idea of categorization, a book can be in only one physical place at a time.

Genre is a form, a type, and a place, but ultimately, genre is a conversation. It is writers talking to writers, writers talking to readers, readers talking to readers, readers talking to writers, and, of course, booksellers talking to each other and everyone else. Whether we want it to or not, every decision we make about where to shelve a book participates in that conversation. That conversation takes place within a historical and a contemporary political context. A conversation about whose stories are valuable. A conversation about how books spread truth or don't. Conversation is supposed to be what we're good at. Talking about books is supposed to be one reason we are valuable. We can be passive about that conversation, trying to shift the responsibility to some imagined "average reader," or we can be active and intentional, directly conversing with the world of books in ways that promote our values, strengthen our communities, and increase access to the world of books.

THE LEAST WE CAN DO

White Supremacy, Free Speech,
and Independent Bookstores

APOLOGY

When Sean Spicer was given prime billing at BookExpo America and Milo Yiannopoulos tried to publish a book with Simon & Schuster, I churned out forty pages of text about free speech, white supremacy, and independent bookstores over the next several months, returning to it now and then as a salve or outlet for my frustration and then just...let it sit. I should have written something even earlier, after I had been in bookselling for ten years and watched Republicans and conservatives profiting—in terms of money and power—off the racist backlash to the Obama administration. Someone should have written something even earlier, as we watched the Bush administration start two endless wars, institute torture as an official American practice, and completely remake American society after the trauma of 9/11. Someone should have written something when Rush Limbaugh's first book was published, before the reactionary racism of right-wing talks shows became fully mainstream. Like so many white, liberal Americans, I thought the gains made during the Civil Rights Movement were secure and that even if there was still a long way to go toward true social and racial justice, at least we weren't sliding back. It's embarrassing. Only the thinnest veils were thrown over the racism of the war on drugs, criminal justice reform, and welfare reform. Even after the Tea Party rose to power almost entirely through the white grievance and racism stoked by Fox News. Even after the Republican Party formally embraced this radical version of themselves. I did not see a resurgent threat and I did not see my complicity in that resurgence.

At most, I was an active participant in a conversation with the Porter Square Books managers group about our relationship to books written by and/or supporting contemporary right-wing, conservative, and/or Republican authors, with some of us arguing that we needed to dramatically change that relationship, and others arguing that the current relationship is correct. Parts of that conversation will appear throughout this essay. But as the Trump administration, Fox News, and Republican politicians enacted more and more racist and destructive policies, we never reexamined that compromise. It just never seemed like the right time. There were always more pressing problems. Once the pandemic hit, we never felt like we had the emotional reserves for that difficult conversation. And I didn't force it. I expressed myself on Twitter and in informal conversations, but I never truly pushed for a formal reexamination of what books we should allow on our platforms, what ideas we want to give space to, and what people we want to be a revenue stream for.

Money is power. The more money you have, the more time you can spend advancing your cause, the more people you can hire to help advance your cause, the more you can donate to other people and organizations advancing your cause. If you have money, you can pay lobbyists, create fake and biased studies to support your ideologies, make misleading advertisements, hire lawyers to litigate cases you think will advance your cause, pay troll farms to harass your opponents on social media. If you can't convince people of your ideas, but you have enough money, you can get those ideas reflected in government policy anyway.

If you have published a book, people will listen to what you say, at least more than they will if you haven't. If people see your book at a bookstore, they will conclude that the book world believes your ideas are worth reading. Whether they agree with your ideas or not, the fact of a traditionally published book tells readers some basic level of value or legitimacy has been reached. Furthermore, publishing a book unlocks other platforms for your ideas: book reviews, media appearances, events, and other publicity. You'll get the chance to point people to your website and social media. If you're lucky, or have some specific supports, you'll even make money.

Donald Trump was president, in part, because the media, publishers, bookstores, book reviewers, readers, and everyone with power and influence in books decided it was okay to sell books by Rush Limbaugh, Bill O'Reilly, Ann Coulter, Laura Ingraham, Michael Savage, Sean Hannity, Tucker Carlson, and all the other right-wing pundits and politicians, monetizing and legitimizing the white supremacist ideas they expressed and providing a platform for those ideas to reach more people. Donald Trump was president because we did not take responsibility for our own decisions. Donald Trump was president because we did nothing when con artists monetized white grievance, white fear, and white supremacy. Most of us took some of that money. Some of us took a lot of that money. Donald Trump was president because the conservative movement over the last thirty years broke our political media's bullshit detector. Donald Trump was president because people like Newt Gingrich, Paul Ryan, Mike Pence, Ted Cruz, and, well, Donald Trump himself were taken seriously, as if they were honestly participating in American political discourse. Donald Trump was president because publishers and bookstores showed readers that we believed those people and ideas deserved to be taken seriously.

Whatever we do going forward, we can no longer pretend that we are innocent. Donald Trump put children in cages. We can no longer act as though book sales do not have ethical and moral components. Donald Trump sabotaged the national response to COVID-19, killing hundreds of thousands of people. We cannot pretend that it does not matter who we help make money. A Confederate flag was waved in the Capitol Building during a violent insurrection that killed six people. We cannot pretend that we don't have some responsibility over what ideas are discussed in public discourse.

Like people in many industries and institutions, booksellers have done a lot of work in the last few years in response to the Trump administration, the Black Lives Matter movement, the #MeToo movement, and other events and forces for social change in our society. We've formed committees, hosted panels, and held training sessions and though all of that is important, I have almost never seen booksellers grapple directly with the economic, social, and moral consequences of selling books by white supremacists, fascists, misogynists, and other believers in objectively dangerous ideologies. Though I will offer some specific strategies, I hope this piece acts as the start of a more sustained conversation about the relationship between bookselling, politics, and free speech. Furthermore, free speech is a concept of ragged edges and many of the decisions we make about what speech is protected or not, what speech is appropriate for what spaces, what speech should be amplified on which platforms, require nuance and context. Since I can't provide that nuance and context for everything, I'm going to focus on speech by Republicans with actual political power, and Fox News and conservative pundits with significant influence over politics and policy.

I apologize for waiting this long to take this small step

within my industry. I apologize for not listening to what many, many people had tried to tell me and all of white America about the threat to our country. I apologize for prioritizing avoiding interpersonal conflict with friends, family, and colleagues over confronting a persistent and deadly threat. I don't know if what I've written here will make a big difference. I don't know if independent bookstores have enough power to make a big difference in the fight against white supremacy, other supremacist ideologies, and fascism in America. But we have some power. And if we don't fight, we can't win.

TO SOME, THIS IS ALREADY A CIVIL WAR

The current state of American governance is not politics as usual. It isn't even the usual "let's find a way to be racist that isn't quite as bad" of most of American legislative politics. It isn't just "partisan bickering" or "both sides have some good ideas and some bad ideas." You may be insulated from the violence surging through our country. You may not spend time in radical right-wing corners of the internet. You may not see the recruiting efforts, the merchandise, the planning, the infiltration of our law enforcement and military by organized white supremacists, but all of that is happening. Some people in this country believe we are in a civil war, in the exact same way that some people believe the apocalypse is imminent, and they are acting like it.

It seems almost ... silly to spend time on this after the violent insurrection of January 6, 2021, but apparently even pipe bombs placed around D.C., men in military gear with zip cuffs and perhaps even assassination plans, evidence of coordination with members of Congress, and six people dead is not enough to convince everyone that we are in an armed and violent conflict. In fact, as I write this Republicans in Congress are acting as if the insurrection wasn't the violent assault we all watched on national television, but a peaceful protest. Some Republicans are just moving on, some are denying various aspects of it, some are spreading misinformation and conspiracy theories about it, and none of the Republican politicians with any kind of power have (to date) suffered any consequences whatsoever. But this is not something that will just pass. It was never something that would just pass. This is not something that will get sorted out in congressional committees. This was never something that would get sorted out in congressional committees. This is not something that will get hashed out in the marketplace of ideas. This was never something that would get hashed out in the marketplace of ideas. And this won't end with the Trump administration, no matter what eventually happens (or does not happen) to Donald Trump himself, just like it didn't end with the Nixon administration, the Reagan administration, or the two Bush administrations.

The complicity of American publishing and bookselling with white supremacy is not the most powerful force supporting and sustaining white supremacy in America. It's probably a minor one. And whatever antiracist and antifascist actions we take within our industry will also be relatively minor compared to actions taken by other institutions and industries. But we should take them, nonetheless. There are no minor actions in a civil war.

THERE ARE NO FREE SPEECH ABSOLUTISTS

The first time I heard the term "free speech absolutist" was in a conversation with another bookseller several years ago about the American Booksellers Association's new code of conduct for events and conferences. This other bookseller's concern was that people would be so afraid of saying something that could be considered a violation of the code of conduct that free speech would be curtailed. Booksellers would choose to remain silent rather than risk whatever punishments were in the code. I understand being concerned with making clear distinctions between speech that is "offensive" and speech that is "harassing" or between speech that makes people "uncomfortable" and speech that makes people "unsafe," but the term "free speech absolutism" doesn't actually interact with those distinctions. Even when used as a kind of shorthand for giving the benefit of the doubt to allowing rather than restricting speech, the term obfuscates the debate by shutting down the nuance around these issues.

I cannot call you up in the middle of the night and tell you I'm going to murder you. I cannot send an email to your boss that claims you were convicted of cruelty to animals. If I am a pharmaceutical company, I cannot say my new drug cures cancer if it doesn't cure cancer. I cannot tell you that I'm a doctor or lawyer or police officer if I am not. I cannot tell the IRS I made no money when, in fact, I made a lot of money. (Well, I can, but I have to speak a very specific language.) I can't say "fuck" on certain media at certain times of day, I can't use TV advertising to try to convince children to smoke, and, of course, I can't shout "Fire!" in a crowded theater. There has never been, there will never be, and no one has ever actually argued for, absolute freedom of speech.

Though some people, like the bookseller I was talking with, certainly use the term in good faith and it certainly sounds like a principled idea, most of the time arguments for "absolute freedom of speech" aren't actually used to advance an idea or work towards the truth. Rather, they are designed to shift the debate away from the ideas themselves while creating space to occupy on a platform. It is, essentially, a kind of rhetorical jiu jitsu that creates publicity and recruitment opportunities, obscures the terms of the discussion, and shifts the focus away from problematic or difficult to defend ideas to vaguer notions of free speech. If there was any doubt, any ambiguity, any space to learn something about personal expression and its relationship to society, it might be worth our time to seriously engage with arguments that include versions of the phrase "free speech absolutist," but there isn't, so we don't.

PROGRESS TOWARD BETTER IDEAS

Rather than thinking of our discourse as "the marketplace of ideas," I think of it as society's scientific method: people offer ideas (trial) and the use, meaning, and veracity of the ideas are examined until a flaw is revealed or a different idea is agreed to be better (error). As with any scientific endeavor, the more trials we have, the more truths we can discover. Protecting free speech allows for the greatest volume of these intellectual trials and errors.

But not all ideas or expressions are actual intellectual trials. Take, for example, the sentence "Cheetahs are a type of tree." This is, obviously, not true. But not only is it not true, it also doesn't help discover any truth. Everyone knows cheetahs are not trees and re-proving the fact that cheetahs aren't trees doesn't help produce some other truth.

Take a more reasonable example from the debate around the Affordable Care Act, the signature legislation from Barack Obama's first term as president. Very broadly, the Affordable Care Act's goal was to lower health care costs through a number of mechanisms while leaving it based in private health insurance. It was modeled directly on the Massachusetts health care program signed into law by Republican governor Mitt Romney. There was a lot of nonsense in the debate around the ACA, but the most nonsensical was the accusation that it created "death panels," essentially euthanasia bureaucrats who would decide whether or not your grandma would get the health care she needed.[42] The substance from which this lie was drawn is the provision that allows for Medicare to cover optional appointments dealing with living wills and other end-of-life care issues. If you can't see how coverage of optional counseling sessions (which absolutely could result in a patient deciding, "Don't you dare unplug me!") could become death panels…well…exactly. But the idea nevertheless gained traction, boosted by the likes of Sarah Palin and former lieutenant governor of New York Betsy McCaughey, and marred the debate long after it was debunked. It was rated "Pants on Fire" pretty much every time it was repeated and named the "Lie of the Year" by PolitiFact.

By lying about "death panels," right-wing critics of the Affordable Care Act sabotaged the discourse around it. Instead of debating things like whether there was enough funding allotted for the rollout of the technology or exploring other improvements to the actual bill, the discourse wasted time and energy on a problem that did not exist. (I would argue that most of that was tactical rather than earnest, as it is a lot easier to get people to oppose the ACA because "euthanasia is bad" than because "people should have their financial lives ruined because they cannot afford to pay their medical bills.") To return to my extended metaphor, the idea that the ACA created panels of bureaucrats that could deny lifesaving care to the elderly was not an actual intellectual trial from which other truth could be learned, and just like proving cheetahs are not trees, we learned nothing from proving the ACA did not have "death panels." To be clear, I'm not arguing that people who claimed the ACA was out to murder grandma should have been thrown in jail for expressing that opinion; I'm saying that we shouldn't have given them platforms to express that idea, that if they wrangled a platform anyway they should have been shut down once they started to express that idea, and that depending on who they were, what their jobs were, and how much power they had, they should have suffered professional consequences for their lies, especially if they kept saying it after it was debunked.

IS COMPROMISE POSSIBLE BETWEEN OPPOSING IDEAS?

Most of the time, we have to act even when we haven't reached consensus about an action, idea, or policy. In those cases, we must find compromise between the proposed ideas in order to move forward with whatever we are doing. Just as we need as many honest ideas as possible for all those trials, we need as many honest ideas as possible from which to explore compromise. For example, "the rich should pay no taxes," is a terrible idea, but we can at least imagine compromises between it and the idea that "the rich should pay taxes commensurate with the benefits they have received from society."

But compromise isn't possible with some ideas. What would represent a compromise between the ideas "Cheetahs are a type of tree" and "No, they're not, you fucking weirdo"? Or perhaps, "I would like to burn your house down," and "Please don't burn my house down." Is a half-burned house really a compromise? If it is possible to find some kind of compromise between the expressed idea and its opposite then it will probably also contribute to that whole society's scientific-method thing. But if it's not, what work does the idea do? And if the idea does no work, why would you have an obligation to include it in your platform?

*

SUPREMACIST IDEAS AND THE POSSIBILITY OF
COMPROMISE

As others have eloquently pointed out, there is no com-promise between "Black people are human beings" and "Black people are not human beings." And we know this, not just because of obvious logic, but because the vast majority of America's social and economic problems and injustices are rooted in trying to create a compromise between "Black people are human beings" and "Black people are not human beings." Can you imagine looking someone in the eye and telling them they need to believe what they are watching is a "debate" or "free exchange of ideas" if one of the possible conclusions is "You are not human"? Furthermore, the process that created this "compromise" is much less like actual compromise and much more like appeasement. To many (to most), this isn't a conversation. It's a conflict. To others, this isn't a debate. It is still a war.

Supremacist ideas, in the form of white supremacy, in the form of misogyny, in the form of xenophobia, are inherently antithetical to compromise. In a white supremacist society, white people do not have to compromise with non-white people, regardless of the issues, ideas, policies, and potential actions. In a misogynist society, men don't need to compromise with women. In a xenophobic society, you don't have to compromise with someone born in a different country. The alt-right, white supremacists, incels, fascists, and a whole lot of people who would consider themselves (and are considered) to be mainstream Republicans don't actually believe in compromise; they believe in getting what they want, however they can.

*

WHATEVER IS HAPPENING ISN'T BASKETBALL

Imagine if a basketball player stopped dribbling and just ran with the ball and dunked it. Now, imagine if the two points counted. Maybe the player is ashamed and never does it again. Maybe that's the end of it. Or maybe the player does it again and gets away with it again. It's a lot easier to score if you don't have to dribble. (Joke about how James Harden doesn't have to dribble.) So more players stop dribbling. Maybe some still do. Maybe a lot still do for a whole host of reasons but those who dribble lose. So now some players never dribble, some dribble every now and then, some dribble most of the time, and some still dribble all the time like they're supposed to. Something is happening on basketball courts, but it's not basketball. That is the state of American discourse. Very broadly, one team is still mostly playing basketball, while the other team just picks up the ball and runs.

There are problems with using sports, or any kind of competition, as a metaphor for the state of discourse because, in theory, discourse should not be a competition. Despite all our differences and disagreements, everyone involved in our discourse *should* have the same goal; to work toward policies that make the world better. Even though we differ on how to make that happen, even though we differ on what constitutes "better," the "winner" or "loser" of the debate is irrelevant to the solution the debate produces.

Over the course of American history various groups, identities, and ideologies have treated discourse as a competition, as something that can be won or lost. The thing about making winning your only goal, is, well, you tend to win. Not all the time, of course, but way more than you would have if your only goal had been to play the best basketball you could. If political representation was based on which party would enact the policies most Americans support, Democrats would have been in power at almost every level of government for a quarter of a century or more. So more and more Republicans have played only to win. When they stopped being able to convince people to vote for them, they stopped trying to convince people, instead shifting their focus to turning out their base by incorporating whatever right-wing nonsense was most motivating at the time and leveraging specific wedge issues (same sex marriage, gun control, abortion) that inspired those voters, then moving on to the next when either the issue was resolved or the voters' focuses changed. (Notice how little we hear about gay marriage now. Notice how once gay marriage was made legal by the Supreme Court, the greatest threat to American society was suddenly transgender rights.) As the cynical techniques worked, the techniques got more cynical. When the information didn't support Republican goals, they spread misinformation. When their actions were questioned they used "whattaboutism" rather than actually defending those actions. They prevented the passage of or refused to support any policy that could be considered a win for the Democrats, even if, like the ACA, that win included plenty of Republican policies and priorities. They gerrymandered districts at an unprecedented level so they could maintain legislative control whether more people voted for them or not. When the Voting Rights Act was gutted, they added enhanced voter suppression to their arsenal, specifically tailoring voting laws to discourage likely Democratic voters.

They still use the gestures and language of rational debate and they certainly argue that their opponents have an obligation to convince them of absolutely everything (even things they may have previously agreed with), but the vast majority of new voters they have gained over the last few years seem to have gotten there through indoctrination by Fox News and the right-wing internet.

What is the value of having ideas from Republicans in your stores if the authors of those ideas aren't actually looking to convince anyone their ideas are correct?

USING THE COURT TO DO ANYTHING BUT PLAY BASKETBALL

Outside of Congressional politics we saw another technique, especially after the advent of the internet. Radical right-wing groups hijacked the mechanisms of discourse not to actually engage in those debates but to simply occupy that space, essentially as a publicity technique. Because the ragged edges of free speech require nuanced debate to navigate, because very broadly most people support free speech, and because as a culture Americans identify "free speech" as a fundamental value, positioning yourself in that ongoing debate about what types of speech have the right or privilege to happen in what types of spaces is an easy way to occupy space in a discourse whether that discourse has anything to do with free speech and whether your point about free speech does any productive work in the discourse. This is why "cancel culture" is such a common talking point from the right. (Which was of course preceded by "political correctness.") It allows them to reframe a debate about sexual harassment in professional settings, or anti-Semitism, or how an estate wants to manage an artist's past use of racist imagery, away from those issues, while, at the same time, maintaining their participation in the discussion around those issues.

To return to our basketball court: Imagine if teams started putting out extra players who just…stand there with websites on their jerseys. Every now and then maybe they wave at the ball or take a step or two in the direction of the play, but they really just spend most of their time arguing with the ref that they should be allowed to be there. Once again, we find ourselves with something happening in the space, but it's not really a basketball game.

POPPER'S PARADOX OF TOLERANCE

Karl Popper's paradox of tolerance, from *The Open Society and Its Enemies*, is a relatively simple idea (especially in the world of paradoxes): If you allow every voice into a space, with no moderation, eventually intolerant voices will make it an intolerant space, resorting to violence if they need to in order to control the space. Whether we're talking about Weimar Germany or the punk rock and hard-core music scenes, when you tolerate white supremacists in your space, your space becomes a white supremacist space. "Unlimited tolerance must lead to the disappearance of tolerance. If we extend unlimited tolerance," Popper argued, "even to those who are intolerant, if we are not prepared to defend a tolerant society against the onslaught of the intolerant, then the tolerant will be destroyed, and tolerance with them."[43] We're actually watching experiments in low-moderation space in real time on social media. Many people, especially women and even more especially women of color, do not express themselves on Twitter because when they do, Twitter allows their timelines to be flooded with death and rape threats, threats against their families and children, and messages that would get someone fired or arrested in virtually any other context. A death threat cannot be answered with rational debate. As Popper says, "It may easily turn out that [the intolerant] are not prepared to meet us on the level of rational argument, but begin by denouncing all argument; they may forbid their followers to listen to rational argument, because it is deceptive, and teach them to answer arguments by the use of their fists or pistols." To put this another way, conservatives and other right-wing thinkers, pundits, and politicians frequently use harassment to stifle the free speech of other people on social media. "We should therefore claim, in the name of tolerance, the right not to tolerate the intolerant." Twitter would actually have much more open discourse and be a much more tolerant space if it actually enforced its own terms of service and refused to tolerate intolerance. (This comfort with intolerance has only gotten worse since Elon Musk took over the platform.)

I can already hear someone arguing that no one needs to be on Twitter (or any other social media) and though that is sort of true (though it conveniently ignores how many jobs, especially in the book industry, require a social media presence) it's also kind of my point. Intolerant acts drive people away and eventually you end up with a purely intolerant space.

BACK TO THE LAB

To circle back to the language of science: Lies, misinformation, bad faith arguments, and expressions that negate the expression of others are like tampering with lab results. We cannot find a cure for cancer if someone mislabels the samples, lies about the results, refuses to change their conclusions after those conclusions have been shown incorrect, or in any other way obscures or diminishes the results of the testing. The discourse around finding a cure for cancer is only productive if everyone involved is primarily concerned with finding a cure for cancer and is willing to be open and honest with their tests and arguments and open to being critiqued and shown wrong in their efforts. Likewise, the discourse around national policy is only productive if everyone involved in that discourse is committed to finding the best national policy rather than having their guy win. Just as science doesn't work if those with power over its application do not believe in science, democracy, in whatever form it takes, doesn't work if a critical mass of those participating in the dialogue do not believe in democracy.

STAMPED FROM THE BEGINNING

Every now and then you read a book and something mysterious snaps into focus. I had always wondered why contemporary Republicans could act like increasing the federal deficit was the single worst sin an administration could commit when Democrats wanted to spend money on social programs yet they themselves increase the deficit all the time with tax breaks, military spending, and wars when they are in power. In *Stamped from the Beginning: The Definitive History of Racist Ideas in America,* Dr. Ibram X. Kendi shows that racist policies and practices preceded racist ideas and ideologies. The ideas were designed to justify slavery, rather than slavery growing out of racist ideas. Because the job of these ideas is to support a specific policy, they aren't held to the same standards as other ideas. They don't need to be consistent over time. They don't need to incorporate agreed-upon facts. They don't need to be internally consistent. They can even include facets that are mutually exclusive.

The Three-Fifths Compromise is a perfect example of the flexible logic of racist ideas. Under the compromise, three-fifths of a state's slave population would count toward the state's total population, increasing the number of representatives the state would have in the House of Representatives.[44] That makes no sense. If slaves are property rather than human beings, why should their number count toward political power? Elbridge Gerry of Massachusetts asked why should "blacks, who were property in the South," count toward representation "any more than the Cattle & horses of the North?"[45] And if slaves do have political value, then, logically, shouldn't they have some rights or inputs or protections within the political system? But the point of the debate, at least from the slaveholders' perspective, wasn't to make sense, but to protect the institution of slavery by increasing the power of the slaveholding states. And that is exactly what the compromise did. The contemporary Republican Party, in large part because of a process that started with Nixon's Southern Strategy (which involved attracting southern Democrats alienated from the party by the Civil Rights legislation), is now the formal party of racist thought, so their ideas are used as techniques for policy and power.

Why argue that coverage for optional end-of-life counseling sessions constitutes a "death panel" when that is obviously not true? Because it grabs headlines, erodes support for the bill, and draws attention away from the potential benefits of the bill in order to deny President Obama a legislative victory and lay the groundwork for a midterm backlash. More recently Representative Marjorie Taylor Greene claimed[46] that legislation to expand background checks for gun purchases and give federal law enforcement more time to vet gun buyers included a gun registry, even though the legislation actually explicitly excluded one. Republicans act as if increasing the federal deficit is like a gunshot wound when they are arguing against funding social programs because it's easier than arguing some people deserve to starve to death in the richest country in the world. Once again, we find ourselves unable to debate ideas because the ideas do not follow the rules that create debate. You can't debate ideas that aren't interested in being true.

*

THE TENTH ARTIST

Stick with me through one more thought experiment to try to bring these threads together and a little closer to the world of bookstores.

Imagine that an art gallery invites ten artists to do a joint exhibition. The tenth artist never arrives to set up the exhibition.

The next morning, the gallery owner comes in and all the paintings in the exhibition have been turned to face the wall. The gallery owner finds a note from the tenth artist that says turning the other paintings around, without getting permission from the other artists, is their contribution to the exhibition.

Obviously, turning the other paintings around is a statement, a personal expression, and perhaps even a critique, and the tenth artist shouldn't go to jail for it. But, though it is the tenth artist's personal expression, it negates the personal expression of all the other artists. It's one thing to say that you believe the back of the canvas has more value than the painting itself, or that the other nine artists do not deserve to be in galleries, but it is another to prevent other people from seeing the paintings.

So what should the gallery owner do? They are responsible for the platform the gallery offers, so they are stewards of the discourse that occurs on the platform. If they think there is value in this particular exchange, they can put in the work needed to make this a meaningful exchange. They can take photographs of the paintings facing the wall, print them out life size, turn the paintings the right way, and hang the negations next to their corresponding paintings. That would preserve the image of negation in a way that would carry most, if not all, of the critique inherent in the tenth artist's action, without actually negating the expression of the other artists. It is a creative way to manage the discourse so that the public can interact with all the expressions and come to their own assessments. (And what the tenth artist should have done to begin with.)

Of course, the gallery owner would be well within their rights to turn all the paintings the right way and tell the tenth artist to fuck right off for being a selfish fucking asshole. Disagreement on a platform takes work to be productive and maybe the gallery owner doesn't want to or doesn't have the time to put that kind of work into their platform at the moment. Given that the tenth artist did not follow the expectations of the exhibition (did not follow the convention of the discourse) and undercut the other artists (actively negated expression in the discourse), why should the gallery owner give the tenth artist a platform?

Now, let's imagine the tenth artist (once again without permission) paints over the other paintings. It is still personal expression, it is still an idea, but once again, it is a negation. The tenth artist's expression erased the expression of the other nine artists. Much like Popper's paradox of tolerance, when negation is allowed to stand on the platform eventually there will only be negation on the platform. To connect back to the nature of compromise, if one expression is a house and the other expression is burning down the house, if the second expression is allowed to stand then there is no more house.

But this expression not only destroys the discourse the gallery owner was trying to create on their platform, it does actual, tangible harm to others. It has cost the nine other artists time, money, and emotional anguish. I think we could all agree they would be well within their rights to sue the tenth artist. I imagine the gallery owner would also be able to sue as they would lose all the potential revenue from selling those paintings. If you were another gallery owner, would you work with the tenth artist? What if the tenth artist claimed they had a right to your platform because their personal expression might be constitutionally protected? What if the tenth artist argued the discourse is only legitimate when he, um, excuse me, when *they* have the right to destroy it?

Now imagine that the tenth artist (again without permission) replaced the descriptions of the paintings with misleading, inaccurate, or deceitful descriptions. You can still see the paintings, but the viewers will interact with them in ways the other artists never intended. This act isn't a complete negation of discourse, but, by preventing the viewers from interacting with the works as they were intended, the discourse has been damaged. To put this another way, honest discourse cannot happen with dishonest materials.

If you were a gallery owner, would you give your platform to the tenth artist? If you know they will undercut some people's ability to express themselves, or will derail the discourse through dishonesty, or might actually do real harm to those others trying to participate? If you would not give the tenth artist a platform in your gallery, why should the *New York Times* give a platform to climate change deniers? White supremacists want to erase the expression of people of color, so why should they be allowed on our platforms? Misogynists want to erase the expression of women, so why should they be allowed on our platforms? All supremacist and phobic ideologies have costumed their ideas in the diction of science, parading bullshit around (even contradictory bullshit) as justification for their ideas, so why should we give a platform to someone who bases their conclusions on IQ testing or argues for gay conversion therapy?

Obviously, having a book on your shelves doesn't erase all the others or somehow prevent a customer from pulling others off the shelf, but shelf space is limited. Every book on your shelves is taking the place of another book that could be there. The same goes for display space, which is even more limited. The issue of display space was a major challenge when Porter Square Books was deciding how to handle the controversy around Jeanine Cummins' *American Dirt*. Many members of the staff and management wanted to act on the critique from Mexican and Mexican American critics who argued that *American Dirt* is a racist book, inaccurately portraying Mexico, Mexican culture, and the asylum crisis at our southern border in ways that damaged the discourse around the issue. Others felt that Cummins had been successful in her stated goals, or, at the very least, that altering our decision around displaying the book in response to those critiques infringed on Cummins's free expression and/or wasn't the type of judgment we were supposed to make. In the end, we compromised, displaying it on the bestsellers display where it could not really be replaced by another title, but not displaying it in other displays, like the new-fiction display, where its space could be given to another book. In other words, beyond the damage done in the wider world, there is an opportunity cost when bookstores choose to stock certain books, just like there is an opportunity cost when the *New York Times* runs a column by a climate change denier or something like Tom Cotton's incendiary piece "Send in the Troops,"[47] which argued for military intervention in BLM protests.

Bookstores might be insulated from most of the negating forces in our discourse, and do not have the same moral obligation to vet specific ideas the way the *New York Times* does, but that does not excuse us for supporting those forces on our platform. Much of this essay is written in anticipation of counterarguments, so I feel like I need to make a stronger argument about why bookstores should care about shit that doesn't happen in bookstores, but at the same time, I think Kayla Chadwick phrases it perfectly: "I don't know how to explain to you that should care about other people."[48] Just because you live in a brick house doesn't mean you get to be friends with arsonists.

EXCLUSION IS PART OF INCLUSION

What you have on your shelves is a statement of what you value, just like every book a publisher publishes is a statement of what they value. There is only so much control over how readers and customers interpret that valuation. What does it feel like for a person of color to walk into a bookstore and see a copy of Sean Hannity's latest book? Is the first thing they see "a commitment to free expression" or "an acceptance of white supremacy"? Do they see "giving space to opinions you disagree with" or "more concerned about an angry old white dude's anger than your fear?" Do they see "this one copy represents a limited platform" or "we're cool with making money off racism"? There are other actions you can take that might earn you the benefit of the doubt from these customers, but even considering the fundamental lack of control one has over how other people interpret one's decisions, regardless of how you frame it, regardless of your specific valuation of the title, when you have a book by a white supremacist on your shelves you are saying, "I believe this book has enough value of some kind to justify its author and publisher making money from sales of it at my bookstore." It says, "I value the potential sales of the book more than I fear the consequences of these ideas or the author's actions."

What about when someone from the LGBTQ2+ community, or their allies, sees a book by, about, or celebrating Mike Pence? Pence supports conversion therapy, which is child abuse, his homophobia contributed to an HIV outbreak in Indiana by disrupting a clean-needle program, his wife works at a school that excludes homosexuals, and he continually supported Donald Trump through all his crimes, including declining to support use of the Twenty-Fifth Amendment to remove Trump after the insurrection. What does someone of Mexican, South American, or Latin American heritage see when they see *The Art of the Deal* (how many bookstores brought this back into stock when Trump announced he was running for president?) or any of the many books that supported him? Do they think, Well, it's important to include both sides, or do they think, This fucker would have put my children in a cage? Muslims? People who come from the places Trump called "shithole countries"? Sexual assault survivors? I don't know the answer to these questions and I don't know how many other booksellers do either, because I have not seen these questions asked.

In *Making Spaces Safer: A Guide to Giving Harassment the Boot Wherever You Work, Play, and Gather*, Shawna Potter argues, "You have to think both holistically and specifically. For instance, don't overlook the little things that make up the overall feel of your space. Don't give a pass to discriminatory statements, art, or 'jokes' on event flyers, tip jars, or band merchandise."[49] One could argue that a single book on the shelf doesn't contribute much to the "overall feel of your space," at least not the way a poster in a music venue would, but faced-out books and displays certainly do. One might argue that even then, the occasional display doesn't mean a whole lot, but as Potter says, "Each instance [of harassment] matters, because they add up."[50] Furthermore, they can act as reminders of and potential triggers of past harassment. Seeing a picture of Sean Hannity on the cover of his displayed or faced-out book is not an act of racist harassment, but it can certainly remind people of past acts of racist harassment and it certainly undercuts any goal the store might have of being a refuge for members of their community. Furthermore,

"A key component of discrimination in our culture is that it minimizes the very real suffering of marginalized people," so be very careful before you argue that something that happens in or is a part of your space is "not that bad" to make sure you have truly examined the act or situation from the perspective of those who might feel hurt by it and factor in how this moment might fit in with a lifetime of accumulated moments. Finally, Potter is very clear about how the idea of "safer spaces" is not supposed to be used. "It's important to point out that, as I use the term, a 'safer space' is not one free of challenging ideas or different opinions. It's not about avoiding exposure to people who are different from you."[51] Potter is speaking primarily from and to the music industry, but I think her ideas are applicable to all managed public and semipublic spaces, including bookstores. As with posters, merch, and other visible aspects of bars and music halls, the books we choose to stock contribute to how safe or unsafe our space feels.

In conversations with booksellers, I've heard it argued that booksellers have an obligation to withhold judgment, that it is not really our job to tell people whether a book is "good" or not, and that it is a violation of our social contract to pass any kind of judgment on books or judge people based on what books they buy. I absolutely agree with the latter idea and very broadly—and when phrased in certain ways—also agree with the idea that booksellers should not dictate which books are "good." But I don't really see why choosing not to stock a book because it is written by a white supremacist is fundamentally different from all the other reasons we have to not stock a book. A customer will have to ask for it at the desk if it's a publisher we don't get good terms from, or if it's about a non-local sports team, or if the book has gone out of print, like the Dr. Seuss books that were pulled by his estate because they contained racist images, or any of the dozens of different reasons why a specific book might not be on the shelves at a particular time. It is also somewhat difficult to hear a principle of nonjudgment from an industry that judged and shamed romance readers and writers for decades.

The fact that the Republican Party and much of mainstream conservative media has collapsed into blatant and aggressive white supremacy, xenophobia, misogyny, and fascism, and that much of publishing treats them as if this is acceptable, is their fucking mistake, not yours. Trump being president does not make his ideas worth your shelf space. Fox News getting ratings does not make the ideas of its pundits worth your shelf space. Just because the Republican Party is the largest conservative party in America does not make their ideas worth your shelf space.

CURATION IS NOT CENSORSHIP

In the same way that we know that "free speech absolutism" doesn't exist, we also know exactly what censorship is. Censorship is the suppression or prohibition of speech, communication, or other information on the basis that such material is considered objectionable, harmful, sensitive, or inconvenient. Censorship is what happens when the government bans books, movies, or other media and punishes the production, distribution, or ownership of that media. As private businesses, bookstores are under no obligation to carry any book they don't want to for any reason. And we know this because many bookstores specialize. Primarily carry books by authors of color and authors from marginalized communities? Not censoring white authors. Only carry sci-fi, fantasy, mystery, romance, cookbooks, nonfiction, poetry? Not censoring other genres. Only carry books by Christian publishers? Not censoring other publishers. Only carry books by authors whose first name is Jonathan? Probably not a very good bookstore, but still, not censorship. Nothing a bookstore has the actual power to do is censorship. Whether argued in good faith or bad, with real critical thought behind it or lazy point scoring, arguing whether a bookstore is censoring a book or author is a waste of time.

As part of those conversations around displaying *American Dirt*, I heard it argued that choosing not to display the book in all the displays it might fit in "stifled" the free speech of the author. Displays are not an expression of accessibility but of amplification. The book and the ideas and speech it contains will still be accessible whether it is on display, on the shelf, or needs to be special-ordered. Putting it on display simply amplifies it and extends its reach. Furthermore, newspapers, journals, and magazines choose which books to amplify by choosing whether or not to review them or cover them in some other way. Books section editors and book reviewers are not accused of "stifling" free speech when they exercise their editorial discretion by not covering, and thus, not amplifying, a book.

Bookstores are platforms. By carrying, displaying, and special-ordering books, the ideas contained within them are provided with an audience. That platform can be pretty large (stacks on the table, face-outs in the shelves, staff picks, shelftalkers, events, and promotion on social media), relatively small (a copy on the shelves), or essentially non-existent (special-ordering books not carried, books listed on industry-wide databases); but as private businesses, bookstores have the right to decide which ideas get to use their platforms and which ideas don't, which books they will try to create sales for by putting them in front of customers, which few thousands of books out of the hundreds of thousands published every year will be right at hand. I mean, that is one way to describe the "curation" that Ryan Raffaelli identified as one of the key components of the independent bookstore resurgence. A bookstore without curation isn't a bookstore, it's a warehouse.

WHAT YOU DON'T LIKE BUT STILL STOCK

Whenever concerns about giving a platform to white supremacists and other demonstrably dangerous ideologies are brought up, someone inevitably argues that bookstores have a responsibility to open discourse and that means bookstores have a responsibility to carry books expressing ideas the booksellers personally disagree with. This point has come up in several conversations I've had and I've struggled to articulate this idea in the moment, but "disagreement" isn't the issue. "Destructiveness" is. Whether I, personally, agree with an idea or not is almost beside the point if it is hurting other people. Furthermore, I, personally, have never argued and have never seen or heard anyone argue that bookstores shouldn't carry books with conflicting opinions, or that they should only carry books whose ideas the booksellers agree with. This response seems to be directed at general assumptions about "social justice warriors," "wokeness," or "cancel culture," instead of any actual argument being made. But even then, disagreeing with the ideas expressed in a book doesn't require you to stock it. Just because an idea or a person conflicts with your ideas does not mean productive discourse will come from interacting with that idea or person. And just because a book exists, it does not mean that including it in your platform makes your platform open and inclusive. You are not obligated to keep a bookseller on staff who does no real work for the store. So why should you be obligated to keep ideas on your platform that do no real work for the discourse?

*

WHAT CAN INDEPENDENT BOOKSTORES DO IN THE SPACE THEY OCCUPY?

Independent bookstores occupy a strange and difficult space in the defense of our national discourse in the age of Trump (an era which is going to outlast him). On the one hand, independent bookstores are respected institutions in their communities. We are drivers of the national literary conversation. Individuals and communities look to us for guidance on what to read, which, at least for readers, isn't that far removed from looking to us for guidance on how to be. But we are also a tiny fraction of the book industry. For all our influence, both short- and long-term, on which books are talked about and which books sell, we actually sell surprisingly few books. Even if every independent bookstore in the country banded together to take some action, in strictly economic terms, it wouldn't amount to a whole lot. The Big 5 publishers would blink, maybe issue a statement, sure, but quickly move on with their publishing plans. Of course, we can't band together to take such actions because, and you'll want to be sitting down for this, antitrust laws make it illegal for bookstores (who are legally competitors) to take many kinds of group actions.

Perhaps the most obvious technique is to refuse to sell books that damage our discourse in the ways described above. But no buyer can read every book their store carries. No bookseller can fact-check every assertion and track down every source in every work that claims to be a work of history. We can't vet every book of political nonfiction to make sure it isn't just a collection of racist dog whistles, conspiracy theories, and white grievance. Nor can booksellers hunt down the identity of every author to make sure they aren't Nazis or abusers or TERFs. So when St. Martin's Press tells us that

Killing Lincoln by Bill O'Reilly is a work of history, we kinda have to believe them.

Or do we?

For me, there is a pretty simple solution. In this political moment, if the author was racist and fascist enough to self-identify as Republican when Donald Trump was party leader, they are racist and fascist enough to be excluded from your platform. If they are racist and fascist enough to be Fox News contributors, they are racist and fascist enough to be excluded from your platform. Will that miss the Gavin McInneses and Richard Spencers of the world? Maybe, but we can't let perfection be the enemy of the good. If we remove nine out of ten white supremacists from our platform, that still counts.

ON BOOKSTORES AND BAKERIES

I've heard the argument from a number of different people that if we use our morals to influence our business decisions, we're no different from the bakers who refused to make wedding cakes for gay people.[52] They used their morals to guide their business decisions and we all condemned it as an act of discrimination. Therefore, if we use our morals to guide our business decisions, we are also committing acts of discrimination.

But there is a big difference between refusing to bake a wedding cake for a gay couple and refusing to stock a book by an author you believe is advancing the cause of white supremacy.

First, gay people don't hurt other people by being gay, but white supremacists (misogynists, xenophobes, homo/transphobes) do hurt other people. The bakers will claim they are hurt by gay people getting married, but they are wrong. The actions of gayness are not destructive. The actions of white supremacy are. A bookstore that chooses not to work with a racist organization or facilitate the bulk purchase of a racist book by a known racist, identifies a set of actions that are doing actual harm to real people and then refuses to support that set of actions.

Second, and more important for this specific distinction, we are not refusing to serve customers because of who they are. Maybe a bakery doesn't have, I don't know, red velvet cake for some reason. They are not discriminating against you if they won't sell a red velvet cake, even if you really want a red velvet cake. But if they sell wedding cake and they refuse to sell you a wedding cake because it would be used in a gay wedding, they are discriminating against you. A white supremacist (assuming they aren't doing anything to make staff or other customers feel unsafe) will be able to buy from us any books we stock. Any books we sell. We are not restricting access to our general services and space or choosing to sell some books to some people but not to others. Deciding what to sell is different from deciding who to serve. Refusing to be a revenue stream for white supremacists is different from refusing to sell the books you do have to people of certain identities.

CUSTOMERS ARE NOT THE ONLY PEOPLE IN YOUR STORE

Our conversation around curation almost always focuses (somewhat reasonably) on how customers will interact with our stock. But customers are not the only people in our stores. Booksellers (obviously) interact with our selection as well and what that selection says about the values and priorities of our stores. Why would a non-white person take a low-paying, emotionally, intellectually, and physically demand-

ing job that also requires them to sell books by white supremacists? What does it feel like to pour yourself into reading and
handselling and event introductions and social media and
everything else that booksellers do to make bookstores successful and have someone above you in the organization tell
you a person who denies your humanity deserves a presence in
your space? What does it feel like to be told Sean Hannity has
more of a right to be heard than you have a right to feel safe?

At the very least, have the discussion within your store.
Find out what all your booksellers think about the issue. How
does the presence of certain books on the shelves impact
them? Do any of those books make them uncomfortable?
What does it feel like for them to sell one of these books? If
they had ultimate power, what would the shelves look like?
Though we focus on how customers feel when they are in our
stores, we shouldn't neglect how our booksellers feel when
they are in our stores. If we want our staff to look like the real
world, if we want booksellers of color, booksellers across the
gender spectrum, booksellers with a range of abilities and
challenges, both visible and invisible, we need to at least ask
them what it feels like to sell books by people who deny their
humanity. Another one of those free speech bons mots goes
"you have the right to swing your fist until it hits my nose." If
someone on your staff feels like they are getting punched, you
owe it to them as human beings and you owe it to yourself
as a responsible business owner who relies on the skills and
expertise of your staff to at least have the conversation.

ALSO A BUSINESS DECISION

Who is going to actually help keep you open in the long
term: the customers and readers who live in your community and seek refuge and resources in your stacks, who

see you as something more than a store, who appreciate how being in your store makes them feel, who engage with you in actual conversations on social media, who have made you a part of their lives in big and small ways; or the asshole who complains because you haven't stacked Hannity (or whoever their favorite right-wing pundit is) high enough? What about the provocateur who manipulates controversy for publicity? What about the right-wing group looking to funnel money to a politician they like by bulk purchasing their book?

Who would show up if the store had a fire or was damaged by some natural disaster? Who would show up if one of your booksellers had a health crisis and needed help paying medical bills? Who would pick up a mass market every now and then during a recession because, even though they don't have much money, it is important to them to keep you in their lives? Who would donate to a GoFundMe? Who would counterprotest in your favor? The people who tweet back and forth with you over the years or the rando who pops into your mentions to say, "Ever hear of free speech?"

In short, who is more likely to give you the money you need to stay in business? Customers who have become invested in you as an aspect of their community (both physical and digital) because of the content of your character, or those swooping in for one book, one bulk purchase, one event, one tactical display of outrage? From a business standpoint, is it worth risking the former to accommodate the latter?

Furthermore, many, if not most, independent bookstores have decided not to stock books published by Amazon. I remember the discussion around whether or not indie bookstores should carry Penny Marshall's memoir and do not remember any significant concern over the possibility that we might be infringing on the First Amendment rights of Penny Marshall or Amazon as a publisher by declining to stock the book. It's usually framed as rational self-interest. Amazon is a direct and active threat to our businesses and therefore we have decided not to provide a platform for authors who chose to publish with them or become a revenue stream for the company, regardless of the content of the books themselves. Why is that fundamentally different from choosing not to provide a platform or revenue stream to people whose actions are a direct and active threat to human lives?

MORE THAN NEGATING THE NEGATERS

Through staff picks, shelftalkers, displays, events, recommendations, conversations with readers, and on all our platforms both physical and digital, booksellers should advocate for marginalized voices and communities, center own voices, guide readers to the books and authors that will help them grow and develop as readers, take risks to bring attention to books that might make some readers uncomfortable, use books to show how big the world is, be willing to lose the occasional sale because you have been honest with your readers about a book or an author, respect your readers' intelligence in what books you talk about and how you talk about them, and talk back to publishers and other media in ways that develop and support that vital national discourse. Every shift, every single shift at an independent bookstore is an opportunity for antifascist, antiracist, anti-supremacist, and anti-misogynist advocacy. What a privilege that is.

Here are a few examples of the kinds of advocacy that we've done at Porter Square Books. In response to the controversy over *American Dirt*, we included a bookmark in every copy in the store that highlighted books by Mexican and Mexican American authors, fiction and nonfiction, that dealt with the asylum crisis at the U.S.–Mexico border. We created similar bookmarks highlighting books by trans authors to

display with J. K. Rowling's books after she started consistently making transphobic statements. Inspired by Roxane Gay,
we also created an event series called Be the Change. Be the
Change found authors writing about social, political, and economic issues important to our community and paired them
with local nonprofits working directly on those issues, often
inviting representatives from the organization to present as
part of the event. A percentage of all sales during the event
were donated to that organization. These are relatively simple, relatively easy ways to raise up marginalized voices while
leading customers to books they might not have encountered
otherwise and supporting the conversation around social,
economic, and political policy in our community.

Does that opportunity for advocacy mean we can't help
readers find fluff? Goof around on social media? Tweet puns
at each other? Talk about movies and sports and music? Of
course not. Being a reader, being a human, includes goofy
shit and bookstores should include that. In many ways, independent brick-and-mortar bookstores are important because
they are one of the few public spaces left in contemporary
American capitalism that allows us to express and engage in
such a wide range of what makes us human.

WHAT SHOULD BOOKSTORES DO?

1. Refuse to stock books written by Republican politicians,
   members of the Trump administration, and Fox News
   contributors, and communicate that refusal to publishers. Refuse to host events for them, staff conferences or
   other off-site events, or facilitate bulk purchases.
2. Refuse to include Republican politicians, members of
   the Trump administration, and Fox News contributors
   in national or regional publicity like the Indie Next List

and regional catalogs, and communicate that refusal to publishers.

3. Be active and intentional in your support of antiracist, antifascist, marginalized, and own voices with your staff picks, events, social media, in-store displays, handselling, and other publicity, marketing, and promotions.

SPACE FOR DISAGREEMENT

Creating a space for productive discourse between opposing ideas doesn't just happen. Simply having books with conflicting ideologies (with each other and with the general values of your staff and community) doesn't mean you're creating a meaningful exchange of ideas. Work needs to be done for people to feel safe enough to hear critique, to confront their own biases, to cope with learning that something they've long held to be true might, in fact, be false. Even an event, or an event series, isn't necessarily going to create that space without preparation and active (and experienced) moderation.

Porter Square Books held an event with Jean Trounstine, author of *Boy with a Knife: A Story of Murder, Remorse, and a Prisoner's Fight for Justice. Boy with a Knife* uses the case of Karter Kane Reed, who committed murder when he was sixteen, to argue for criminal justice reform around the sentencing of juvenile criminals as adults. The family and friends of the victim organized a protest at the event.[53] Before the event, one of the store's managers spoke separately with the author and the protesters, essentially acting as a negotiator, listening to what both sides needed to feel heard and safe. They agreed that the protesters would stay outside, chanting and holding signs, during the event, but that they would not try to prevent anyone from coming in. After the event, a small number of representatives would have the opportunity to converse with the author. The event went off without a hitch. After the audience filed out, the manager led the representatives of the protesters into the store and stayed in the space during the conversation. It was, I would say, a very successful event and exchange.

But that successful exchange didn't just happen. It took work on the store's part, both before and during the event, to create a space where people could exchange opposing ideas. Furthermore, this was easier for us that it might be for many stores because of who handled the event. The manager who handled this situation is a fifty-something white man and a former lawyer. Because of his identity, he leveraged just about all of our society's unjust biases when it comes to respect and authority to maintain control of the situation despite the strong emotions involved, while using the negotiating skills he acquired as a lawyer to further facilitate the exchange. But even with those advantages there were plenty of tense moments. If you don't know how your bookstore could create that space for disagreement, if you don't have the time, energy, or expertise to create that space, or the resources to hire someone who can, well, maybe your bookstore actually isn't the right public space for those types of conversations.

TAKING OUR EYE OFF THE BALL

Honestly, in the time it takes me to write this sentence, the whole context for this piece could change. Who knows what's going to happen between when I finish this and when someone reads it? Maybe Trump is in jail. Maybe the Republican Party is in absolute shambles. Maybe we have a Green New Deal. Maybe we have Medicare for all. Let's get totally wild and say that maybe we start paying reparations. Maybe white supremacist and fascist ideas don't seem like a threat. Historically, progress has often been followed by setbacks.

Reconstruction was followed by Jim Crow. The Civil Rights Movement was followed by the War on Drugs, welfare reform, criminal justice reform, and other explicitly or indirectly segregationist policies to create the system that Michelle Alexander calls "the New Jim Crow." President Barack Obama was followed by President Donald Trump.

White supremacy is persistent. We are here now because too many people, too many white people, saw a few big wins as proof of final victory. We took our eye off the ball. We must be as persistent as white supremacy. We must remember that our society didn't get this way by accident, that we don't "just happen" to live in a white supremacist state, and we won't "just grow out of it." We got here actively and so cannot be passive if we want to move forward.

THE LEAST WE CAN DO

For all the importance, for all the significance, for all the literal lives on the line as we fight for justice, I'm struck by how little, ultimately, I'm asking of my colleagues. For many of us, I'm not even asking you to lose that many sales. A couple dozen over the course of the year. The occasional hundred-copy bulk purchase. The occasional fifty-copy event. A loss, sure, but nothing that would stand out in a year-end statement. The work of advocacy doesn't really need to be new work. You just might need to redirect, refocus, and be more intentional with the staff picks you already write, the hand-selling you already do, and the events you already host. Maybe you need to do a little work to find books or authors outside your comfort zone, but there are plenty of resources out there for that. Depending on your store, you might want to develop a script for booksellers to use if customers ask about books you don't stock (though, honestly, I'd just say, "We're out of stock right now"). You might also want to develop a process for handling belligerent customers, but you should probably have one anyway.

I don't know if, at this stage, deplatforming white supremacists and fascists from indie bookstores will have much of an impact, especially in the context of shit like, you know, violent insurrections. For all our influence, for all our value to our communities, the big publishers (who are the problem) wouldn't be impacted much at all. But I'd rather fight and lose than not fight at all. If, as a bookseller, I can't push the needle toward justice, at least I won't be holding it back. Maybe, ultimately, all these efforts end at our doorsteps and all we've done is create spaces slightly more free of white supremacy. That feels worth it to me. That is important to me. To me, that seems like the least we can do.

HOW TO READ EXPERIMENTAL WORKS OF LITERATURE IN TRANSLATION (AND OTHER WORKS YOU THINK ARE TOO DIFFICULT FOR YOU)

I'm not going to try to convince you to read experimental works of literature in translation and other books described as "difficult." I'm going to assume that, since you're reading this, you're interested in reading those books or you already read them and are curious about what I'm going to say. I'm assuming you're committed to overcoming "the one inch tall barrier," to borrow phrasing from Oscar-winning director Bong Joon-ho. If my assumption is wrong and you're reading this to be convinced, the "how" will contain some answers to the question "why?" So here are some techniques, tips, and perspectives for reading experimental works of literature in translation and other books you think are too difficult for you.

JUST FINISH THE BOOK: A READER'S FIRST DRAFT

Unless there is literally a test on the book or you have to write a paper for class, there's no downside to grinding through a difficult book. Don't worry about "getting it," don't worry about "appreciating it," don't worry about giving your partner a coherent answer when they ask, "So what's that book about?" Don't worry about knowing what's going on, who is doing what, or what it all means. Just get to the end. Do whatever you need to give yourself that serotonin click that comes from closing the book.

A writer often doesn't know a whole lot about a book when they start it. The writer might have an outline or know the broad story arc, but generally has to write to learn how their characters get from point A to point B. And that's if they know where point B is. As they continue to draft, edit, rewrite, edit again, they get to know the book. They add details and use those details to build connections and complexities. And the more they read what they've written, the more details they remember, making it easier to build more connections and complexities. They become experts in their own books. Reading a book can result in a similar development of expertise. On a first reading, you don't know what point B is, limiting your ability to appreciate point A.

So a first reading of any book is going to be limited. If the book is in a familiar genre and the author adheres to the conventions of that genre, you'll get a lot more of what the book has to offer the first time through because you already have a certain level of expertise. Same goes for books of any type or genre that are intentionally simple or overt with their themes and goals. But if the book is not overt or not in a familiar genre or the author does not adhere to conventions, you'll need to accept that you will miss a lot on your first pass through. You'll produce a reader's "shitty first draft." But that first reader's draft is still important. A writer can't write a better second draft without a shitty first draft. You can't have a second read without the first.

*

CONFUSION IS, SOMETIMES, THE POINT

Books are laboratories of thought and emotion. They are our practice fields, our training runs, our flight simulators. If you're reading a challenging book and you are confused, there is a chance, especially if the work is overtly experimental, that you're not missing something. You are confused because the author is trying to make you feel confusion, in the exact same way that thriller writers intend to make you feel thrilled, horror writers intend to make you feel scared, and erotica writers intend to make you feel horny. Every human emotion and experience has a place in art, even emotions and experiences that don't fit easily into conventional narrative structures, like confusion.

But how do you tell the difference between an author using the tools of writing and narrative to sow a sense of confusion in the reader and an author who is, themselves, confused in either what their goal is or how to achieve it? Signs that an author is being intentional in their creation of the experience of confusion include: the sentences are internally coherent; the facts of the world are consistent with its own rules, even if the rules allow for chaos and free play; there are direct references to or interactions with the idea of "confusion" or any of its synonyms; and the work of sorting out the confusion inspires other ideas beyond a basic understanding of what's going on.

Like books that interact with the emotion of confusion, books that interact with the experience of being overwhelmed are often considered difficult. Rodrigo Fresán's trilogy *The Invented Part*, *The Dreamed Part*, and *The Remembered Part* are intentionally overwhelming. In the trilogy's first book, *The Invented Part*, an aging writer tries to use the Hadron Collider to merge with the Higgs Boson to become an entity capable of rewriting reality. From that premise, the story is able to go, well, pretty much anywhere, through science, pop culture, literature, the mechanics of storytelling, and the mechanics of being. In *The Dreamed Part*, the writer, having failed to join with the Higgs Boson, interacts with an organization preserving dreams against the mysterious White Plague while suffering from his own insomnia. It also wanders through pop culture and science fiction, explores the life and career of a vastly more successful writer than our protagonist and features a long consideration of Brontë's *Wuthering Heights*—perhaps the longest passage devoted to a real book in another work of fiction that I've ever read. In *The Remembered Part*, which I haven't read yet, "The protagonist-narrator...returns to find an answer to the question: how does a writer remember? In particular, how does a he--a writer who no longer writes but can't stop reading and rereading himself--remember."[54]

There are times when these books are absolutely exhausting. They can make you feel like you've ridden a roller coaster one too many times. But the world is exhausting. The world is overwhelming and so some writers choose to explore the experience of being overwhelmed, perhaps even by making their work overwhelming. It's not that far from "overwhelmed," to "what the fuck is going on?" to "confused." So if you feel "confused," perhaps the author was aiming for an adjacent emotion or an emotion like "overwhelmed" that can be a source of your feeling of confusion.

As with feeling confused, it's entirely possible for poor execution on the writer's part to make a reader feel overwhelmed without giving them the tools to make something productive from that feeling. With emotions that grate against our expectations of narrative, it can be difficult to be certain you're experiencing what the author intended. But in the absence of certainty, why not just assume the confusion is intentional and see what results? If nothing else, this will likely help you get that first read under your belt. And if you get to the end and still decide the confusion is the result of a failure of some kind, the effort you've made still counts. The work of understanding still counts. You'll still have given yourself an intellectual and emotional experience through interacting with the book. Imagine you set yourself the goal of being able to do a hundred push-ups in a row by the end of the month and when the month ends you can only do eighty-five. The strength you built to do eighty-five push-ups in a row is still your strength.

Jon Fosse's *Septology* is rooted in an existential confusion. There are two main characters both named Asle, both relatively successful and highly respected abstract expressionist painters, both aging with long gray hair tied back in ponytails, and both always carrying a brown leather single-strap satchel. One, the narrator, is a recovering alcoholic and the other is a suffering alcoholic. They are so similar that a former lover of the suffering alcoholic mistakes one for the other. There are long passages of memories and, at least in the first few volumes, it was often difficult if not impossible to know which experience belongs to which Asle. Most of the story seems to be told in that part of the Rothko painting where you can no longer tell whether orange is bleeding into red or red is bleeding into orange. If your goal is to keep the two Asles clearly defined, it can be profoundly confusing. I believe that specific confusion is intentional because Fosse is exploring the boundaries between individuals and the possibility that the boundary between ourselves and others is far more porous than we like to believe. You are not supposed to know where one Asle begins and the other ends because there is a chance it might be impossible for you to know where you end and the rest of the world begins.

"Foreignness," "otherness," and "I don't belong here," are also experiences. For many people, foreignness and otherness are facts of life, even if they live where they were born. For many people, foreignness and otherness are life-threatening conditions they need to manage as carefully as a chronic illness. But for me, a white, neurotypical, typically abled, cisgendered, straight man born in the United States who speaks American English as my first language, I have been conditioned—and in many ways the world around me is structured—so I never feel foreign, even when I enter spaces that were not constructed for me. This creates an artificial sense of universality, a belief that my experience is "human" experience. But my experience is not universal. Works in translation, especially those that don't have an American angle and don't operate in English-language narrative traditions (and even more especially those that are explicitly anticolonial) can be powerful ways for white dudes like me to experience "otherness" and break that illusion of universality. Okay, so I lied a little bit when I said I wasn't going to try to convince anybody about the specific value of reading works of literature in translation, but this specific issue—the mistaken belief in the universality of white dude experience—is a direct source of the unbearable whiteness of publishing and one of the buttresses of white supremacy in our society. Or, to put this another way, white dudes need to read books that make them feel excluded so they can feel the fact of other valid human perspectives.

SOMETIMES, THE LANGUAGE IS THE STORY

Not only do we experience the world through language, language itself is one of our experiences. We experience joy in words themselves. Some books celebrate that joy. Some books revel in that joy. Some books are less about communicating a series of events or the experiences of characters and more about the words themselves, how they "feel" in your mind, what they evoke beyond their direct meanings, what connections are created by how words sound, what it means to play with your words. With some books, the entire plot, theme, story's main idea is contained in and expressed in every single sentence as you read it.

David Markson's *Wittgenstein's Mistress* is a good example of this. In the "plot," the last woman on earth types out her thoughts while just kinda living her life, but the "story," the meaning, the significances of the book is mostly contained in the specific thoughts themselves. Though there certainly is interplay between the specific thoughts and the "plot," and there is an exploration, perhaps even critique, of the act of writing your thoughts for others to read, nearly every individual sentence or paragraph in the book can be isolated and interpreted as its own flash fiction or aphorism. Fernando Pessoa's *The Book of Disquiet* has a similarly thin plot in service to the prose. Somewhere between a diary and a devotional, *The Book of Disquiet* has a narrator and in some ways a protagonist, and though we learn something of this person's life, this "character's" narrative job seems to be pulling the work itself into fiction and out of philosophy or aphorism or some other nonfiction genre. I have tagged dozens of sentences and passages in the text and though they all circle around, support, explore, and describe Pessoa's idea of "disquiet," they all, also, stand alone as complete ideas and beautiful sentences. For example, "Since we cannot extract beauty from life, let us at least extract beauty from our inability to extract beauty from life. Let us make of our failure a victory, something proud and positive, complete with pillars, majesty, and spiritual acquiescence." (p. 159)

Of course, any book can be read this way, so if you're struggling to finish a challenging book because you can't make sense of the plot or don't understand the motivations of the characters or can't keep track of the characters themselves, don't try to make sense of the plot, understand the motivation of the characters, or try to keep track of them. Read the book as if the language is the story. Look up the words you don't know; think about how the history of the word influences its meaning in this specific context; explore the connection between words that sound the same, especially if they are near each other in the text; be on the lookout for puns; read quickly until you come to a sentence that catches your attention and then really dig into it as an independent entity; pay attention to how one sentence flows into another, especially when they don't seem to carry any plot information; read out loud; treat individual sentences or paragraphs as independent aphorisms or even poems.

We think of "stories" as a series of events that happen in a place or a number of places, to a person or a number of people and though that may be true (or true enough for us to have meaningful conversations about, around, and through "stories,") not all books are stories in that sense, or, at least, not all books are only stories. Another way to "read as though language is the story," is to think of the book as an environment. Rather than creating motion from one event to the next, "books as environments" are linguistic spaces that allow for a broad range of independent thinking. They use evocative scenes, images, and language to inspire readers to think ... really anything. Some books like this, like José Revueltas's *The Hole*, are more explicit by focusing some of the "story" part of the book on the fact of setting and environment, while others, like Osvaldo Lamborghini's *Two Stories*, are so linguistically distant from any kind of happening that it's hard to read them any other way. The point is not so much to follow a plot or excavate a specific theme, but to follow the footsteps of your own thoughts, spending time in the personal memories the books evoke, the flights of fancy, the daydreams, the tangential considerations. It's like walking through a city. Sometimes you follow established paths, sometimes you see the sights, sometimes you think explicitly about what you are seeing, but sometimes the walking and the city create an internal intellectual and emotional space for you to think and remember other aspects of your life and the world your life occurs in. Some books are cities made of language. In those books, your thoughts are the story. (More on that later.)

HARD BOOKS TEACH YOU HOW TO READ THEM

Reading is not a pure skill. It is rooted in expectations and agreements—expectations and agreements that are built and shaped by the culture you learned to read in. But not every book operates within the common reading expectations of its culture. Some are written in opposition to them. These books can be challenging because not all the tools we bring to the project are the tools the project requires. But even when works are written in opposition to dominant reading expectations, they are still written with an awareness of them. So authors often include an image or scene or bit of dialogue or something that realigns your reading expectations with those of the book, often giving you specific phrases that describe the experience.

The Incompletes by Sergio Chejfec opens with the narrator seeing his friend Felix off at a port in Buenos Aires. From the setup, we might expect a picaresque adventure novel as we follow Felix's world travels through the letters and notes he sends back to the narrator. But the book wanders off into a foggy forest of mysteries, digressions, character sketches, displacement, architecture, and alienation, almost all of it taking place in one setting, Moscow. Rather than globe-hopping, the story mostly stays put. In some ways, Chejfec is perfectly overt about what type of story he is telling; the title is *The*

Incompletes after all, but given the initial premise, I can see how readers would be frustrated. Relatively early in the novel, Felix checks into a strange hotel in Moscow; a hotel whose architecture and receptionist would fit in an Edgar Allan Poe story. He is shown a room and this is what he finds:

> At first glance the room seems to be an arbitrary mix of prison cell and bedroom. There are two windows, one down by the floor and the other up high, almost like a skylight—looking out of either will require effort on Felix's part. When he manages, after several contortions, to get close to the lower window, he will see the small hours of the night in a jumble of stillness, silence, and cloud that will last until morning. From there, an artificial panorama of streets opens up, as if the hotel were a ship listing to one side. The parallel and somewhat juxtaposed profiles of houses can be seen, unsteady in the faint light and fuzzy behind a thin layer of fog that is either just forming or about to lift. Beyond that, a street, visible due to the light reflecting off the wet pavement leads away from the Hotel Salgado in a straight line. (p. 30)

The image of Felix contorting himself to look through the two windows is a metaphor for the reader reading *The Incompletes*. The prose style, narrative pace, and focus on obtuse, even foggy, images, means the reader is going to have to contort themselves to see anything, and even then what they do see will be obscured, refracted, and reflected. Furthermore, this image of Felix at the two windows shows that Chejfec isn't interested in giving the reader any clarity and that rather than seeking to make sense of every image it will be more satisfying for the reader to appreciate the fog itself. You contort through text not to see clearly, but to be contorted while you see.

Slipping by Mohamed Kheir is set in an off-center version of Cairo during the Arab Spring, where the gaps and forgotten spaces open into magical alternative worlds and unexplained phenomena. Reading *Slipping* is like walking across a sand dune with the ground constantly shifting beneath you. Its translator, Robin Moger, describes the book this way: "Ironically, though much feels ungraspable and unreal in *Slipping*, it is a book that teaches you how to read it: it's a book about not knowing what's going on."[55] You could think of *Slipping* in the same way you think about a first-person limited-perspective mystery novel. You don't understand what is going on because the characters don't understand what is going on. Like following a detective who slowly pieces together a mystery, we learn as the characters learn, we discover as the characters discover, we gather our footing as the characters do, and though Kheir doesn't provide the certainty of the traditional detective story, he does bring us along from a sense of being completely lost and crushed in a crowd to a kind of comfort with the powerlessness of the individual making their way through a city.

Do "teaching you how to read the book" scenes always happen near the beginning? Of course not. Sometimes they don't happen until the end. In *An Untouched House*, it is the end. Sometimes the "story" the book tells is not the depicted events, but what happens in your mind when you finally learn what the book expected of you. The "story" is what you feel when you get the key to the treasure chest. The "plot" is not a sequential progression from one event to the next or through the changes a character undergoes over the course of those events, but the re-searching, returning, and re-turning of the reader through those events and characters when the reader learns the intellectual and emotional context for those events and characters. The climax is not an event, but the first thought you have after your own particular version of "Holy fucking shit, that's what this fucking book is about?!" The "story" isn't what happens to the characters, but what happens to you.

*

TURN OFF YOUR INNER CRITIC AND APPRECIATE DIFFERENCE

Along these lines, a lot of what makes works in translation "difficult" isn't sophisticated language or complicated plots, or challenging ideas and concepts, but the simple fact that storytelling works differently in different cultures and languages. Some cultures see coincidence as a fundamental fact of life. Some cultures expect digressions in their stories. Some cultures have different understandings of ideas like "realistic" and "closure." And books written in different languages from different cultures have different expectations for what it means to tell a story. With these books, it is less about learning how to read them (especially since they might not try to teach you) so much as it is letting go of your assumptions, expectations, and preconceived notions of what a book and a story "should" do.

Writers often talk about silencing their "inner critic," the voice inside their head that tells them something they're writing is bad. Sometimes you need your inner critic, of course, but listening to it constantly can completely arrest the writing process. If you only let yourself write perfect sentences, you'll never write anything. Readers have an "inner critic" too. As with writers, this inner critic is useful. You should be critical of the books you read. But again, as with writers, sometimes you need to turn the critic off so you can open yourself up to different types of books than you're used to. Sometimes you need to actively remind yourself that "different" is not the same as "bad."

*

FIND AN ANCHOR

Sometimes you just can't wrap your head around the book you're reading, especially on a first pass. Instead of trying to "get," the entire work, I look for a specific event or image or even just a sentence that I can wrap my head around to act as an anchor for the rest of the book. Maybe this anchor speaks to the book's general themes or is a passage that teaches you how to read the book or is in some way important to wrapping your head around the book as a whole, but it doesn't need to be. It can just be a passage or sentence that you think is beautiful or that you really like for some idiosyncratic reason.

Some anchors can be a specific sentence. Ariana Harwicz's *Die, My Love* is an unsettling book. One source of the unsettlement is simple enough: We watch a woman and mother misbehave in ways typically associated with men. We do not necessarily expect men to put their personal drives aside in service to the needs of anyone else. We are ready to apologize for them for drinking too much, sleeping around, and neglecting their children as part of the nature of masculinity. But we are conditioned to believe that a woman and especially a mother doing the exact same things is acting "unnaturally," against her very nature, even "monstrously." I think this double standard is a central theme in *Die, My Love*, but something else seemed to be going on, something that shifted the emotional weight of the critique around for me in uncomfortable ways. There was Harwicz's more overt feminist critique and there was something else, a jagged edge of some kind. Then I smashed my face against this sentence: "I heard the chainsaw." With that sentence as an anchor, I read the rest of the book as a horror novel, because it seemed to have the pacing and diction of a horror novel. This gave me a specific lens through which to view the events and the style, a handle for that "something else" I was struggling with. I don't know if Harwicz intended to frame her narrative in the pacing of a horror movie, but that doesn't matter. What matters is the anchor gave me an additional way to understand, or even contain, how the book was unsettling to me.

Other anchors can be an image. When you think of "experimental works of literature in translation," you probably imagine a book like *Baron Wenckheim's Homecoming* by László Krasznahorkai. "The Emperor's New Clothes" crossed with *Gravity's Rainbow*, *Baron Wenckheim* is a doorstop of a novel with long, cycling sentences and paragraphs that go on for pages and pages in which a destitute yet famous aristocrat returns home in part so his family can be rid of him and in part to meet his high school sweetheart. Its central theme is the inherent futility of life in the face of time. It can be a slog of a book and, given its interaction with the inherent hollowness of certain efforts, difficult for many readers to get through. For me, the real story came together over the image of a bed. The residents of the Baron's hometown believe he is bringing vast wealth with him, and prepare elaborate citywide celebrations and spectacles, including restoring an old residence to its past glory. As part of that restoration a lavish bed is assembled for him. But the Baron does not have vast wealth and he has no interest in participating in the prepared spectacles or sleeping in the lavish bed. So the bed is dismantled. The carpenter tasked with disassembling the bed thinks, "I can pull [the screws] out, but they're not the same screws anymore, they're used screws, no matter how I unscrew them, you can see they're not what they were when they were first screwed in . . ." (p. 435) On the one hand, the image of the bed is another expression of futility; whatever you build will eventually be dismantled. But to me, the detail about the screws changes the direction of the energy, showing that construction has an impact no matter how long the creation survives and that deconstruction can also be creative. I read this relationship between creation, de-creation, and impact on the world as one of the greatest images of the novel-writing process I've come across in fiction. With that image I saw the idea of "futility" in the book much differently. In writing this book, in this way, Krasznahorkai isn't asking us to slog along with him for over five hundred pages, but to create along with him. The building and rebuilding, the retracing of steps, even the two-steps-forward-one-step-back grammar of the sentences I now saw not as an articulation of futility, but as a demonstration of the answer to futility: The bed is not the point, the building of a bed is the point. And so the life is not the point, the living of the life is.

Other anchors can be a general presence throughout the text. The rain appears early in Marie NDiaye's haunting novel *That Time of Year*, about a family that stays in a vacation town one day later than they normally do. "And now a misty rain was falling, and the teacher had no coat to put on." The teacher's wife and child vanish into the tourist town and his search for them through the bureaucracy and authority of the town is a healthy mix of Kafka, Poe, and Jackson. The rain follows him throughout, expressed sometimes directly and sometimes through the dampness of his clothes, all the way to the end and the final catastrophic storm. Whatever Ndiaye intends the rain to communicate or symbolize, its repetition gave me something to expect, even look forward to in the text, almost as though the rain was carrying me through the story. Furthermore, through the rain I was able to notice my own noticing, to see the results of my own reading, to get a little jolt of accomplishment every time I thought, Here's the rain again. This means something.

What can you do with an anchor, once you've found one? First, mark the page so it's easy to find. If it ends up being a recurring image, mark at least its first instance. Printing or writing out a copy to keep handy as you read (even as a bookmark) could be helpful. You could compare it to other scenes. You could look for similar or exact phrases from the anchor in other parts of the book. You could note similar details in other scenes. You could revisit it as new information comes to light, seeing if subsequent details or events change your understanding. Does a color feature in your anchor? Note whenever that color shows up again. Or a place name? Or a character?

Some of us as readers don't need anchors. Sometimes I am simply happy to drift along. Sometimes I won't be looking for an anchor until I've found one. But sometimes we need something more stable. Even if we can't "get" the book, some of us need to "get" something from the book to feel satisfied reading it. Breaking off a chunk of the text that speaks to you and tethering your reading to it is one way to "get" something.

TAKE NOTES

The physical act of writing something down (or underlining it or highlighting it) helps you remember it, makes it easier to find it if you want to refer back to it, and clarifies your own thoughts. Just because you're not actually writing a paper or preparing for a test doesn't mean you can't use the skills you developed in school to help you with the reading you're doing now. Furthermore, there is a "fake it till you make it," element to this. The physical acts of study tell your brain to study. They are triggers or signifiers or maybe even switches that help turn on the part of your brain that studies, interprets, remembers, and critiques.

*

LOOK SHIT UP

While you're taking notes, you might as well look shit up: words, etymologies, historic events, people, places, concepts. Not only will that help you understand the book, it's not like that information expires once you've finished reading. It's yours. Forever. (Or at least as long as you remember it.)

SOME BOOKS ARE WRITTEN TO BE REREAD

Some books are written to be reread. The author has layered more details, more images, more ideas and themes, more references, more in-jokes, more connections, more possibilities than anyone can appreciate or even notice on a single pass. Sometimes you need to get to know a book—you need to read it enough times to know what happens, who the characters are, and to remember specific details—before you can really connect with the book's full potential. Not fully grasping these books the first time through is not a failure on either your part or the author's; it's part of the nature of the work.

THERE IS NO SUCH THING AS AN A

The drive that too often sabotages a first read of a challenging book is "I want to get an A." Years of a very specific type of education have trained us to read for the test and we continue reading for the test even when there is no test. So when we don't feel like we'll pass, when we don't feel like we'll get an A, we become frustrated, we decide the book isn't for us, either because we're not smart enough or the author is being an asshole. We give up. We don't finish that "reader's first draft." Maybe we give up on the author. Maybe we give up on the genre. Some books will be out of reach at first, second, or even more reads and that is okay. There is no test. There is no teacher in your brain grading you. There is no such thing as an A.

THIS TAKES WORK

Sometimes you're going to have to work really fucking hard to get something out of a book. Okay. Life can be really fucking hard. Sorry to go all "dad advice" on you, but sometimes the hardest things to do are the most rewarding to have done.

LISTEN TO AND TRUST YOUR BRAIN

Humans evolved to use patterns of language to communicate with each other. Books are one technology that uses patterns of language to communicate with each other. If you are literate, you have the tools you need to begin making sense and meaning out of anything you read. Trust your brain. If you feel a tickle in your brain that something is there in the text, then there is almost certainly something in the text. Follow that tickle. This isn't quite the same as saying everything you think about a book is correct, but that the tickle in your brain is always a valid place to start an investigation. Furthermore, even if critical investigation shows your original hypothesis to have been wrong, that hypothesis is still valuable because it led you to the investigation and to a better theory, interpretation, or conclusion.

Furthermore, memory is a funny thing. You can't always remember the things you remember, if you know what I mean. Sometimes you need to encounter a specific phenomenon to trigger a memory. To make things more complicated, sometimes a memory can only be partially triggered or vaguely triggered or the fact of the memory can be triggered without any of the actual memory coming to consciousness. There is a lot going on under the hood and you don't always have access to all of it all of the time. Sometimes it will take several triggers for the relevant memory to arrive. Sometimes you'll need to see a pattern a handful of times before it clicks. Sometimes you'll know "something" is happening but it will take a while to actually put the pieces together and articulate what that "something" is. Sometimes it won't hit you until long after you've finished reading and thought your brain had moved on. The path may be long, you may not end up where you expected, you might even discover that something you thought about the book turned out to be completely wrong, but your brain will always lead you somewhere and you will always get something out of that journey. Trust yourself.

NOT EVERY BOOK IS FOR EVERY READER

So you've done all of the above and the experimental work of literature in translation you're reading still isn't doing it for you. Have you failed? Did the book fail? Not everyone likes every type of candy. If you don't like, I don't know, circus peanuts, does that mean circus peanuts are a failed candy or that you are a failed candy eater? (Okay, maybe circus peanuts are a failed candy, but you see where I'm going.) You don't have the same interests I do. You don't have the same history, the same community, the same family, the same talents, the same limitations. Sometimes you're not going to like a book for many reasons or for no reason and that doesn't mean there is something wrong with the book or you. At this moment, this book isn't for you. And that's fine.

Not liking something is part of the process of liking other things. It is how you come to know yourself, how you discover and expand your palate, how you add to the resources you draw from. Not liking some books is simply a natural part of being a reader. And just because you don't like a particular experimental work in translation doesn't mean you won't like any experimental works in translation. Sure, some are thick, sloggy, ponderous tomes, but some are slim and fast-paced. Some use long words and even longer sentences but others play around in other aspects of plot, setting, and character. Some work right at the very edge of our ability to make sense, sometimes even challenging the very idea of sense, while others work on less absolutely fundamental concepts like the nature of character or the relationship between plot and setting. You may not connect with the experimental works in translation that I do, but that makes sense because you and I are different people.

PERSPECTIVES, NOT SKILLS

Building true expertise in writing books takes a lifetime. It is a perpetual process of training your brain to see patterns, track details, and imagine beyond your own experience, all while developing idiosyncratic processes to assist in that seeing, tracking, and imagining.

Most of what I've shared in this piece are perspectives and attitudes rather than techniques or skills because some of the skills of reading, some of the skills of that "something more," can't be directly taught, but are intellectual and emotional intuitions that grow, develop, and deepen through use. In a lot of ways, a trainer or coach can't really teach you to run a marathon, they can only teach you the techniques and perspectives needed to successfully develop the ability to run a marathon into your body. That's what I've tried to do here. Give you the techniques and perspectives to train the ability to read experimental works of literature in translation and other difficult books into your mind. If you want to read "more books like X," the best way to do so is, well, to read more books like X. The only way to get better at writing is to write, and so, really, the only way to get better at reading is to read.

THE ENDING OF *AN UNTOUCHED HOUSE*

In some ways, *An Untouched House*, by Willem Frederik Hermans, is a profoundly strange war novel, as the war itself is almost always just out of frame. In other ways, *An Untouched House* is what we've come to expect from modern war novels, a book perfectly at home with *Johnny Got His Gun, Catch-22*, and *Slaughterhouse Five. An Untouched House* is concerned with the pointlessness, futility, and horror of war, directly opposing the narratives of nationalism and honor that have traditionally supported going to war. Until the very end of the book, of course.

Last chance to jump off the spoiler train. If you haven't read *An Untouched House* and you intend to, I highly doubt this final moment will have the same impact if you know it's coming.

Okay. Here we go.

The protagonist is a Dutch partisan who "chances upon a luxurious, intact estate in an abandoned spa town."[56] When the Germans retake the town, he lies and manipulates in order to stay in the house as its German owners return, insinuating himself into their lives. He spends time with them in the house. He builds connections. The house becomes something of a home. The book seems to be about the aspects of human life beyond the scope of war, the fundamentals of home and hearth that unite all of us no matter what flag you happen to be marching under or whose orders you've most recently taken. For all its ability to destroy, there are some things war cannot touch. The Dutch take the town back and discover the Germans living with the protagonist in that estate. Everything we've read up until this point, including the title itself, suggests some kind of, if not reconciliation between the German family in the estate and the partisans, at least an act of mercy, something that shows our ability to see the humanity in our enemies.

But there is no reconciliation. There is no mercy. The Dutch soldiers brutally murder the German family. The protagonist does nothing to protect the people who had taken him in. Though the murders are violent and gruesome, they're not the shocking part. This is:

> "I turned and stared at the house. It still looked perfectly intact, although here and there the lace curtains had been torn from the windows. I ran back up the steps and hurled a grenade in the hall.
>
> "We were marching through the gate when the explosion sounded. The partisans saw this as the final joke and crowning glory. They started to tug on me and jostle me, asking if I was willing to swap the cameras for anything. I felt that I was going to become very popular.
>
> "I looked back at the house for the last time. All of the windowpanes had been blown out of their frames. I saw bundles of dead raggedy reeds hanging down from the broken ceilings that had depicted heaven. I looked deep into the house's diseased and dying maw.
>
> "It was like it had been putting on an act the whole time and was only now showing itself as it, in reality had always been: a hollow, drafty cavern, rancid and rotting at its core." (pp. 87–88)

Hermans literally throws a bomb into the central metaphor and image of his work in the final pages. We have not been reading about the limits of war to corrupt our humanity, but about our ability to adapt to any environment in order to survive. It is about how easy it can be to become an entirely different person, sometimes many different people, as your environment changes. It's not just that we haven't been reading the type of war novel we thought we were, but that we might not have been reading a war novel at all. It's only at the end that we learn we need to read with a level of cynicism, that we need to be as critical of the protagonist as we would be of a used car salesman, and that we need to think of the war that surrounds the story less as an aspect of the plot and more as an aspect of the setting. With the correct tools for reading it, *An Untouched House* transforms from a well-executed but relatively typical war novel into a work of genius.

An Untouched House is a difficult book. It moves at an atypical narrative pace, it is almost diametrically opposed to the conventions of its genre, it doesn't create the emotional payoffs most readers will expect from its plot, it doesn't provide historical background or context for readers who aren't familiar with the course of World War II in the Netherlands, passages of it read more like a closed-house domestic drama than a war story, and it blows itself up at the end. At times, I found it downright unpleasant to read. But I'm sure Hermans wasn't intending to please his readers. He was intending to shake their assumptions about war, human nature, and community, to unsettle them from their reading habits, and to make them question themselves in uncomfortable ways. Assuming those goals, I think *An Untouched House* is a profoundly successful book. It is important to enjoy books, to be pleased by books. It is important to be entertained, and to read for relaxation and escape. But I believe some ideas, some experiences, even some emotions are only accessible through the hard work of reading experimental literature in translation and other difficult books. With a commitment to trying, a few skills, and the right perspectives, anyone who can read, can read books like *An Untouched House*.

TEAMMATES IN THE GAME OF BOOKS

Lessons for Writers from a Writer Who Sells Books

Everyone in the United States should do two years of service: one the kind of nonprofit and conservation work we usually associate with "a year of service," like maintaining trails, cleaning up national parks, working in underserviced communities, that type of thing; and one working in retail or food service. "Everyone should be required to be spend a year working retail," sounds like a joke, but I am dead fucking serious. A lot of bullshit ideas about how our economy and society work are generated by people who have never done the ground-level, person-to-person, last-link-in-the-chain labor upon which so much of our economy rests.

Retail and food service can be physically, intellectually, and emotionally challenging. To be successful in retail you need to be an expert in whatever you sell, able to troubleshoot your point-of-sale and any other technology in your store, find solutions to logistical problems you did not create, answer for problems, mistakes, and failures that happened long before you had control over the product or situation, and manage the emotions of complete strangers, some of whom do not see you as fully human. And you are expected to do that with smiling deference. You are expected to smile despite almost always being the lowest paid and least-empowered person in the organization. Working retail is an education in a specific topic, in problem-solving, and in emotional literacy, an education that you almost always have to learn on the job and for which you can get fired if you don't learn quickly enough.

More specifically, I think everyone who works in publishing, especially writers, should spend time working in a bookstore. After all, readers generally buy books from bookstores, rather than from publishers and writers. (Many self-published authors are their own publisher and bookstore and if you've got that kind of set-up, great.) The process of creating a book, the labor of making a book, for everyone involved in the publication, is so vastly different from the process and labor of selling a book that the former contributes almost nothing to understanding the later. And vice versa. Though you can find data on how many copies books sell, it's at the bookstore that you actually see why and how books sell. You see what covers draw people in, what displays people interact with, which shelftalkers and handsells move units, which trim sizes get relegated to out of the way places because they don't fit on the shelves, and what media coverage actually motivates readers. You see what publicity materials get to customers and in what contexts. You can see what events lead to sales. And you see that die-cut covers are almost always terrible because they rip, forcing bookstores to send damaged copies back to publishers, so that those books never get put out in the number a store wants. (Just wanted to get that out there.) I'd argue one of the fundamental failings of most MFA programs and other formal writing education is the lack of professional development around the logistics and labor of actual bookselling. A bookstore internship program might solve that shortcoming.

I identified as a writer and even published some pieces before I was hired at Porter Square Books, so I've always seen myself as a writer who sells books. I believe this gives me a

relationship to the craft of writing that helps in both reading books and selling them. I can see what writers are trying
to do, read generously along with those goals, and then use
my own storytelling skills to describe the books to readers
in ways that not only get them to buy but also set them up
for a positive reading experience. It would be a little over ten
years between when I started at Porter Square Books and
when I published a book of my own. That was enough time
that I could approach my first novel as a bookseller. I could
use what I had learned about bookselling to understand the
hows and whys of my book. These lessons have nothing to
do with writing a book, nor will they guarantee your book
becomes a bestseller. Instead, they will provide perspectives
and approaches for after your book is out in the world that
will benefit your mental health and help your long-term career as a writer by improving your relationship with independent bookstores.

THE SALES OF YOUR BOOK HAVE NO DIRECT CON-
NECTION TO THE QUALITY OF YOUR BOOK

Publishers know how to sell a ton of books. The proven techniques for a book to sell well are: be selected for Oprah's
Book Club (with diminishing returns on the various other
celebrity book clubs); be interviewed by Terry Gross, host of
Fresh Air on NPR (with diminishing returns for various other
forms of coverage on NPR); tap into a previously unidenti-
fied cultural current; be a celebrity with existing fame; be a
viral recommendation on whatever social media platform is
currently impactful; get a great review in the *New York Times*
articulated in a specific way so it taps into contemporary
cultural currents; win the Pulitzer Prize or the Booker Prize
(with diminishing returns on other book prizes); have the

book made into a movie or TV series; and be adopted by a number of advocates in bookselling. Do publishers know how to guarantee one of those things happening for your book? No. I've seen publishers and authors angling for one (or many) of those conditions to happen for excellent books and just completely whiff on all of them. I've seen utterly mundane shit blow up because one of the above happened. I've seen works of genius that should have been the topic of conversation in literary circles completely bomb. Sometimes Oprah and Reese pick great books and sometimes they pick what I consider to be garbage. Same goes for the prizes. I've seen celebrities write great books and I've seen celebrities affix their names to ghost-written hack work, and both books have had the same relatively high sales. I've seen pornographic fan fiction become an international phenomenon despite demonstrating an obvious lack of knowledge of the sex it depicts. I've seen authors who toiled in obscurity writing books their few readers absolutely loved suddenly break through with a smash hit that makes buy-a-boat money and sometimes the buy-a-boat book is significantly different from their previous work and sometimes it's not. This isn't a polemic. Fine by me if you like the books I don't. What sells, sells for the reason it sells and writers don't learn a whole lot that's applicable by delving into the whys and hows of specific hits and flops. To put this another way, capitalism just isn't equipped to say anything interesting about the quality of a book.

There are many different ways to phrase this idea and you should find whatever phrasing will stick in your head. For me, I've landed on, "Don't take the sales of your book personally." I think the only bestseller list my book made was the Porter Square Books Bestsellers of 2015 and it wasn't in the top ten. All told, sales of my book landed north of three thousand copies, which, for a debut novel with a complicated relationship to genre and some atypical formatting, published by a small press, is pretty damn good. (I did not buy a boat.) A lot of books I don't think were as good as mine sold a ton more and a lot of books I think are much better sold less. Disconnecting your sense of your own writing from how it sells really isn't an artistic statement or an anticapitalist position or anything so dramatic; it's just a healthy relationship to some of the fundamental facts of your vocation.

YOUR BOOK IS YOUR BOOK TO YOU AND ONE BOOK AMID THOUSANDS TO ME

This is one of those ideas that we all know at an intellectual, factual level, but don't always internalize at an emotional level. We know it, but don't always feel it. Your book is the most important book in the world to you and you have every right to market, publicize, promote, and advocate for it. You have every right to ask a bookstore: to stock it; if they would like you to sign copies for them; to participate in a preorder campaign for it; or to host an event or promotion for it in some other way. And you know what? Your book deserves all of that. But so do thousands of other books. You can certainly ask bookstores for help in selling your specific book, but they might say, no, not as a statement about your book in particular, but because they are responsible for selling thousands of different books by thousands of different authors and just can't make specific efforts for every single one.

I took a pretty hands-off approach to my first book at Porter Square Books. Part of that was not wanting to make my co-workers feel obligated to recommend it if they didn't like it. In order for handselling to work, customers need to trust that booksellers are being honest about what they recommend and why they recommend it. For example, though we'd done this once for another author who had a direct connection to the store, I didn't ask for my book to be a store-wide staff pick. There are lots of readers and Porter Square Books community members who would never be interested in my weird-ass detective novel and it didn't make sense to me to leave them without picks for a month. Same for social media in general. I probably could have made it all *Exaggerated Murder* all the time for its first few weeks but that didn't feel professional to me as a bookseller or as a writer. I did my writer's job when I wrote the book and I decided to leave it to other booksellers to handle selling it. As an additional benefit to this hands-off approach, it was more meaningful to me when it was staff-picked by a Porter Square Books bookseller. Do I think our relationship played a role? Yeah, probably. But I can enjoy his validation much more knowing I did not pressure him for it.

REJECTION BY A BOOKSTORE IS LIKE ALL THE OTHER REJECTIONS WRITERS FACE

If you know how to handle rejection by editors, agents, and publishers, you know how to handle rejection by bookstores, because the reasons for the rejection are essentially the same. A bookstore might choose not to stock your book because they don't think it will sell, because they don't think it's a good fit for the store, because they don't have a section it would succeed in, or because the buyer just isn't connecting with the pitch. It doesn't mean your book is bad or that the store's buyer thinks it's bad, just like an editor who rejects your book for publication doesn't necessarily think it's bad. All of those ideas apply to events, online promotions, or anything else you might think of as a way to generate sales for your book.

Putting a manuscript out there means you're going to get rejected by publishers. That is just a fact of writing. Unfortunately, that doesn't change when the manuscript gets published. Putting your book out there means you are going to get rejected by bookstores.

YOUR PUBLICITY FOR YOUR BOOK WILL ALWAYS* CREATE MORE ATTENDANCE AT EVENTS AND MORE PREORDERS THAN A BOOKSTORE'S PUBLICITY

Authors and publishers reach out to bookstores all the time to promote events and books and bookstores are often happy to help. Whenever a bookstore promotes a specific event they promote the fact that they put on events to their community. Whenever a store promotes a specific preorder, they promote the general fact that they accept preorders. Depending on the store's marketing resources, these partnered publicity efforts can comprise a significant part of the store's publicity.

But when a bookstore talks to their community, they talk to their entire community, including a lot of readers who would never be interested in your book. When you talk to your community, you are talking to readers who have a relationship with you and so are more likely to preorder your book or attend an event. This is not to say that bookstore-led publicity is pointless, but that announcement tweets from a bookstore aren't going to put the same butts in seats as your newsletter or message in a group chat. My launch at Porter Square Books was very well-attended and the largest of my solo events. This makes sense as there was significant overlap between my community and the store's community. But even for a bookseller who had been full-time for ten years, those communities didn't overlap completely. There were plenty of events, even events I hosted, that had much higher attendance.

The odds that a bookstore knows your book well enough to effectively market it, to effectively connect it to readers in their community who might be interested is ... well ... pretty small. I generally finish between fifty and a hundred books a year and start but don't finish several dozen more. I know booksellers who crush many more and some who don't read quite that much. From bookish media, staff picks from other booksellers, and booksellers talking about books, I can answer questions and even recommend another fifty to a hundred new books per year. Another couple dozen reach a level of saturation that I can figure out if a reader is asking for them with very little identifying info, but I don't know enough to recommend them. So out of the hundreds of thousands of books published a year, I can plausibly competently promote two hundred of them. The odds that any number of booksellers at a particular store have read your book, even when they are hosting an event for it, are pretty small, especially if you don't have an existing relationship with the store or with specific booksellers. That doesn't mean we won't work hard to sell your book, it just means we simply won't have the same level of knowledge of the book as you do to draw from in those efforts so we won't be targeting your book's most likely readers.

*UNLESS YOU HAVE AN ADVOCATE AT THE BOOKSTORE

Advocates, booksellers who have read your book and commit to supporting it, can lead publicity campaigns that put butts in seats and move units by talking to the specific parts of their community who would be interested in the book in ways that motivate action. They can use their expertise selling books in general to sell yours specifically. They can tailor their specific pitches to specific customers. They can use their reputation for good taste within their community to confer inherent value to your book. So how do you get advocates for your book at bookstores?

As with the other techniques for selling a ton of books, there is no guaranteed way to garner advocates, but the first step is to get booksellers to read your book. And the first step in getting booksellers to read your book is identifying those who are likely to read it. You need to find kindred spirits, booksellers who already advocate for books like yours. This used to be a lot more difficult but with social media and with booksellers active on just about all the platforms there are public records of booksellers' reading tastes and advocacy. If you're not sure if a bookseller is a good match for your book, it never hurts to ask via email, DM, or through someone at the bookstore with a publicly available email. If they say yes, great, send them the galley and remind them in a note or something that you connected with them. I have definitely been flummoxed by a galley appearing in my mailbox until a note reminded me that I, in fact, asked for it. If they say no, you've saved yourself or your publisher a little money for a galley and postage. And they might also say, "No, but I know someone who would." Furthermore, if you are traditionally published, even at a small press, someone is being paid to sell your books to booksellers. Someone is responsible for helping you find those advocates. Sales reps and publicists get to know individual booksellers over the years and send galleys specifically to them.

From there, the other techniques publishers use to capture the attention of a reader apply: the copy, the blurbs, the publisher letter, and the cover all play a role. In fact, after years of reading publisher copy and other blurbs and looking at covers, I've learned the techniques, or even codes, publishers use to express the character of a book through a few phrases of description or an image on a cover, and so can tell, with a certainty most general readers don't have, whether or not I'm likely to connect with a book. (Yes, you should judge a book by its cover. A lot of people worked really hard to tell you something important about the book with it.) Finally, booksellers know publishers and so who you publish with will greatly increase or diminish the chances a specific bookseller will give your book a chance. If you're with a publisher I trust, I'll probably give your book a try. If not, well, so many books come out from those publishers I trust and want to support that the chances I'll get to your book aren't zero, but they're not much higher.

THE FIRST TIME I TALK ABOUT THE IMPORTANCE OF RELATIONSHIPS

Regardless of all that ambiguity, I can say booksellers are far more likely to read a book by an author they have a relationship with than any random galley that shows up in a back room. These relationships aren't necessarily friendships, though they can be, as much as acknowledged connections through social media, in-person events and gatherings, and other correspondence. Some of the writers I advocate for I consider friends, while others might struggle to remember me, while many others fall somewhere in between. Regardless of what type of relationship I have with a writer, I always take a moment to at least consider a galley when I come across it, and even if I don't end up reading it, I remember that it exists. I have definitely sold books by telling a customer that, though I haven't read the specific book they're holding, I know the author, and I know the author writes the types of books the reader just asked about.

Building professional relationships with booksellers isn't that different from building relationships with other authors. You start with those kindred spirits, with those targeted galley mailings, you tend connections that start on social media. You follow up with booksellers you met on your first book tour or when you attended an event at their store. There are also more formal avenues for building relationships with booksellers. First, if a publisher or publicist asks you to participate in a dinner with booksellers, fucking do it. At conferences, trade shows, and other book industry gatherings, publishers will often take a number of booksellers out to dinners we absolutely cannot afford on our wages. We eat, drink, talk; I order fancy cocktails. Sometimes these are thank-you gestures and it's just booksellers and publicists, sales reps, and other people who work at the publisher, but often a few writers are brought along to be introduced to booksellers. So many relationships start with food and drink. If you are given this opportunity, take it.

At a booksellers' conference in 2014, Graywolf Press organized a dinner to promote Leslie Jamison's debut essay collection, *The Empathy Exams*. The conference took place at the end of January and the book was published in April. There were five or six booksellers along with at least one publicist for Graywolf and Jamison. I knew most of the booksellers, either from similar conferences, the internet, or both. A few of us were pretty established as booksellers on social media. There is a wonderful picture of all of us smooshed into a selfie, smiling brightly at the camera. A lot of other stuff happened over the course of that conference, but the practical effect of that dinner was that not only did I read *The Empathy Exams*, but I read it in light of the relationship that was created at that dinner. I staff-picked it and I think several other people at that dinner did too. It ended up being on the Indie Next List, a national promotion that highlights twenty books nominated by booksellers around the country. It also ended up being a surprise smash hit and established Jamison as a major contemporary voice in American essays. A lot of different currents flowed into that success and though the most significant one was the stellar review in the *New York Times*, that dinner, and the enthusiasm and relationships it created, was certainly one of them.

Next, more and more bookstores and publishers are looking for conversation partners for their author events. Often finding the conversation partner is the bookstore's responsibility, so bookstores try to build a cadre of authors frequently willing and able to participate. If you're able to be a conversation partner or in a bookstore's cadre of authors, do it. It creates and maintains a relationship with the bookstore, of course, as well as with the other authors. These events are also extra publicity for you.

Finally, be a customer. Shop somewhere consistently. Attend events. Ask for recommendations. Buy staff picks. Be a community member who also happens to be an author. Though there's a lot you can hope for from bookstores for your book specifically, there isn't a whole lot you can expect. But I don't know how you can expect even that little if you do all your book shopping on Amazon.

YOU ARE NOT READING, YOU ARE PERFORMING

Authors have caught on that standing at a podium and reading for half an hour directly from your book isn't usually an effective way to make sales. If you are in front of a microphone, you are there to perform. This doesn't require theatrics. You can still make the "read a little from the book and then answer questions" format work, you just have to read with some emotion and energy, make eye contact with the audience (even during a virtual event) and choose passages from the book that work for whatever format you're in.

For my tour for *An Exaggerated Murder*, I selected several passages of varying length and mood, including a darker, artier passage, a lighter, funny passage, and a passage that had a bit more meat from the plot. I devised a couple of different ways to let the audience choose which passage I read to garner some early engagement. I also chose passages with relatively little dialogue in an otherwise dialogue-heavy book and made sure the chosen dialogue was only between two characters. I printed out the passages, single-sided, double-spaced on 8½ x 11 paper to make them easy to read. I took out phrases that work in print but sound repetitive when spoken and added identifying words and phrases because the audience most likely would not have the book in front of them. I kept the printouts in a three-ring binder with some lined pages for notes. I prepared a spiel to give at the end of events, encouraging people to shop that night. Stores can only host events if shopping happens at them, so even if, for whatever reason, attendees didn't want to buy my book, I encouraged them to buy something. I didn't always get the opportunity to give the spiel, but I had it ready. I grabbed a bookmark after every performance and taped it to the binder, creating a nice memento.

A great performance can only create so many sales, but it will create fans. Giving a great performance for the dreaded two-person audience is going to have an impact on those two people. They'll read your book and they'll read it generously because the emotions of the event will be a part of their reading experience. They'll share your book as an evangelist who wants to spread the joy of the event and garner the social capital for having "discovered" you. They'll slowly contribute to that base of sales that gets you from book one to book two. Of course, the dreaded two-person audience is actually the two people plus the booksellers. No matter how big or small the audience is, you are always performing for booksellers. A great performance can make booksellers fans, too. A great performance can create relationships and advocates.

*

THE GIRL BEHIND THE CASH REGISTER

A nn Patchett's first book tour was not a runaway success. As is the case for many debut authors, attendance wasn't particularly high. But whether she was reading for five people or one person or no people, she always made time to connect with "girl behind the register," as she said in a talk to independent booksellers. She would chat with them and just acknowledge the fact of their humanity. She would sell her book to the booksellers. She credits these connections as part of what kept her career going at the beginning, because "they did read the book and handsold it."[57]

Connecting with "the girl behind the cash register" doesn't require much effort. Some authors bring cookies or treats to their events, while others send thank-you notes afterward, and while both of those gestures are lovely and appreciated and memorable, really just acknowledging the booksellers at the store when you're there and thanking them for the work they've done to support your book is all that's required.

BOOKSELLERS WORK WITH YOU, NOT FOR YOU

D o not treat booksellers like your staff, even at your event. We are allies in the project of your book. You are not our boss in the project of your book. Booksellers are more than happy to do whatever we can to help sell your book, to make whatever accommodations are required for a successful event, to make sure you feel welcomed, supported, and celebrated in their store. You don't need to help put away chairs—in fact, the booksellers would probably prefer you don't help with the chairs. You don't need to put the signed copies of your book on display—in fact, definitely ask before doing anything to a display. And we'll do a lot of things someone who does work for you would do. We'll get the books for you to sign, we'll flap the covers, we'll take your coat, we'll get you a drink. If you have specific protocols for handling events or you have an actual fucking rider, we'll get everything done and be happy to do it.

But it is one thing to do those tasks in partnership with someone who sees and appreciates the effort and another to do those tasks for someone who thinks they are my boss. This isn't about being nice or bubbly or slathering us with gratitude or anything like that; just notice our humanity and talk to us as human beings.

BOOKSELLERS REMEMBER AND BOOKSELLERS GOSSIP

Does this sound threatening? Maybe it is. Booksellers know each other. We talk to each other. If you're a jerk, it'll get around.

THE SECOND TIME I TALK DIRECTLY ABOUT THE IMPORTANCE OF RELATIONSHIPS

Unlike most writers, I had as direct a connection to the sales of some of my books as possible, because I literally sold copies of my book. Like literally accepted payment, printed out a receipt, put it in a bag. The whole deal. And not like, working an event or conference or whatever when they knew they were buying the book from the guy who wrote it. I also processed online orders and preorders. Ultimately, there were two types of people who purchased my first novel:

people who had a relationship with me and people who didn't. There were, of course, friends and family, colleagues at Porter Square Books, other booksellers who knew me from conferences and the internet and such, and customers who knew me well from the store. People who we would naturally think of in terms of relationships. But there was another group that I think is instructive. For a lot of readers, the simple fact that I worked in the store they happened to be in at that moment created enough of a connection that a lot of maybes turned into yeses. I know because I would watch them pick up my book—yes, it was kind of like spider sense and also yes, I really tried not to watch them but could not tear my eyes away—turn it over, and read the back long enough to get to my bio and they'd make a demonstrative gesture, some physical version of "Oh!" or "Ah!" or sometimes even "Huh." Then they'd bring the book up to the register, set it cover down, point at the bio, and say, "Is this you?"

In general, people are hungry for relationships the way they are hungry for food. Partnerships, families, and friendships, sure, but also acquaintances, work friends, friends of a friends, the people we see every time we commute to work, "I know a guy" guys at local businesses, and internet friends, as well as transitory relationships like the person on the train reading your favorite book, or ordering the same drink as you at a bar, or wearing a T-shirt from a concert you attended. All of these feed our hunger for relationships too. But that hunger isn't just about consumption, it is also about tending. To be fed by a relationship requires giving as well. Head nods to strangers who are fleeting friends, likes on social media, attendance at parties, and, of course, buying a book from the person who wrote it.

So what does this actually mean to a writer? First I think you, as a writer, need to decide how important sales are to you in relation to everything else in your life. Yes, you want to sell enough copies of book one to get to book two, but there really isn't a universal minimum for book contracts. If an editor or publisher believes in your talent and sees you as a potential long-term investment, then your threshold for getting that next contract is probably pretty low. Debut but midlist authors on a one-book contract at a Big 5 publisher are probably going to need to move more units. But being a "writer" and being an "author" are different things. You can be one without being the other. Personally, for reasons I don't know if I can fully articulate, it is important for me to be a published author. I can't help you decide for yourself, but I do think you need to ask yourself how important being published is to you.

If you want to sell enough books to stay published, you need to make sure as many people as possible who you have any kind of relationship with know your book exists. I did a lot of that through my own social media of course, but every event I had, every display the book was on, including the staff-pick display at Porter Square Books, contributed to spreading awareness along the spectrum of relationships. This is one reason why your publisher/publicist is on you to get on social media. Sure, another reason is that it outsources some of the publicity work to you and outsources it in a way that they don't have to pay for, but the other reason is that social media allows you to create and tend to an entire spectrum of relationships, from your closest friends and family to the people you meet at conferences and wish you saw more, and to your fans. This is not me saying you should feel obligated to produce more content or be on social media more than you have determined is healthy, or that you need to do everything your publisher asks you to do in promoting and selling your book. But it is me saying that you will contribute to sales of your book if you use the relationships in your life to support it.

Ultimately, you don't have a whole lot of power over your book once it is out of your head and bound into covers. You can't make bookstores stock it, you can't make newspapers review it, you can't make Terry Gross interview you on *Fresh Air* and you can't make Oprah pick it for her book club. You can't even make your publisher do everything you think they should. For most of the most impactful things that can happen to your book you just kinda have to write the best book you can and hope. But you can control how you treat people. You can treat the people selling your book with respect. You can be a person other people want to see succeed, someone booksellers, readers, and other writers root for. With so much powerlessness in the world of books, with so much powerlessness in the world, why not take this modicum of control? The world may not give a shit, but you can control yourself, and you can be a person who creates, tends, and rewards relationships.

WE ARE TEAMMATES

Too often, writers (and booksellers, to be honest) see the world of books as a zero-sum game. If someone buys your book, it means they didn't buy my book. If someone buys a book from your store, it means they didn't buy a book from my store. Though customers certainly choose one book over another and one store over another, the perspective that all gain is balanced by an equal loss is destructive, oppressive, and, of course, bullshit.

There are more than enough readers to go around. I mean, there used to be over a dozen bookstores in Harvard Square alone. We don't need to see each other as competitors in a contest of resources. If there's one thing that has become crystal clear to me as a writer who is a bookseller and a bookseller who is a writer, it is that writers and booksellers are on the same team. Sometimes working together as a team will lead directly to sales for your latest book and sometimes it won't. But I think it will lead to more sales overall for all authors and at all indie bookstores. And a world with more indie bookstores and better-fed authors is a better world.

Working retail, you see people at their best and their worst. You see people when they're tired and frustrated and angry, and, for whatever reason, can't think of any other way to cope with their emotions than taking that negativity out on someone less powerful. You see people for whom the opportunity to exercise power over another person is almost as important as getting whatever it is they're buying. You see people in the midst of mental health crises. You see people who realize what they've done and can't apologize fast enough. You see people who realize what they've done and just don't have it in them for the emotional work of acknowledgment and apology. You see random acts of kindness and generosity.

Whether it's fair or not, whether you want it or not, whether you have any actual power to affect a situation, working in retail and food service means you are occasionally the difference between someone having a good day or a shitty day. You are that difference no matter what type of day you're having. You're that difference and you've been on your feet for hours, you've walked several miles, carried boxes, pushed carts, de-escalated conflicts, and solved customer service problems, and, odds are, you weren't paid particularly well for it. And then you've had to watch the news and see politicians talk about the working class as if coal miners in West Virginia are the only people who put in hard days of honest work for their bread.

Guaranteeing more people work ringing up purchases and waiting tables won't solve all the problems created by convenient definitions of labor, if for no other reason than those who most need to see the world through the lens of waitstaff or cashiers are also the most able to weasel out of it. Nor will working as a bookseller guarantee your book becomes a bestseller. It certainly hasn't (at time of writing) guaranteed it for me. But something important happens in that last link in the chain. You can strategize, plan, plot, run your algorithms, do whatever else you can think of from the office, but whether we're talking about bagging a stack of books or bringing a pizza to a table, ultimately, we're talking about people as temporary teammates working together toward a shared goal. And ultimately, writers and booksellers share many goals. By working together as teammates, we can achieve those goals, creating a vibrant book culture and a thriving book industry.

TELL ME EVERYTHING YOU'VE EVER THOUGHT AND FELT IN THIRTY SECONDS

On Connection, Intuition, and the Art of Handselling

was walking either to or from the Javits Center in Manhattan during BookExpo America when I fell in next to Paul Yamazaki. Paul is the buyer at City Lights in San Francisco, the store founded by Lawrence Ferlinghetti, and an absolute bookselling legend. I'd only spent time with Paul once before, during a tour of Oxford, Mississippi, as part of a booksellers' conference. We grabbed a drink at a bar just off the main square. There was someone else there and, though I can't remember who it was or if they were even another bookseller or a publisher, I know it was someone Paul knew a lot better than I did. I remember doing very little talking and a whole lot of listening. Paul might have known of me as a reader through my write-ups that had appeared in Indie Next Lists, or from social media, or even through my novel. Paul probably would not have said he knew me all that well, but he knew me well enough to recommend *Confessions of the Fox* by Jordy Rosenberg, describing its writing as, among other things, "like Foucault." What else could I do? I bought it as soon as I got home and read it right away. At some point, probably at several points, I thought, I'm gonna sell a million of these.

When I approach someone with a recommendation because I think of a book that complements the two they're carrying, or because I overhear something, or I get a vibe from their tattoos or a band T-shirt, I make the sale approximately 50 percent of the time. If we're talking about someone I've recommended books to before, that 50 percent jumps to 70 percent or higher. When someone approaches me for a recommendation, that percentage jumps again to 80 to 90 percent, maybe even higher, with the misses almost always happening because they're asking for something in one of the few genres about which I don't know enough to recommend specific titles. I have no idea how those numbers compare to other booksellers. I wouldn't be surprised if most are around that 80–90 percent for customers that approach them, because, well, those customers almost always intend to buy a book. Those are sales to lose.

Not every bookseller approaches customers the way I do and not every bookstore encourages it. Furthermore, this data can be difficult if not impossible to track with any long-term consistency. Often customers buy the recommendations right away, but not always. Maybe the purchase happens after I've gone on break or it's made online later that day. Maybe I'm great at recommending books, maybe I'm average at it, and maybe I'm terrible at it. It's hard to know.

All that said, when I decide to advocate for a book, when I think it's good enough or important enough that I want to actively push the needle for it, for the author, and for the publisher, when I want to have a direct and tangible impact on sales, either through a staff pick, through talking about it on social media, by looking for likely readers, or all of the above, I can move units. Primarily through my advocacy, Porter Square Books has sold almost 150 copies of *Translation as Transhumance*, a book-length essay about the nature of translation published by Feminist Press and written by Mireille Gansel, a French-language translator essentially no one in the United States had heard of. Porter Square Books has also sold over two hundred copies of *Ducks, Newburyport* by Lucy Ellmann, a thousand-plus page stream-of-consciousness novel set not quite entirely in the mind of a woman and mother who supplements her family's income by baking in her home kitchen. (I got a tattoo to celebrate it.) I've sold eighty-two copies of *Signs Preceding the End of the World*, the debut novel in English by Yuri Herrera, eighty copies of *The Long Ships* by Frans G. Bengtsson, a Viking adventure story originally written in the 1950s, and fifty-nine copies of *A Ghost in the Throat*, a translator's memoir of working with a classic Gaelic poem whose author is all but lost to history. (All of those totals being *and counting*.) Which I guess is a long way of saying that, wherever I am on the spectrum of booksellers, over the course of many years I've learned a thing or two about handselling.

There are two storylines in *Confessions of the Fox*. In one, a scholar named Dr. Voth, a trans man working in academia, is trying to publish something that will give his career a vital boost while also navigating the advances of a colleague who turns out to be more interested in sex with a trans man as a novelty than as part of an actual romantic relationship. Dr. Voth's world seems vaguely dystopian (but that might be because I've never worked in academia) and he is poised to descend into a career-threatening stagnation while also sloughing through oppressive personal ennui. Then he makes a discovery: the secret journal of Jack Sheppard. Jack is a real-life English folk hero famous for breaking out of prisons, often with the help of his partner, Edgeworth Bess. The fictional journal reveals a history-changing fact: Jack Sheppard was a trans man, and perhaps the recipient of the world's first top surgery.

The second storyline is, of course, the journal itself. Jack tells his story of discovering his gender identity, the risks he took to affirm it, the relationships he built along the way, and his criminal escapades and daring prison escapes, which are based on those of the historic Jack Sheppard.

As I say in my staff pick: "One part sexy rogue's tale, one part intellectual exploration of the nature of history, one part examination of how people are marginalized by the powerful, all wrapped up in a tale of frustrated love and surveillance, this wild novel wriggles through genres, tones, and themes like a Dickensian pickpocket disappearing into a crowded London street. You won't read anything like it this year. One of my favorite books of 2018." Like, let's fucking go, right? How could I miss?

But I did. A lot. I didn't sell nearly as many copies as I expected when I staff-picked it, even though it was 20 percent off for the month. The store only sold seventeen copies of the book in hardcover. Not bad, but well below my expectations. The paperback has done a bit better in the three and a half years since it came out, at ninety-eight total Porter Square sales, but I think that reflects how often, rather than how well, I recommend it. I put it on lists, I recommended it online, I brought a stack to our Grown-Up Book Fair and the one holiday pop-up we did. The 50 percent of sales when I approached customers was a lot closer to 25 percent and that 80–90 percent dropped too. When a customer approaches me for a recommendation, I usually give them two or three choices, and more often than not with this book, when they made their purchase, *Confessions* was left behind. Maybe it's the academic setting. Maybe it's because Jack is British. Maybe this would have been a smash hit if it starred Billy the Kid.

If you approach me for a recommendation, I start with questions. What type of book are you looking for? Who is the reader you're looking for? What have you liked in the past? What have you disliked? What was the last great book you read? The last book you didn't like? Why did you like it or dislike it? Your favorite book? Pretty standard technique.

Sometimes readers give precise answers, telling me a handful of other titles and specific details about them. That precision makes it much easier to come up with recommendations and, more important, for those recommendations to be successful. If I know what you want is sophisticated neo-horror with a flavor of *The Secret History*, and it would be great if it were in translation, I'll be able to bring you to *Jawbone* by Mónica Ojeda, translated by Sarah Booker. But most of the time, I don't get that level of precision. Most of the time I get a version (or several different versions) of one of the most frustrating phrases a bookseller can hear: "I just want a good book."

I think about books all the time. What I'm reading, what I'm going to read next, what I just read, what I might not finish, and how I would describe all of them to potential readers. I doubt many other people, especially people who are not booksellers, think about books as much as I do, or spend so much of that thought on ways to describe those books and the experiences they inspire to other people. Why would they? There are lots of important things in my life that I only think about when I'm using them or buying them. Which means many people, even many people who identify as readers, don't have much practice describing books and the experiences they can create. They don't know the subgenres, or sometimes even the genres. You can't ask for what you can't name.

So if that initial round of questions doesn't elicit much useful information, I ask follow-ups. What mood are you looking for? Are you looking for a happy ending? Does the plot need to move quickly, or are you looking for something that lingers? How comfortable are you with sex or violence? What movies or TV shows do you like? Dislike? I try to find the specific emotions and experiences you're looking for so I can bring you to the genre you'd ask for if you knew it by name. "Something light" can describe many different books and genres. "Something light" with crime is a different desire than "something light" with robots, "something light" with wizards, "something light" with sex. I often try to get beyond the simple facts of the plot, though, because even within more specific subgenres, like cozy mysteries or military sci-fi, there can be dramatic differences between books that otherwise have similar plots. I use those questions not just to learn about your interest in plot and themes, but to tease out the narrative tone you're looking for, the pacing, the intensity of the different emotions you're hoping to experience.

Though it mostly takes the form of questions and answers, this isn't always just an input/output exchange. This is a conversation between two people about books. Sometimes a customer tells me more about why they're buying the book, or about the person they're buying it for, or about another book they've read, or I'll tell them something interesting about the author or share a facet of the book that I think is important in order to have a positive reading experience. Sometimes it's this tangential information that drags a great recommendation from my mind. There is more going on in our brains than we are conscious of and sometimes we need something outside our control, something unintentional, to access it.

If I don't have an immediate recommendation, I'll start walking through the stacks, conversing while I look at the books. This can be a memory retrieval technique. I'll know I have a good match and though I can't remember the title or the author I have a sense of where it is in the store. Sometimes I'll remember what display it's on or even remember the specific shelf. Often the physical act of moving among the shelves triggers the memory: I'll start walking one way and then turn on my heel because I've remembered the book I'm looking for is in an entirely different part of the store. It's like how you often only remember a phone number or PIN when you make the pattern with your finger on a keypad.

Other times, I'll have no fucking clue what to recommend and walking the shelves is also a stalling technique. It keeps the conversation going long enough to get some of that tangential yet ultimately vital information. Sometimes I'll see a good recommendation while I'm running my eyes over the spines. Sometimes seeing a book that would be a terrible recommendation for this customer makes me think of one that would be great. That little bit of extra stimulus is what my brain needed.

However I get there, I almost always get there. I have been in bookselling long enough, I have read enough, I have absorbed enough from other booksellers, from social media, and from customers that I almost always find something, no matter what the reader is looking for, no matter how little information they give me. If they ask me for a recommendation, I almost always put at least one book in their hands. I could say something cheesy, like, "There's a book for everyone," but that's not true. There are dozens of books for everyone. Not just in the world—I mean in the store right now. But *almost always* isn't *always*. There are a few sections I can't do anything with. There are readers who have read far more in the ones they're asking about than I have. "You're doing great," I'll say, to buy myself some time if they've read everything I've recommended, or maybe, "So I'm on the right track." If there's another bookseller who knows the section better than I do, I'll pass the customer off. But if not, I'll be honest if I realize I can't help them. I'll say, "This is where the types of books you're looking for are," and leave them to it. If you want someone to trust you when you have a recommendation, you have to be honest when you don't.

In the fall of 2022, I had a lot of success handselling *When I Sing, Mountains Dance* by Irene Solà to anyone who had witchy tattoos and seemed like they'd be up for a recommendation. I just handed them the book and told them to read the back, and when they got to, "He dies. The ghosts of seventeenth-century witches gather around him, taking up the chanterelles he'd harvested before going on their merry ways," they often decided to buy it. I'm always on the lookout for people wearing the Hold Steady T-shirts, because *Jack Ruby and the Origins of the Avant Garde in Dallas* by Robert Trammell could be described as the book version of a Hold Steady album. Craig Finn's "Charlemagne" and "Hallelujah" would be right at home with the trodden-upon but still vibrant, seedy but still charming, denizens of Trammell's fictional Dallas bar the Quiet Man. Online, I recommended *A Song for a New Day* by Sarah Pinsker to someone interested in speculative fiction, rock music, books like *Daisy Jones and the Six* and *A Visit from the Goon Squad*. They emailed the store back to tell us they had actually just been about to buy *A Song for a New Day*, but it was out of stock at their local bookstore.

I've been trying to remember other examples of the spontaneous handselling that happens when a customer approaches me, to show you tangible results of that conversation, but I can't. The process that generated the handselling described above is intentional and critical. It is a much longer intellectual process, so it leaves a deeper impression. Most of the time when I have one of those conversations, I move right on to the next task in the queue. If I think about it again it's because I've found a spare moment and I try to figure out whether the recommendation landed. But even then, it's on to the next thing almost right away. More often than not, when someone comes back to thank me for a recommendation, I need to ask them what I recommended. Handselling relies on all the books I can remember and yet I only rarely remember on-the-fly handselling itself.

The first step in recommending a book to someone I approach is deciding whether I should even approach them. Often, I'll have overheard something that triggers a recommendation. I overhear stuff all the time—people talking on the phone, to the person they're with, to themselves—and a stray phrase just clicks. Seeing someone carrying a couple of books creates that click as well, but I've also approached people because of a tattoo, a T-shirt, a tote bag, even just a general vibe. Something about how they are being in the bookstore hits me and I think of a book. Then I have to decide whether to approach. Sometimes I'll get a sense they want to be left alone. If I have any doubt, I'll err on the side of not, especially when the reader is a young woman, who almost certainly endures far too much unsolicited attention in public from strange men. I don't really have a formal system for deciding whether someone is approachable beyond that. (I'd be very surprised if anyone does.) I try to assess everything I can observe about them in the few seconds a human can look at another human without drawing their attention. Are they looking back and forth from their phone to the shelves? Do they seem to be scrolling through a list? When they're looking at the shelves, does their gaze move methodically along the alphabet, or does it drift around? Are they dancing their fingertips across the spines? Are they looking up at signs around the store? How much do they seem to notice other people, either when they're browsing or when they're chatting with whomever they're with? Are they chatting or conversing? Do they seem cool? Sometimes those distinctions are obvious, but often they're not. Ultimately, sometimes I have to guess, and much of the time I'm not sure what it was that made me decide I could approach this person, but not that person.

And ultimately, I'm wrong a lot. So I almost always offer an explanation, or even an apology, when I approach someone. I'll say something like, "Sorry to bother you, but I saw your T-shirt and I thought of this book," or, "Excuse me, I see you're carrying X and Y and wanted to make sure you knew about Z." Even, "Pardon me, sorry, this might sound weird, but I got this general vibe from you and it made me think of this book." Sometimes, "I don't know if you're looking for a recommendation, but if so, I loved this book." Or I'll hedge my bets even further by asking if they need help finding anything and decide by how they respond whether to offer a recommendation.

Whether someone approaches me or I approach them, whether I've already got a book in mind or come up with one or three on the fly, there is a gap between me and the reader and between the reader and the book. They can't tell me everything they've ever thought or felt in thirty seconds. They can't tell me every book they've ever read and every thought they've ever had while reading them. I can't tell them absolutely everything about every book I might recommend, every possible hook or trigger or interpretation. To deploy a cliché, they, as human and as reader, contain multitudes. But so do I. When I hand them a book, it's like a spark of electricity leaping across a synapse. Those cells never actually touch, yet they still connect. I can never know your multitudes, just as you can never know mine. Furthermore, we often have to discover our own multitudes as we respond, react to, and learn about the world around us.

When a reader leaps across that fundamental gap by taking a risk on a book I recommend, we share something beyond an exchange of information; we share a faith in the ability of people to share something whether they know anything about each other or not. And when a reader loves a book I recommended to them, that risk and faith are rewarded with meaningful connection.

Recommendation algorithms attempt to erase this gap. They are designed to gather massive amounts of information about you over time and feed that data through formulas that, through brute computing strength, will return better matches than anything a lowly human brain could come up with. But no human life can be contained in collectable information, nor can any human's reading habits be collect-ed in clean data. The experiences of reading are too deep, they engage with aspects of our being that are difficult or impossible to quantify, and the values of those experiences change over time. Furthermore, algorithms can't elude the opinions of human brains entirely. Some person needs to de-cide what makes a book light or dark, what makes this book speculative but this other book dystopian, what distinguishes thrillers from crime fiction, and that person is not around to talk to you if you understand those terms differently. This is why suggestions from algorithms are often either totally bor-ing, recommending a near exact replica of what you already bought; or irrelevant, making recommendations based on atypical purchases made for atypical reasons; or nonsensi-cal, returning recommendations you would never in a million years take because your understanding of "tense psycholog-ical thriller" is different from what a few other people have crammed into a book's metadata. Ultimately, not even Ama-zon or Google can know everything about you, and so when those algorithms make recommendations as if they did, the recommendations often fail.

Handselling books isn't just important because you buy something or you are more likely to appreciate what you buy; it's also important because it validates and centers the spark that is such a vital and joyous part of being a human being with other human beings. It is a brief tangible moment in which you are not alone, not isolated. Over time, conver-sations with customers can accumulate into an interesting type of relationship, a kind of micro-community built through books and recommendations. Some of these customers at-tended the launch for my first novel, including Arielle, who brought her daughter, the event's youngest attendee. Ever since I recommended *I Hotel* to her when she was a student in the area, Kim comes to the store to get books from me whenever she's in town. Rachael moved to Alaska, but her partner's job brings her back to Boston every now and then. When she happened to be walking by Porter Square Books: Boston Edition and saw me in the window, she came in and bought a few of my recommendations.

After getting a couple of recommendations as part of bookseller bundles, including one for *Saint Sebastian's Abyss* by Mark Haber, one customer (another Rachael) described on Twitter feeling "very seen and maybe a little attacked and that's fine."[58] I responded that that is a potentially perfect description of a good recommendation. Being *seen* describes both recognition and understanding. Used in this context, it isn't just about recognizing that someone exists, but somehow seeing enough of them in the right way that you understand parts of their identity, personality, and character in ways they may not expect other people to recognize. *Attacked*, in this context, describes aspects of yourself being seen that you maybe didn't see yourself or perhaps didn't want others to notice. It describes a moment of vulnerability, a passing through of your defenses, but in a way you ultimately appreciate. Maybe you get something you didn't know you needed or weren't quite prepared or able to ask for.

Whether we phrase it in terms of being "seen and attacked" or as making connections, this bridging of the gap between people is proof that, despite all that fundamentally separates us, we are not alone. We may all be individuals locked inside our skulls, but we're all individuals locked inside our skulls together. "Third places," places that are neither work nor home, like bookstores, other shops, libraries, public parks, and festivals, are important in part because of how they let us be together at the exact volume we, as individuals, need at that moment. You don't need to talk to a bookseller or anybody else when you're in a bookstore if you don't want to. If you just want to be around other people who aren't your family, you can do that. And if you want to make a more direct, more active connection with someone, you can do that too.

Not every recommendation is successful. I can misunderstand what a customer tells me about themselves as readers or about the type of book they're looking for. I can misremember key aspects of a book or just have a very different interpretation of it than another reader. Furthermore, there are readers who have good reasons to doubt a bookseller like me has the experience and perspective to connect with them.

One time I asked a customer if she needed any help. She said she was looking for books for an older teenage girl who was questioning her gender and sexuality. I said I'd be glad to help and maybe even took a step toward a book that popped into my head. She held up her hand. She said she meant no offense, but it was really important that these recommendations didn't come from … you know … a man. Though she didn't articulate it specifically, and I certainly didn't press, it felt clear to me that she didn't think a man like me could share enough of the experiences the reader was going through to recommend the right books for this moment in the reader's life. Whether she believed that herself or thought the person she was buying for believed that, I don't know, but it amounts to the same thing. For this recommendation, she needed a bookseller to share a significant part of their identity with the reader she was buying for. And you know what? That's fine. I called in one of the women I work with.

I wonder if this need for some shared identity is part of the reason I didn't sell *Confessions of the Fox* as well as I thought I would. I usually brought it to readers who were already carrying a queer or trans book or two, most of whom presented themselves in queer-coded styles. I can't know how any specific person I approached identifies, but I read the vast majority of customers I handed *Confessions of the Fox* to, both spontaneously and in the context of solicited recommendations, as queer. I'm a white guy with a beard and glasses, wearing either a bookish T-shirt or a plaid button-up, in a bookstore. To my knowledge, no one has ever read my identity as anything other than the cisgendered heterosexual man that I am. Perhaps because I described it as "sexy," some readers were concerned it presented a fetishized version of the trans experience. Maybe they were afraid I wasn't aware how frequently queer characters are killed off or how often they are presented as stereotypes in books and other media. Rosenberg is certainly aware, and I think he successfully subverts those occurrences, but you won't know that until you've read the entire book. There is ample history of readers with privileged identities championing books about marginalized identities, from *The Education of Little Tree* to *Hillbilly Elegy* to *American Dirt*, that are inaccurate and destructive. So as with the customer looking for recommendations from someone who is not a man, I can't really blame people for not taking a risk on *Confessions of the Fox* when I handed it to them.

When I recommended *Saint Sebastian's Abyss* to Rachael, she specifically pointed out "unhinged art criticism [and] friendship!!"[59] as reasons my recommendation connected. But that's not why I recommended that book to her. I know Rachael really well, so I knew there was a good chance she'd enjoy the prose style. The obsessive focus of the narrator on one particular piece of art created an equally obsessive narrative voice that I think dipped, by the sheer weight of the obsession, into brilliant satire. I knew she reads weird shit, and, if nothing else, Haber's commitment to the bit makes this book weird shit.

Often, when someone comes back to tell me about a successful recommendation, they mention aspects of the book I hadn't thought of when I handsold it to them. You can draw a couple of conclusions from this. You could argue I just get lucky, and there would be an element of truth to that. You could also

argue that the reader's desire for a good recommendation influences their reaction to the book, leading them to find ways
to like it, and there would be some truth to that too. But I think
good recommendations and meaningful connections happen
too often and, for me at least, too consistently for successful
handselling to rely on generously assessed lucky guesses.

First of all, I need to know of a shit ton of books. Of course,
I read a shit ton of books, compared at least to the average
reader, but my ability to handsell would be catastrophically
limited if I relied only on books I read. I broaden my mental
bookcase by paying attention to what other booksellers at
Porter Square Books recommend and talk about, either with
customers in the store, through their staff picks, or through
their recommendations on social media or with each other
on Slack. I pay attention to what booksellers from other stores
and what authors and book reviewers talk about on social
media. Finally, on every shift I walk around the store and just
look at the books. Essentially, I browse the store as if I were a
customer. I look at the new releases tables, the seasonal displays, the bestsellers, the staff picks, and the stacks. I look for
authors I recognize and books I've heard people talking about.
I notice what's been faced out and put on display on book
stands. And I also try to spend a little time with books that
just catch my eye, finding out who published it, reading the
summary, seeing who blurbed it. This is one reason I sometimes need to walk through the stacks to find a recommendation: I'm aware of the book because I found it that way. All
these different sources create a ton of information and I wish
I had some tip or trick to explain how I retain it all, but I don't.

But it doesn't really matter that I know a book if I can't
think of it when I'm actually talking to a customer. A customer isn't going to wait several minutes for me to think of
something. I have to be able to pull the book off my mental
bookcase within seconds. Athletes, dancers, musicians, paint-

ers, and other professionals who rely on repeated physical actions practice them over and over. This process develops muscle memory, a level of proficiency in which people don't need to consciously think about the movements to execute them. I think the concept applies to intellectual processes as well. Chefs train their palate to know when a dish "tastes right." Painters train their eyes to know when a color "looks right." Musicians train their ears to know when a note "sounds right." At this point in my career as a bookseller, I've had to retrieve books from that mental bookcase so many times over the course of thousands of exchanges that I don't need to do any conscious thinking for potential books to pop into my brain after just a few seconds of conversation.

How someone says they'd "just like a really good read," often contains far more information than the sentence itself. Nobody talks only with words. They talk with their voices, their faces, their hands. Sometimes their tone suggests they want something they feel ashamed about. They want a romance but feel romances are "guilty pleasures." Another tone or piece of body language suggests they're looking for the kind of book that works well for book clubs. Another suggests they just want someone else to make the choice for them. How they take a book from me, how they hold it, their facial expressions as I say this or that, often tells me more than their words. I don't really sense my brain drawing conclusions, but I've absolutely shifted recommendations mid-phrase in response to how I'm interpreting social cues. I've stopped in my tracks and put a book back on the shelf. I've emphasized aspects of the book that seemed to be getting positive reactions. A book can be absolutely perfect for a reader, but they won't buy it if I don't show them the potential connection in a way they understand, and I can't do that if I don't listen to everything they are telling me.

The attention I pay to books in my life plus my talent for remembering books creates a mental bookcase of titles I can draw from, but I don't entirely understand how that talent works. Observing social cues helps me better understand exactly what the customer is asking for, but I can't say for certain how I understand. Thousands of conversations with hundreds of readers over almost two decades of bookselling have helped me develop the ability to pick titles from that mental bookcase, but in the moment I am very rarely certain why a specific book arrived in my thoughts and it is often only while I make the pitch to the customer that I discover the reasons for the potential connection. Even this long into my career, even this late into this essay, there is mystery.

I didn't have a formal definition for intuition when I started this essay. I just knew that handselling didn't work without it. At least not for me. I spend a lot of time in my own head making rational arguments. I think about politics, critical interpretations of books, ideas of bookselling, bullshit at work, housing policy, hockey strategy, and other random problems, subjects, things. Is it healthy to spend so much time arguing in your own head for a federal policy that incentivizes rewilding personal lawns? I don't know. But I do think I know what "rational" thinking feels like, and handselling doesn't feel like that. It feels and has always felt like intuition even though I had no idea what intuition was. But I have a picture of it now as something composed of intellectual muscle memory, semi- and subconscious banks of information, reading social cues, and trust in what appears in my mind even when I can't explain its appearance. Intuition is one of those concepts that can be difficult to explain or discuss rationally because it does not use the same mechanics that "rational" thinking does. We know more than we know. We develop expertise in a stunning range of skills, abilities, and techniques. The world is varied and so we have varieties of intelligence to cope with the world. Intuition is one of them.

For all the variability around handselling, I have one bit

of actionable advice for booksellers. When in doubt, recommend a book you love. This works for a few reasons. First, it is an answer to the paradox of choice. When someone "just wants a good book" and walks into a bookstore, they are faced with thousands of choices. Depending on who they are as a reader and how prepared they are for the visit, they might be overwhelmed. The sheer range of available choices makes the act of choosing stressful. Saying, "I'm not sure this is the book you're looking for, but I love it" offers a solution to their feeling of being overwhelmed. Second, excitement is contagious. When people see that someone else is excited they want to be excited too. The opportunity to share excitement, even in the somewhat distant way a recommendation offers, is sometimes enough to make a book worth trying. I mean, if a bookseller loves it, it has to be good, right? Third, of course, you want to sell the books you love.

Finally, the recommendation itself adds value. When you recommend a book to a reader, you create a story. It isn't just "I wanted to buy this, so I did," or even "This caught my eye." It's "I bought this book because Josh recommended it." Now there's a plot. There are characters. There is meaning. And that story stays with the book for as long as the book stays with the reader. Regardless of who the book is recommended to, the fact of a recommendation adds its own value.

I don't get thanked for recommendations very often. Even the most loyal supporters of a community-focused bookstore don't visit that frequently. I can go months without seeing a regular. And even if I do see a regular who got a great recommendation from me, that doesn't mean they'll say something, even if, when they finished the book, they intended to. I'm still waiting for a reader to thank me for recommending *Confessions of the Fox*. But I have been thanked for other recommendations. I've been thanked for *I Hotel* by Karen Tei Yamashita, *Signs Preceding the End of the World* by Yuri Herrera, and

Feebleminded by Ariana Harwicz. I've been thanked for recommendations I was desperate to know about and thanked for recommendations I completely forgot. I've been asked to pass on thanks to other booksellers. I've been thanked the next time that customer came into the store and I've been thanked years later. I've been thanked in person, via email, and on social media. Most of those thanks are, of course, very practical—I'm being thanked for recommending a book the customer ended up loving—but I believe there is a less practical, less tangible, less consumerist undercurrent to that gratitude as well.

Goran Petrović's novel *At the Lucky Hand* (translated by Peter Agnone) is set in a fictional world that allows people reading the same book at the same time to physically meet in the setting of the story. It is a vibrant and imaginative exploration of the idea of a community of readers. Though Petrović uses this world to tell a sad story of classism and the tension between reality and fantasy, I think his thought experiment gives body to a more positive truth. Books help us be together. It means something when a bookseller sees you in such a way that they can connect you with a book. Being seen is a felt experience, being connected is an emotion, and for readers, being seen and connected through books can be especially powerful. You can't buy trust. You can't buy intuition. You can't buy real recognition. You can't buy connection. You can't buy community. But you can buy a book. And when you trust a bookseller to use their intuition to handsell you a book, you get all those things for free.

THIS IS MY MASK

My Bookselling During the COVID-19 Pandemic

AT TIME OF WRITING

I don't always feel like I've understood something until I've written about it. I turn to poetry, with its flexible grammar, complicated relationship to what we consider "rational," and ability to somehow evoke the unsayable with words, when I need to understand how a person or event made me feel. Similarly, I used my blog to cultivate my understanding of political, economic, and social events.

Sharing what I already think was only one motivation for writing about bookselling. I also wanted to learn about it through the effort of writing and researching the essays. "Write what you know," like so many dollops of writing advice, is both correct and incorrect. I've never understood that advice as a restriction of content but as an invitation to education. You start where you are and you write at your own ignorance. I write to organize. I write to understand. I write to compartmentalize. I write to learn. And I need to better understand what happened, what I felt about it, and what I've learned as a result of the COVID-19 pandemic.

I hoped this piece would be composed in the spirit of assessment. I was supposed to consider the facts of my life as a bookseller during the pandemic after it was over. Though I wrote contemporaneously, I planned to edit and rewrite, looking back from the conclusion. A couple of times, it did look like we knew the ending. I wrote several passages after I had been vaccinated as though I could see the end. But the pandemic lurched on. Things I thought I knew in 2021, it turns out, I did not know.

I'm stuck.

As a person, I want to understand what I experienced in the eighteen or so months that would constitute the height of the pandemic. As a writer, I know a book about bookselling written in the last couple of years would feel incomplete without something about COVID-19. As a bookseller, I know the pandemic has been so challenging, even traumatic, for booksellers, that we need to have reparative conversations about it.

I could, of course, just start afresh on a new essay. Writers abandon projects all the time. I abandon projects all the time. But this lurching on, this treading water, this sense of "we should be fucking done with this shit already" is a central part of the experience of COVID-19. Retail and service workers in particular have been slogging through a boggy limbo, seeing cases rise and plunge and rise again, watching our leaders in government stop leading, being told by customers that enforcing safety measures is essentially a form of slavery. Because a limbo is part of the experience of COVID-19 for me, I want to preserve it. I want to understand it.

The phrase "at time of writing," has taken on a new significance over the last few years. So much is happening so quickly all the time that we are so exhausted by the things happening we have no energy left to reflect on them. And when you reflect on an issue or incident, almost as soon as you've articulated your thoughts and reflections, they're irrelevant because the landscape and context have already changed, perhaps dramatically. In some ways, if you're working on anything remotely contemporary, the caveat "at time of writing," is essential. The term itself has become something of an anchor for me. Maybe I couldn't understand all the changes taking place, but through that phrase I could wrap my head around the pace of those changes. Over the course of the pandemic, other terms have also become ubiquitous. "Pod." "Social distancing." "Getting back to normal." These have also become anchors for my understanding of the experience.

In a lot of ways, this essay isn't even a definitive record of my bookselling during the pandemic. Every time I read this over I remember something else I haven't touched on. I realize I haven't said anything in this essay about the unprecedented surge of book buying after the murder of George Floyd, a kind of nationwide retail therapy for white liberals that pumped a lot of capital into independent bookselling, but also burdened many bookstores and especially Black-owned bookstores with customers who were used to getting what they wanted when they wanted it, no matter what. I haven't said anything about how incessantly the phone rang during the pandemic. Fucking relentless. We had to develop entire workflows to cope. I still sometimes flinch a little when the phone rings.

Some booksellers had similar experiences, many others did not. My hope is that this personal process of growing toward understanding will provide structure, or material to help other booksellers and people engage in their own process. And this will get to you in some form months after I last touched it. The world will either look like a slightly different version of the one I write from today or it will look very different, the cascade of tragedies will have continued unabated or will have abated. Or, maybe, some good shit will have happened. Given how I am struggling to see the past, I don't have much confidence in my ability to see the future.

*

+LOCKDOWN

For a few weeks in March and April 2020, no one was allowed in the store. No customers. No workers. From home I manipulated online orders so they could ship directly from warehouses, helped with a daily newsletter, generated social media, and messaged my way on Slack and email, with everyone else, through the most turbulent few weeks in the store's and perhaps the industry's history. I think we threw out three full schedules, all while the manager making the schedules was stuck in Utah because she was visiting her parents when travel was shut down. I'm trying to remember those weeks, but they seem to live entirely in those sentences. I can see my desk with my laptop, I can see the online IndieCommerce order display, which, at the time, was essentially just a list of titles, ISBNs, and quantities. I can see the printouts with the notes about which books were in which warehouses so I could figure out which ones needed to be removed so any order could ship at all. At the time, that information was not integrated. I had to feel something during those sixty-plus-hour, seven-day workweeks. There must have been reactions to suddenly finding myself with a desk job. And some of it, honestly, wasn't so bad. I liked making videos. I liked writing for the newsletter. I liked, and still like, doing office work from home.

Perhaps I was just "doing" at a pace that didn't allow for any "feeling." So maybe it didn't feel like anything. Maybe that was a good thing. Maybe the order-by-order, decision-by-decision, problem-by-problem-solved focus protected me from some of the emotional impacts of these early days and weeks of the pandemic. I was not thinking about the thousands of people dying every day. I was not thinking about the potential risk to the bookstore. I was just editing that order so the "send to warehouse" button popped up. I was doing another take of the video of my reading from *I Hotel*. I was just answering questions on Slack, writing about books for the newsletter, debating store policies.

Eventually, some control over COVID's spread was attained and business owners were allowed to work in their stores. Porter Square Books had a twelve-member ownership group at the time. When many small businesses in Massachusetts had to make due with one or two people, we had a dozen legally allowed to work in the store. Even though some co-owners couldn't come in because of the higher risks to themselves and their families, we could have one or two one-person shifts in the store every day. Living within walking distance of the store and not having any extra risk factors for COVID-19, I was one of the owners who worked the six-to-ten-hour shifts fulfilling online orders. I became a warehouse worker: picking orders, packing them, shipping them, all of it alone. At most, I would see a co-worker in passing as they left or as whoever was receiving, once we started receiving again, passed from the front of the store to the back of the store or rolled out a cart for shelving.

In a lot of ways, this was still better than sitting at a computer at home every day. It was still drudgery, still devoid of the energizing aspects of pre-pandemic bookselling. It was still lonely. But at least there were tangible results. I could take books off shelves. I could match special orders. I could fill mail tubs. I was still working seven days a week, still doing a lot of that computer work at home, but I could actually see the results of some of my labor.

Eventually, the state lifted additional restrictions, more out of impatience than triumph, employees were allowed back in stores, and then, again more out of impatience than triumph, customers were allowed back too. Lockdown, such as it was, ended. We had to think of more ways of doing business. Some people worked at the register, as "with customers" as possible with Plexiglas barriers, while others worked exclusively in the back, only coming out to gather books for online orders. We found ways to keep our community happy. We kept our book-sellers as safe as we could, and to the best of our knowledge no one caught COVID-19 while working at the store. We paid everyone based on their pre-pandemic schedule throughout the entire lockdown whether they worked that schedule or not. By just about any rubric you could think of, Porter Square Books had a successful lockdown.

And yet it doesn't feel like a success. In some ways, it doesn't even feel like survival. Perhaps it's because people are still catching and dying of COVID. Perhaps it's because most of the other booksellers I spent the most time with during the height of the pandemic have left. I can't turn to another book-seller and say, "Hey, remember that night in December 2020 when we laughed about the name Bonnie Cockman for, like, an hour?" Perhaps it's because of the missed opportunities to use the crisis as a creative force to make significant changes in how we live, work, and sell books. Or maybe it's because, at this moment, I'm still so tired from that time that I don't really and truly feel as though I've actually gotten out of lockdown.

MASK

In order to be—or at least feel—safe reopening the store for in-store shopping, we enforced health and safety protocols. Some were decreed by the state or the city, and others we de-signed for our specific space. Leaving our doors open as long as there were customers inside, regardless of the weather, to allow air circulation was a vital component of that safety. If you have an open door, people will walk in, no matter what else is happening in the world and no matter how many signs you have up, where those signs are, or how big they are. (You might assume people walking into a bookstore would always read the signs. You would be wrong.) So a new responsibility was created. We called the job "front door." During a "front door" shift I would stand at the front door, count people in and out using a stitch counter to keep to our occupancy limit, and recite the new Pledge of Allegiance: "Mask on, over the nose, sanitize your hands on the way in, and please limit your visits to about fifteen minutes," and I did my best to enforce all of that. I also fetched curbside orders. (Would the occasional person just walk right in during the five or so seconds it took me to grab an order even though there was a chain across one side of the door and a line of people along the wall? You know it.) When I had to queue people outside because the store was at capacity I would try to, you know, be a libromancer. I'd ask people what they were looking for and grab it if I could. I gave recommendations. Eventually, we got a laptop near the door so I could actually look things up and sell books right there. I worked the line. I tried to make people feel that the time they were simply standing around wasn't completely wasted. I made some sales. I got some laughs. I did my best.

As we planned reopening and as we designed this role, a lot of booksellers requested to not be scheduled for it. We'd all seen videos of people losing their shit over having to wear a mask. When we were still only doing curbside pickup, a man flipped the plastic folding table at one of our booksellers. The bookseller wasn't physically hurt and that was the only violent incident, but there is a world of difference between zero violent incidents and one violent incident. A mark was left, not just on that specific bookseller, but on everyone. Still, there were no other "viral" moments and my time at front door was almost conflict free. Our community, for a whole host of different reasons, wore masks and followed the rules.

Furthermore, I am a white, masculine, cis, affable man. Blond hair. Blue eyes. Appley cheeks. On the stocky side. I look like "the guy who works at the bookstore." People don't start shit with me. Honestly, people having psychotic episodes don't start shit with me. A few people stormed off after I wouldn't let them in for whatever reason. A number grudgingly pulled their masks up when I reminded them, in much more professional terms of course, that masks only work when they cover all your fucking breathing parts. More people actually thanked me for my recitation than complained about it because of what it said about the store's commitment to safety.

And then, on a beautiful summer day, a white woman, thin the way some people are just thin, with bobbed ashen-brown hair, likely in her early sixties, was standing in line holding a beech leaf in front of her mouth. A. Beech. Leaf.

I said, "Oh, do you have a mask with you today?" because I am almost pathologically patient.

She looked me directly in my eyes and said, "This is my mask."

This. Is. My. Mask.

I gave her one of the disposable masks we kept at the door. (See above about patience.)

Imagine trying to explain to someone from another planet that people refused to wear masks during a respiratory virus pandemic. Imagine having to say, "People risked their lives and the lives of everyone they spent time with because they—grown-ass adults—needed to perform that 'you are not the boss of me' schtick." Imagine having to say people compared wearing masks so they could shop indoors to being a slave. Imagine having to say, "There were protests."

You would have to start with the way President Donald Trump downplayed the threat of the pandemic, both in terms of its severity and its potential duration, convincing many of his followers the whole thing was actually a hoax. Of course, you couldn't stop there, because it would make no sense that people wouldn't trust the recommendations of scientific experts, so then you'd have to explain how the anti-vaxxer movement and those trying to prevent the policy changes needed to deal with climate change undercut the public's trust in "experts" in general and on specific scientific issues. You would probably need to talk about Gamergate to show how media can be undercut by coordinated action. So you probably need to discuss the general media environment that would allow such nonsense and be vulnerable to such actions at all, which will bring you to Fox News, Ronald Reagan's deregulation of media, the myth of the liberal media, and then back to the Republican Party's unaccountable dishonesty and duplicitousness over issues like deficit spending, WMDs in Iraq, and climate change. Luckily, all of that would help explain how Donald fucking Trump could win a presidential election, so you'd get a running start on that one.

Crises are never just themselves. The stress they put on society exposes other flaws and weaknesses. Smaller problems that seem or have been manageable are no longer manageable. There is a crisis in the media, of course, in that we do not have a journalistic ecosystem that can actively sort truth from bullshit, or honest disagreement from tactical rhetoric. There is the crisis of our two-party system that is compounded by the crisis of our Republican Party, which is itself a continuation of our crisis of white supremacy. The conflict over masks is just a particularly visible expression of this cascade of stresses and crises.

The masking crisis also revealed that many people believe they have absolute power over anyone they happen to be paying. To some, buying dinner at a restaurant is not just buying a meal, but also buying agency over the staff. They are not just buying the service provided, they are also buying power. The COVID-19 pandemic didn't cause this attitude, nor was it the only source of conflict over masking. But it did change the context of these exchanges in ways that supercharged this attitude. People not only felt this power, they felt new permission to wield the ever-loving fuck out of it. If you've worked in retail or food service for any length of time, someone has treated you like a vending machine. The pandemic and the crisis over masking just empowered more people to kick the vending machines harder.

Crises can be opportunities. From the struggles and challenges, new solutions and new ways of doing things can be discovered. We could have used this to interrogate our relationship to the people we pay, we could have explored how it relates to race and class, to long-standing social and cultural structures, and to more recent changes in technology and mores. We could have used this attack on the dignity of workers to defend and elevate the dignity of workers. Instead, our systems of power did just enough to keep the ledger of death at a level that we could absorb and absolutely no more than that.

POD

In the summer of 2020 when pandemic restrictions were beginning to ease, another bookseller and I had been trying to get a joint writing project going for a couple of weeks, but just couldn't get our schedules together. One day we were working together and decided to just hang out after our shift to work on our project. I knew at least one of the other booksellers on that shift did some writing too, so we invited everyone else to stay and write with us. One did, so we had a little writing group. We did this informally a few times and pretty much every time we invited other booksellers to stay and write with us, they did.

Once it was clear people were getting something out of

this, we formalized it a bit more. Since in-store shopping was limited to four hours a day, customers were only in the store for half our shift. This meant we could all take our breaks at the same time. Meeting during our break, rather than after our shift—which we did sometimes too—meant this group didn't extend anyone's time inside at the store. We put on roughly half an hour of music, sat somewhere we could stay spread out like in the kids section, and wrote until the music stopped. We didn't share or critique. It wasn't about producing a written work. We just got words out together as a pod.

Once the entire staff was allowed back in the store, I had an instant pod, a group of five-ish people I could share indoor space with, without adding much more risk of exposure than we took on being at work in the first place. What many people never had, worked really hard to create, or took their chances without, I had built into my life through my job. I wonder what state I would have been in without it. I wonder what risks I would have taken. I wonder how much I would have drunk.

The shared struggle of working in a bookstore during a pandemic, combined with the support and connection of being able to make real eye contact, see body language in person, hear tone of voice unadulterated by Wi-Fi connection and headphones, created two or three close friendships, people who were relatively new additions to my life who I could not imagine my future without.

The pod meant it didn't add risk for people to gather on my porch or in my backyard. The pod meant it didn't add risk for some of us to share car rides or go on hikes. The pod meant it didn't add risk for a friend who lived an inconvenient distance from the store to occasionally crash at my place. The pod meant a few of us could stay after our shifts, watch All Elite Wrestling, and drink a couple of beers.

"Add risk," is the key phrase. This pod was never truly safe. Just about every member had roommates or lived with a partner who had to work with the public like we did or didn't live with a partner but spent time with them or had to accommodate family members. This isn't a critique of the choices any of us made, just an acknowledgment that as safe as things were, there were still very real risks. If any of about five booksellers, and certainly two other booksellers, had caught COVID during this time, I almost certainly would have too. And if I had gotten it, they would have. It's a strange bond. It never felt like a deadly risk, and that probably speaks more to how we internalize abstract threats than anything else, but, ultimately, that's what it was. Through that risk, co-workers and friends became pods.

T-SHIRT

When in-store shopping shut down, bookstores around the country found themselves unable to sell nearly as many books as before. The customers that only occasionally shopped with them, but didn't feel a strong connection, migrated to Amazon. I suppose this is one of those coincidences that does not imply causation, but at one point while articles were circulating about how Americans were buying more books than ever, and while Amazon was seeing massive increases in profits, sales at Porter Square Books were down 20 percent. Many different currents fed into how shopping changed during the height of the pandemic, but it was profoundly frustrating to read about a return to reading in our country while people were buying far fewer books from us and other indie bookstores.

To a store of any kind, there are two types of people: those who shop at the store and those who don't. There are two general courses for increasing retail sales: Get the people who aren't shopping with you to start, and get the people already shopping with you to spend more. It is accepted knowledge that it's less expensive—in terms of time, money, and effort—to get existing customers to spend more than it is to create new customers. I know I'm more likely to convince someone who's already buying two books to buy a third than to make a sale to someone who wasn't planning on buying anything. So stores found ways to get their existing customers to spend more. Sometimes they directly asked people to shop, other times they solicited donations, and many, if not most, started selling T-shirts and other swag. I don't know if selling T-shirts kept any stores from closing or even kept any booksellers employed who would have been laid off or furloughed, but it was cash coming in with relatively low overhead and that always helps.

But something else happened with T-shirts. I bought at least half a dozen from other stores and I know a lot of other booksellers did too. Seeing that crystallized one of my fundamental frustrations with how we, as a society, handled the pandemic and, honestly, how our economy operates in general. While booksellers around the country were spending money they probably didn't have supporting each other in a kind of ad hoc mutual aid society by way of Bonfire, the wealthiest people in the world—many becoming richer every single second of the pandemic—were, at best, doing jack fucking shit to help anybody and, at worst, lobbying for premature reopening, getting their workers classified as "essential," exploiting the Paycheck Protection Program, and, in general, continuing to use their wealth and its attendant powers to make sure everyone else suffered. Those with the least did as much as they could. Those with the most fucked off to space. T-shirts are great and the community of booksellers is great, but seriously, fuck Jeff Bezos, fuck every venture capitalist, fuck every billionaire, and fuck everyone who has the political power to actually help people but allows billionaires to happen instead.

Wait, this is about T-shirts and how the word helps me understand the pandemic. This is about a demonstration of camaraderie. This is a celebration of bookselling. This is one of those feel-good stories, the kind the local news use to restore our faith in humanity, to help us look on the bright side. But it's one thing to look on the bright side and another to paper over tragedies built directly on the status quo with heroic—yet temporary—inspiring—yet limited—triumphs. This is about all the great booksellers around the country. The friends I've made in my years of bookselling. How social media creates space for and then supports new types of relationships and friends. Wait. This is about T-shirts. This is about bookstores. This is about capitalism. This is about a plague.

CURBSIDE

When the state of Massachusetts was in total lockdown, Porter Square Books became an online-only store that fulfilled all of its orders through wholesaler warehouses. I clicked a button and sent the order to Pennsylvania or Tennessee or sometimes even Indiana, and the order was packed and shipped by workers there. When the lockdown was eased and owners were allowed back into the store, we changed our model to a combination of wholesaler and store fulfillment. Eventually we added a local delivery option that was free above a certain purchase threshold and PSB booksellers were driving all around Cambridge and Somerville dropping off bags of books. Eventually, regulations loosened up a bit more and our business shifted again to include shipping, local delivery, and curbside pickup.

Not that we really had a curb. Porter Square Books is in a strip mall with a wide sidewalk and a patio between us and the parking lot. We didn't really offer "curbside" pickup so much as "at the front door," pickup, but by the time we added the option, "curbside" had entered the pandemic lexicon. At times, we had the doors closed and you had to call a phone number when you arrived. It wasn't the store's usual phone number because we needed the calls to bounce to booksellers' cell phones so we wouldn't tie up the regular number with pickup calls. Eventually, we had the door open and a table in front of it, sometimes with the phone set up, and sometimes just watching the door. We changed again when customers were allowed in-store. As we understood the pandemic, as it got safer and more dangerous, we constantly adapted, changing our business model a handful of times over the course of a year or so.

To me the ability of Porter Square Books, so many other bookstores and businesses, and so many people to accommodate the safety requirements of the pandemic while still providing goods and services, proves we had the resources needed to endure a much longer and more effective lockdown. Delivery services were added. Laws were changed in Massachusetts so bars could do curbside cocktails. We had streaming entertainment. We got professional sports going relatively safely. We eventually learned a ton of outdoor activities were safe. By and large, Americans were ready and able to do what people in countries like South Korea and New Zealand did to save thousands of lives. There was no way we were going to completely avoid tragedy. There was going to be death in March and April 2020 no matter what we did. But it would have been not just possible, but frankly easy to save many more people than we did.

On the one hand, I don't want to end so many sections of this essay on the mass grave dug by American capitalism and all those in political power who support it, but on the other hand, when you see a mass grave, it's hard to land anywhere else.

*

GETTING BACK TO NORMAL

"There are five fucking people in the entire store! How the fuck is one of them standing exactly where I need to go?!" Everyone who has worked for any length of time in a bookstore knows that if you have one book left to shelve someone will be standing exactly where it goes. As exasperating as that moment was, it was also a nice bit of normalcy. I was spending my shifts either counting people in and out at the front door, checking people out at the register behind plexiglass, or processing online orders at one of the computers in the office, and doing very little actual libromancy. Even though it was a mild inconvenience, I appreciated this dollop from the beforetimes.

But as nice as moments of normalcy were, I don't know if there was a more destructive phrase or idea than "getting back to normal." Whether it was sending students back to school, prematurely reopening bars and restaurants, or dropping mask requirements, "getting back to normal" killed tens of thousands of people. Perhaps more.

And this is before asking whether the "normal" so many powerful people were so desperate to get back to was worth getting back to in the first place. Shouldn't we always try to make the world better than it already is? Could we have dramatically improved public transportation when so few people were using it? Could we have put in more and safer bike lanes while so few people were driving? Could we have identified the permanent value of public outdoor spaces and redesigned our cities to create more of them and improve the ones we already have? Could we have examined our relationship to work and offices and if we decided fewer people needed to congregate in formal offices in order to make our economy run, could we have experimented with new uses for those less or even unused spaces? Could we have identified some of the underlying economic and social forces that made some of us far more vulnerable to the pandemic than others? Of course we could have. But that was never the goal of those in power so we didn't.

If you think about it, a "normal" holiday shopping season is pretty fucking terrible. Cramming 50 to 70 percent of all retail shopping into six weeks or so strains supply chains, puts exhausting demands on every person working in retail and delivery, and quite often results in stressful experiences for customers. Stores run out of things. People are disappointed. Kids cry. Adults cry. I think holidays and celebrations and rituals have their place in society, including Christmas, but do we have to do our shopping in the most batshit way possible?

The pandemic gave us an opportunity to do Christmas differently, to try something that wasn't normal. To, at the very least, spread out our shopping so people gave what they wanted to give with less stress. And some people did change. Some people shopped early, shopped differently, planned different types of celebrations that weren't wholly dependent on getting to a specific place at a specific time. Many people put saving lives over having a normal Christmas. But many people chose normal.

As a writer, reader, and general lover of language, "normal" as a goal doesn't make sense. "Normal" is neither good nor bad. It describes a relationship, not a value. By definition, once something happens enough or is happening long enough, it becomes "normal," whether we like it or not. We will always "get back to normal" because we will always adapt to the most common situations. I suppose I could listen to the argument that there was inherent value in returning to our most recent "familiar" or "comfortable" as a base to build from, but that wasn't the argument being made. We were asked to die for "getting back to normal."

*

SOCIAL DISTANCING

I don't remember exactly how the connection was made, but at some point in June or July of 2020 a bunch of PSB booksellers, as well as my partner, were all excited about reading *Where the Wild Ladies Are* by Aoko Matsuda, translated by Polly Barton. By this time, experts were certain that outdoor activities, where exhaled virus particles could disperse into the atmosphere, were essentially safe. So we organized a book club in my just-big-enough backyard. We drank. We ate a shit ton of BBQ. We had a party. We hosted another store book club later for the new translation of *Beowulf*. This time we gathered in the store itself, had the party, even made T-shirts, and took a picture.

I hosted another party the Saturday after the 2020 election. By then it was clear Joe Biden had defeated Donald Trump, and even though there was still a long way to go for Biden to actually become president, I had some sparkling rosé and Porter Square Wine and Spirits had just restocked their champagne cooler. Though it had been cold the preceding few days, the weather was warm enough that we could sit outside in the early evening for a bit. A handful of us spread out in my backyard, had a few varieties of bubbly, and shot the shit for a few hours.

The election led us to the holiday shopping season. The holidays in retail always make booksellers a little loopy, but with the pace of online orders and the surrounding stresses we had December 7 energy in mid-November and got to December 18 energy pretty damn quickly. (Those who know, know.) One night we came across an order with the last name Winograd on it and one of us pronounced it "Wine-o-grad." A few of us had the following Sunday off. The weather cooperated again and we celebrated an ad hoc holiday called "Winograd" (the second Sunday in December if you'd like to celebrate this year). We gathered in my little backyard, in pockets six feet apart, and drank five or so bottles of wine.

One the one hand, "social distancing" sounds like one of those sneaky terms designed to tell the truth so that those who hear you assume you mean the opposite of what you actually said. "Social" is about being together. It is about shaking hands, patting backs, giving hugs, whispering in ears, laughing, and talking. It is about closing distances, not maintaining them. And that is true, of course. I remember when I saw the bookseller who had been trapped in Utah for the first time in months. Neither of us are particularly huggy people, but even non-huggy friends hug if they haven't seen each other in a while, especially when those months had been so challenging. Having to wave to her from six feet away felt like running into a brick wall.

But a lot of connection can still happen from six feet away. Cities started to create more public outdoor spaces. Parking and streets were taken from cars and turned over to restaurants, parks, and other places for people to gather. By reclaiming a few thousand square feet here, a few thousand square feet there, cities were able to improve the quality of life for thousands of their citizens, not just in terms of enduring the pandemic, but also going forward. We had other resources for enduring a much longer and more effective lockdown. Sure, watching a concert online with a chat open with your friends is not the same as watching a concert in person. Same goes for watching movies using a virtual party platform, or a game night, or any of the other online gathering sites, but they're all something. Something we would not have had if this pandemic happened ten, maybe even five years earlier. And even then, we could have parties and game nights and concerts as long as we did it outside and kept our distance.

A lot of things about social distancing sucked but not as much as being dead. Once again, the story of social distancing is a story of unmet potential. It is the story of "normal" fucking things up again. It is the story of powerful people making decisions with absolutely no imagination.

ONLINE ORDERS

M ore work. Fewer sales.

That was the difference between being tired and being exhausted. A lot of work goes into every sale at a bookstore; buying, receiving, shelving, maybe answering a question, maybe helping the customer find the book, but even at its most labor-intensive, there are still parts of in-store sales customers do themselves, such as bringing their books up to the register so they can be run through the point-of-sale system and removed from inventory, and transporting the book to its final destination. They also take the books out of the store right away so our space isn't filled with books no one can buy because they've already been sold. When a store is open, we are essentially "processing" dozens of orders simultaneously. But for an online order, we do everything we do for an in-store order, plus take it off the shelf, plus take it to a register so it can be removed from inventory, plus manage the order if it can't be completed right away, plus prepare it for shipping or storing it until the customer picks it up. Furthermore, when people are shopping in the store they often buy, you know, what's in the store. If we don't have a specific book they want, yeah, many will special-order it, but many more will just buy something else they can have right now. When shopping online however, damn near every book has the "add to cart" button so even though overall sales were down, the number of titles we had to special-order skyrocketed and special orders all take a little more work to process than books already in stock. Furthermore, during the pandemic, Porter Square Books did everything we could to limit the number of people physically working in the store at any one time, so significant portions of the online ordering process were done from home. This added an additional layer of complexity as we designed workflows to keep grinding through hundreds of orders a day. There was so much staff time required to get through orders that we actually had to hire new people to keep up. In retail, there's usually a direct correlation between how busy you are and how much money you're making, but during those early months of the pandemic that particular relationship was severed. All that extra work was for fewer sales.

It was near the end of the 2020 holiday season, right before sales starting tailing off because books were running out of stock, deadlines to ship orders had been passed, and the supply chain was reaching its third or fourth breaking point. I worked a lot of late nights because I was salaried, as well as being a co-owner who earned a percentage of the store's profits each year, the evening manager, and living relatively close to the store,. I had a long-standing nightly ritual with my cat Circe. Around ten o'clock, when my partner was getting into bed, I would join her to read, chat, and hang out for a bit before getting up for the rest of my night. I would pick Circe up and put her on the bed, because she only had three legs and couldn't jump that high. She would lie on my chest and purr for about ten minutes before getting back up for the rest of her night. With this exception, she wasn't an affectionate cat. After the third or fourth night in a row of me disrupting this ritual by coming home long after ten, Circe met me at the front door and yelled at me for fifteen minutes.

It is easy when we're sitting at our computers or holding our phones to forget that nearly every aspect of online shopping doesn't happen online. It requires physical labor. It requires human beings to use their bodies to move an object from one place to another, objects with size and weight, objects that inflict wear and tear. There is work that is hard that rewards through its difficulty and there is work that drains your life. I woke up still exhausted one morning at this time and my first thought was, Oh, this is why people used to die by forty-five.

Once Porter Square Books was open for in-store shopping with no restrictions, online orders fell steadily. Most people who had been in-store shoppers came back. But not all of them. And not all of the customers we served over the course of the pandemic were pre-pandemic in-store shoppers, either because they lived too far away or they just hadn't heard of us yet. So although we're not at the relentless grind of the early pandemic, we still process dozens of online orders a day, a pace that would have been unimaginable before COVID. This means that even though I am able to have conversations with the community again, I still spend the majority of my floor shifts sitting at a computer processing online orders. Ultimately this is good for the store. I like that these sales help us pay booksellers more. I like the profits I earn from these sales. So the challenge, once again, comes back to expectations of timeliness and our understanding of convenience. Because there are expectations and understandings that would allow Porter Square Books, and all retail, really, to pay living wages and be profitable without grinding up their employees.

POD: TAKE TWO

The schedule-created pods presented a challenge too. Porter Square Books has always organized our schedule around morning and evening shifts, as many stores do, and as with all groups of humans over, say, three members, some stratification grew out of that organization. Over the years, some conflicts grew out of that stratification. I'm not saying having two shifts literally caused conflicts, but the fact that some of us would only see each other for a few hours a week meant that any sharp edges caused by differences in personality, general beliefs, bookselling philosophies, miscommunications, whatever, weren't dulled by familiarity. Furthermore, we had slightly different day-to-day experiences, which sometimes led to slightly different priorities and goals. During the pandemic, by scheduling in pods to prevent additional risk of exposure, we could go months without seeing some of our coworkers. Virtual meetings are better than nothing, but they simply cannot contain or accommodate the small talk that reminds co-workers that, even if they aren't friends and even if they have their differences, they share something through their work. Connection is lost when you can't share a quick complaint or tiny triumph. The project management program Slack kept the wheels moving but we discovered far too late than many of us had different expectations for how it should be used and for what counted as polite and respectful on it. Some of us already had a fair amount of experience communicating through text and emojis and some of us had to learn on the fly.

Booksellers care about bookselling and when you care about bookselling, you have ideas about it because you're thinking about it. It isn't weird for different booksellers to have different ideas about how to be booksellers, about what our responsibilities are and what the right ways to meet those responsibilities are. It's even less weird for booksellers from different generations, different backgrounds, and different lived experiences to have different ideas about how to be booksellers.

I don't know, and I guess I can't know, if the differences of opinion and bookselling philosophy would have led to the same level of conflict our "pods" experienced without the stresses and stratifications of the pandemic. When you have fundamental disagreements with someone over a shared project, over something you are both passionate about, there are going to be conflicts. Furthermore, before the pandemic, the election of Donald Trump as president and the Republican Party's embrace of white nationalist fascism changed the stakes of bookselling. And it's not like the other conflicts created or intensified by contemporary conservatism paused for the pandemic; the conflict over policing and the Black Lives Matter movement, the assault on trans rights, the assault on voting rights, and, eventually, the assault on reproductive rights through the Supreme Court's overturning of Roe v. Wade, all continued throughout the stresses of the pandemic and all raised the stakes of every decision booksellers and bookstores made, whether booksellers confront those stakes or not.

Not everyone in the Porter Square Books management group agreed with my belief that indie bookstores should actively deplatform white supremacists by not stocking their books, which led to a number of very challenging conversations when my chapbook making that argument was published and we struggled to decide what relationship the store would have to it. We'd faced fundamental differences before around *American Dirt* and bulk orders for books contrary to our community's values, and found consensus. The consensus didn't settle those fundamental differences, of course, since, well, really nothing could, but it at least created situations in which everyone felt their ideas were valued and everyone was comfortable with the results. They were difficult conversations but they were productive. How many of the challenges of the pandemic conversations would have happened anyway, because the stakes in bookselling are higher than they used to be and how many of them were created because those conversations took place in entirely new-to-us media? How differently would I have argued if I weren't also frayed by the stresses of the pandemic? How differently would I have listened? Or even more practically, what would we have done differently if we knew at the beginning that Slack and Zoom were going to be the primary modes of communication through a year and a half of challenging decision-making? Maybe nothing. Maybe everything.

VACCINE

"Vaccine" should have been the conclusion. And maybe it still will be. Maybe we'll get to the point where COVID is managed through a yearly shot like the flu, though, as of March 2023, that hasn't happened yet. The right-wing response to the pandemic—despite the fact the vaccine was developed during their guy's administration—combined with the existing anti-vaxxer movement meant that we never reached the level of vaccination required to eradicate the virus. Nor were the masking, gathering, and traveling restrictions strict enough or maintained long enough after the vaccine started making its way into the population for it to have maximum impact on containment. The continued spread allowed for mutations that diminished the efficacy of the available vaccines.

My post-vaccine time was defined by a couple of oases; after the first vaccine and before the rise of the Delta variant and after my second booster and before the rise of Omicron. In these oases, I went to a wonderful wedding, grabbed dinner and drinks indoors a couple of times, went to a private showing of *Dune* for a friend's birthday, visited a museum, and attended an annual holiday party I had sorely missed the preceding two years. During that first oasis, there was a real sense of relief, a sense that I hadn't been killed by COVID, a sense that we had made it through, a sense that even if we hadn't handled the pandemic very well, science bailed our asses out. And then people chose not to get vaccinated, were unable to get out of work to get vaccinated, thought they had to pay for vaccines even though they were free, all while roll-outs were botched, and restrictions were lifted way too soon. We watched the light at the end of the tunnel recede just as we were getting there. I was more emotionally prepared for the arrival of Omicron after my Delta booster, ready to watch those in power make the exact same mistakes again, ready for journalism to fail in sorting out the bullshit from the actual debate, ready for people to continue to wave their disbelief in science and disrespect for the health and well-being of others like a national flag.

By the end of the second oasis, I couldn't be angry any-more. I couldn't even feel rage. It was too obvious what would happen. Expectation had snuffed the spark I needed to feel anger. Instead, I felt a dull, almost pulsing, frustration be-cause it was clear "vaccine" would be another term in the long limbo of COVID-19.

TURNOVER

Porter Square Books has always had better staff retention than most retail and even most independent bookstores. There is some turnover, of course, as people who start in their early-to-mid twenties figure out what they want their lives to look like and decide they can't do that on the wages Por-ter Square Books can provide. But even those who always saw bookselling as temporary tended to stay a year or more. Some stuck around part-time much longer. It's something to be proud of.

There are metaphors that feel natural to describe what it felt like being a bookseller at the height of the pandemic, and though they feel accurate they all draw on a diction of violence and that doesn't sit right with me. Even something less violent, but still physical, like describing processing online orders as going down into the "mines," though closer, still doesn't feel fair to those who actually go down into mines. Chatting with other booksellers, sure, we were "in the trenches," we were in the "order mines," but in an essay, where I have to consider the depth of the words I use, I need to do better. I want a word that describes the type of experience that creates comrades.

I don't remember the exact date, but by the fall of 2021 or maybe the spring of 2022, every single hourly employee I had gone through that grind with, as well as two managers, had left. A third manager left at the beginning of 2022. At one point, I had a full six-hour shift that was just me and a bookseller who had started that week. With most of them, individually, there were reasons for leaving outside of Porter Square Books or the pandemic. This person got offered a dream job. That person's partner moved to the West Coast. This other person got a higher-paying job in publishing. Not being a manager who handles personnel I never asked any of them directly about their decision. Maybe those outside elements really were the primary reasons all those people left and it was just a coincidence that all of those reasons happened at once. And I also knew, through the whisper network, that Porter Square Books was relatively supportive during the pandemic, doing our best to create and maintain as safe an environment as possible for all of our employees. We did well enough that a number of booksellers left other stores when we were hiring specifically because we seemed to be a better place to work. I still think we are.

But taken together, it is impossible not to ask questions.

To wonder what we could have done better. To knock your head against scenarios that seemed unavoidable at the time. Bookselling and publishing have historically devoured the young people who bring so much energy to them, who bring ideas and passion and commitment, because, economically, bookselling and publishing don't pay what those ideas, passions, and commitments are worth. Sadly, too many powerful people in the industry don't value them even as they profit from them.

Still, I think Porter Square Books is exceptional and despite the strains of the pandemic we have done a good job in valuing and supporting our booksellers. But it might not have been enough for the grind of the pandemic. However I tried to maintain our community of booksellers it wasn't enough. Was this turnover connected to the stress the pandemic put on existing conflicts? Were those relatively high wages still not enough for what we asked? Did our efforts to accommodate everyone end up creating more burdens than they eased? Did the space get poisoned so it no longer felt like a good place to work? Was there something we could have done to detoxify it? Sitting at my desk now, in whatever phase we consider the pandemic to be in, I hope we don't have to confront those questions again, because I don't know the answer to them.

Since the pandemic we've increased our starting pay, changed the structure of raises so our booksellers get more money sooner, raised the amount of vacation time long-serving booksellers can take, and created a pathway to co-ownership for nonmanagement booksellers. Would these changes be enough if the natural conflicts that arise in groups of people committed to the same goal, but with different opinions, get put into the pressure cooker again? Would they be enough if another table gets thrown? If all of the energizing work is sucked out of the job by a lockdown? Or is there something

else, or many somethings else, that I'm not seeing? Maybe.
Probably.

I went back and forth about including "Pod: Take 2" and
"Turnover" in this essay. On the one hand, as the marketing
director, the public image of Porter Square Books is my primary responsibility. I know the phrase "no publicity is bad
publicity," but what people think about Porter Square Books
matters to me, both at an emotional and on a financial level.
A lot of books we sell, we sell because of our public image.
An image, biased as I may be, I truly believe we've earned. On
the other hand, I can't tell the truth about this time in my life
without talking about these conflicts and this turnover. Of
course, being honest about my experiences and supporting
the store's public image don't need to be conflicting goals. No
bookstore, no business, no person is perfect. We all fuck up.
We all do things that aren't really fuck-ups but aren't getting
it right either. What we do after we fuck up is what counts.
Is our primary goal learning from the fuck-up and using the
lessons learned to do better? Or is our primary goal making
the fuck-up disappear? The latter creates precariousness, vulnerability, perhaps even bitterness for those involved, while
the former creates experience, change, maybe even wisdom.

ESSAY

I started this essay complaining about how the staggering
endurance of the pandemic leaves us unable to actually assess it. I don't know how I feel about it because it's not over.
I've argued that missed opportunities defined the pandemic,
that the crisis gave us opportunities to change that we did
not take. But maybe those opportunities haven't really passed.
2022 was one of the strongest years for organized labor in decades, maybe in my lifetime. Some businesses have preserved

work-from-home or hybrid schedules. Many cities preserved
at least some of their extended public outdoor spaces. In the
summer of 2022, the Biden administration passed the largest investment in combatting climate change in America's
history, and despite it being far too small for the actual scale
of the problem, it's finally a start and one that could create
a platform for truly significant acts. The Biden administration also took small steps to mitigate the student debt crisis.
Speaking of students, young people and especially teenagers
and high school students, have been active on issues of gun
control, LGBTQ2+ rights, and climate change at a volume
I've never seen before.

Is this a way to shoehorn a kind of "it ain't over till it's
over" optimism into an otherwise profoundly frustrated
piece? Is this a "well, we really don't know the outcome of
the COVID-19 pandemic" get-out-of-jail-free card? Is this like
one of those white lies we tell because we're afraid of hurting
someone? Maybe. Maybe. Maybe.

Over the course of the pandemic, independent bookselling has been building momentum toward significant changes. Motivated by the Trump presidency, motivated by events
at bookseller conferences, motivated by the pandemic itself,
motivated by the other cultural and political changes in
our society, motivated by the natural cycles of generational change, motivated by individual booksellers asking questions and pushing for changes, independent bookselling is
going to look, be, and mean something different in the next
few years than it has over the past few years. The pace of
change isn't inherently limited to the bad shit. The conversations we're having about bookselling are already different
as I write the last words of this essay than they were when I
first began thinking about it. They look likely to change more
between now and its publication. Essays written in the spirit
of expectation and speculation, out of hope that certain con-

versations and certain questions will become pervasive in the industry may appear outdated because, in the next few months, the momentum may carry independent bookselling past my expectations and speculations. Something new is coming to bookselling. Something exciting. Or rather, many somethings new and many somethings exciting. A crisis is always an opportunity and I am hopeful bookselling, at least, will make good on this one.

ACKNOWLEDGMENTS

Over the years, the number of booksellers, sales reps, publicists, authors, editors, and readers who have helped me become the bookseller I am today is so great I would be afraid of leaving someone out if I started naming names even if I weren't writing these acknowledgments in the brain fog of new fatherhood.

If we have ever been on a panel together, ever chatted in between workshops at NEIBA's Fall Conference, Winter Institute, or BookExpo America, ever shared a virtual or real room for a booksellers' round table, ever sat next to each other at a publisher dinner, ever sang karaoke together, or grabbed a drink at a bar or several bars after some bookish something, you are in this book.

You are in this book if we have ever exchanged emails, tweeted back and forth, exchanged occasional words about bookselling, about what it means to bring the written word to the public. You are in this book even if you have left bookselling or books altogether and know that I am showing my gratitude to you specifically by doing everything I can to help make this a sustainable industry, so that everyone who wants to make a living being a bookseller can.

And of course a special thank-you to my colleagues, past and present, at Porter Square Books. I still learn from you every day.

*

Portions of "A Reader's Introduction to Bookselling" appeared on my blog *In Order of Importance*.

An early version of "The Indie Brand Paradox" appeared on my blog *In Order of Importance*.

An early version of "Advocacy and Stewardship, Peace and Destiny: Indies Introduce, *Faces in the Crowd*, and *The Haunted Bookshop*" appeared on my blog *In Order of Importance*.

NOTES

1 https://www.bookweb.org/about-aba
2 https://www.theguardian.com/technology/2022/jan/18/ama-zon-wrongful-death-lawsuit-illinois-tornado-warehouse
3 https://wordsrated.com/amazon-print-book-sales-statistics/
4 https://www.reuters.com/legal/litigation/amazon-copied-products-rigged-search-results-promote-its-own-brands-docu-ments-2021-10-13/]
5 https://www.press.uillinois.edu/wordpress/rip-michael-s-harper/
6 https://opencountrymag.com/in-conversation-with-lan-sa-mantha-chang-director-of-the-iowa-writers-workshop/
7 http://sewaneewriters.org/faculty/ayana-mathis.html
8 https://www.salon.com/2012/05/27/exclusive_the_paris_re-view_the_cold_war_and_the_cia/
9 https://americanstudies.yale.edu/
10 https://www.smithsonianmag.com/arts-culture/peter-mat-thiessens-lifelong-quest-peace-180950444/
11 https://blog.leeandlow.com/2020/01/28/2019diversitybaseline-survey
12 https://en.wikipedia.org/wiki/Race_and_ethnicity_in_the_United_States
13 https://blog.leeandlow.com/2020/01/28/2019diversitybase-linesurvey/
14 https://blog.leeandlow.com/2020/01/28/2019diversitybase-linesurvey/
15 https://www.publicbooks.org/how-the-new-york-times-cov-ers-black-writers/

16 https://www.shelf-awareness.com/issue.html?issue=4208#m55872

17 https://edwardlowe.org/open-book-management-at-work/#:~:text=Letting%20your%20staff%20see%20into,and%20allocating%20resources%20more%20sensibly.&text=Open%2Dbook%20management%20helps%20your,like%20bottom%2Dline%20business%20owners

18 https://www.youtube.com/watch?v=Veo-z4bPYqE

19 https://www.shelf-awareness.com/issue.html?issue=4187&share=true#m55591

20 https://twitter.com/nolafleurdelit/status/1512859922307981315

21 https://twitter.com/iamragesparkle/status/1280891537451343873?lang=en

22 https://www.nytimes.com/2021/04/29/technology/amazons-profits-triple.html

23 https://en.wikipedia.org/wiki/Strand_Bookstore

24 https://thebaffler.com/capital-offenses/hanging-by-a-strand-oconnor

25 https://thebaffler.com/capital-offenses/hanging-by-a-strand-oconnor

26 https://en.wikipedia.org/wiki/Strand_Bookstore

27 https://twitter.com/strandbookstore/status/1319686649798905856/photo/2

28 https://www.opensecrets.org/personal-finances/ron-wyden/net-worth?cid=N00007724

29 https://www.nytimes.com/2020/10/26/books/the-strand-bookstore-nyc.html

30 https://web.archive.org/web/20200122154536/https://thebluenib.com/a-poor-imitation-american-dirt-and-misrepresentations-of-mexico/

31 https://davidbowles.medium.com/non-mexican-crap-ff-3b48a873b5

32 https://tropicsofmeta.com/2019/12/12/pendeja-you-aint-steinbeck-my-bronca-with-fake-ass-social-justice-literature/

33 https://www.nytimes.com/2020/01/27/opinion/american-dirt-book.html

34 https://www.lrb.co.uk/the-paper/v42/no4/christian-lorent-zen/goldfinching

35 https://www.nytimes.com/2016/01/03/opinion/sunday/mur-der-isnt-black-or-white.html

36 https://www.nytimes.com/2020/01/19/books/review/ameri-can-dirt-jeanine-cummins.html

37 I know there was some weirdness around potentially publishing an early draft by accident, but I'm using the review as it appears now assuming this is the definitive version.

38 https://lareviewofbooks.org/article/white-writers-omission-of-race-jess-rows-white-flights-race-fiction-and-the-american-imagination/

39 https://www.nytimes.com/2020/01/17/books/review/ameri-can-dirt-jeanine-cummins.html

40 Matthew Salesses, *Craft in the Real World*, p. 14

41 https://newrepublic.com/article/158166/book-publish-ings-next-battle-conservative-authors

42 https://www.politifact.com/article/2009/dec/18/politifact-lie-year-death-panels/

43 https://en.wikipedia.org/wiki/Paradox_of_tolerance

44 https://en.wikipedia.org/wiki/Three-fifths_Compromise

45 https://www.aaihs.org/a-compact-for-the-good-of-america-slavery-and-the-three-fifths-compromise/

46 https://twitter.com/RepMTG/status/1368943858990657536

47 https://www.nytimes.com/2020/06/03/opinion/tom-cot-ton-protests-military.html

48 https://www.huffpost.com/entry/i-dont-know-how-to-ex-plain-to-you-that-you-should_b_59519811e4b0f078efd98440

49 pp. 25–6

50 Ibid, p. 4

51 Ibid, p. 11

52 https://en.wikipedia.org/wiki/Masterpiece_Cakeshop_v._Col-orado_Civil_Rights_Commission

53 https://www.bookweb.org/news/protesters-picket-author-ap-pearance-porter-square-books-33623

54 https://www.openletterbooks.org/products/the-remem-bered-part

55 https://www.portersquarebooks.com/interview-robin-mo-
    ger-translator-july-staff-pick-slipping

56 https://archipelagobooks.org/book/an-untouched-house/

57 https://www.shelf-awareness.com/issue.html?is-
    sue=1645#m14722

58 https://twitter.com/handsrm/status/1517331180282122243?s=2
    0&t=3FIvOdgwUO8PNfUDSRI4qA

59 https://twitter.com/handsrm/status/1517331088263237635?s=2
    0&t=3FIvOdgwUO8PNfUDSRI4qA

J osh Cook is a bookseller and co-owner at Porter Square Books in Cambridge, Massachusetts, where he has worked since 2004. He is also author of the critically acclaimed postmodern detective novel *An Exaggerated Murder* and his fiction, criticism, and poetry have appeared in numerous leading literary publications. He grew up in Lewiston, Maine and lives in Somerville, Massachusetts.

Printed by Imprimerie Gauvin
Gatineau, Québec